THE EDUCATION OF DESIRE

THE EDUCATION OF DESIRE

MARXISTS AND THE WRITING OF HISTORY

HARVEY J. KAYE

Foreword by Christopher Hill

ROUTLEDGE

NEW YORK   LONDON

Published in 1992 by

Routledge
An imprint of Routledge, Chapman and Hall, Inc.
29 West 35th Street
New York, NY 10001

Published in Great Britain by

Routledge
11 New Fetter Lane
London EC4P 4EE

Copyright © 1992 by Routledge, Chapman and Hall, Inc.

Printed in the United States of America

Library of Congress Cataloging-in-Publication Data

Kaye, Harvey J.
  The education of desire: Marxists and the writing of history/Harvey J. Kaye; with a foreword by Christopher Hill.
    p. cm.
  Includes bibliographical references (p.) and index
  ISBN 0–415–90587–7–ISBN 0–415–90588–5
  1. Marxian historiography.   I. Title. D13.K315 1992
335.4'119—dc20   92–11609
                                                                              CIP

For my sister, Phyllis,
and my "brothers,"
Ron Baba and Henry Giroux

CONTENTS

FOREWORD

Harvey Kaye is easily the world's greatest authority on "the British Marxist historians." His 1984 book of that title dealt with Maurice Dobb, Rodney Hilton, Eric Hobsbawm, Edward Thompson, and myself. Since then he has edited two volumes of essays by Victor Kiernan and one by George Rudé, as well as a volume of *Critical Perspectives* on Thompson (with K. McClelland). The present book reprints revised versions of articles on Thompson, Kiernan and Rudé, and on A. L. Morton, Leo Huberman and John Berger. The outstanding British historians still to be dealt with are Dona Torr, the inspiration of us all, and John Saville.

Harvey pays due tribute to the Communist Party Historians' Group which flourished from 1946 until the early fifties, under the benign guidance of Dona Torr. The discussions within that group of committed Marxists were the most stimulating intellectual experience I have ever had: anything I have written since derives from them. They were wide- and free-ranging, totally undogmatic, often agreeably fierce.

In the present book Harvey stresses the importance of Gramsci for many of us. Gramsci's work is of course of the greatest significance for all historians, but I do not remember his being discussed in the Historians' Group. Harvey quotes a review which I wrote in 1958 of *The Modern Prince and Other Writings,* edited by Louis Marks. I rather think that was my first serious acquaintance with Gramsci's writings. The only interest of this is that the members of the Group had arrived independently at some of the ideas which Gramsci had so effectively presented. Harvey notes Victor Kiernan's shift from Leninism to a Gramscian position, which I suspect took place after he left the C.P. and so the Historians' Group. He also comments on the importance of Gramsci for the evolution of Rudé's thinking; and it is perhaps significant that Rudé was only intermittently a member of the Group, since he was a victim of the McCarthyite era in England and had to go into "exile" in

Australia and Canada to find an academic post. (Louis Marks would have had an academic career in a freer country.) Those of us who had tenure before the cold war heated up were lucky to retain our positions: there was no promotion and no recruitment of Marxists into the profession in the fifties.

Especially valuable in the present work is Harvey's generous appreciation of A. L. Morton. Leslie never held an academic post: he was too politically active. He did not write for academic historians; he wrote for and was read by a much wider public than any of us could aspire to. But his standards were those of high scholarship, as his collected articles show. The Historians' Group in its early days spent many sessions discussing with Morton revising the first edition of *A People's History of England,* and in these discussions Leslie gave as much as he got. He taught us all something—though not enough—of the necessity of writing comprehensively for a wide audience. He was a very great scholar and a marvelous man.

I also find fascinating Harvey Kaye's discussion of Leo Huberman and John Berger, not hitherto included within his canon. This reaching out to less academic history is a welcome innovation, already present in Harvey's book, *The Powers of the Past: Reflections on the Crisis and the Promise of History,* published in 1991. Here he surveys the present state of history in Great Britain and the U.S.A., noting the contrast in both countries between popular interest in history as a subject and lack of interest in the work of academic historians. He rightly blames the latter. He also pillories the deliberate ideological pressures of Reaganism and Thatcherism, with their tame historians, recruited from renegade ex-socialists or promotion-hunters.

Thatcherite history is a sentimentalized and half-baked version of the history against which my generation reacted in the 1930s. This assumed that the most important theme in history was the evolution of "freedom" and "democracy," slowly broadening down from precedent to precedent until it reached perfection in the British constitution. All we had to do was to export it to less fortunate nations, and history could "come to a full-stop," in the immortal words of that great send-up of English historical humbug, Sellar and Yeatman's *1066 and All That.* Those were the days when England was just ceasing to be top nation; similar fantasies are popular in the U.S.A. today.

Academic historians no longer accept that sort of history, perhaps because they no longer generalize; but it underlies the Thatcherite demand for revision of the history curriculum for schools so as to stress our "achievements" whilst forgetting little items like colonial aggression (from Ireland onwards), British and American pre-eminence in the slave trade, our role for centuries as the bully maintaining world order—all underwritten with the unique Anglo-Saxon gift of self-deception and humbug. Mrs. Thatcher told the French (who had invited her to celebrate the bicentenary of 1789) that the rights of man were not invented in France but by the Magna Carta barons (!) and that England's peaceful revolution of 1688 was a much nicer way of doing things than the French. She failed to congratulate the French on learning regicide and republicanism from the English in 1649, and terror from the English in Ireland.

Harvey thinks radical historians have been too quiescent in face of vulgar Thatcherite perversions. He calls for a revival of popular narrative history which will tell a very different and truer story, admitting the vices as well as the virtues of our past. He quotes Edward Thompson: "stability, no less than revolution, may have its own kind of terror." It is a challenge which we have not yet faced up to. Since Morton's *People's History* there has been much innovative work on history from below, on women's history, and on the history of empire. It will be a big job to synthesize this material in a new narrative that nonprofessionals will read. But Harvey Kaye is right: it must be done.

Christopher Hill
Sibford Ferris
Oxfordshire
January 1992

PREFACE

There are so many people to thank for their contributions to my work on Marxist historiography and theory during the past decade. But questions of space insist that I limit my acknowledgments here to those whose help has extended over the several pieces included in this volume. Thus, I should first record my appreciation of the aid, advice, and influence of Christopher Hill who is, as E. P. Thompson once said, "Master of more than an old Oxford college." Both my very first book, *The British Marxist Historians,* and most of the present one have depended upon Christopher's willingness to listen to, or read, my ideas—*and* to respond with corrections, criticisms and suggestions—about the intellectual and scholarly tradition with which his writings have been bound up and of which he has been so central a figure. Indeed, it seemed to me only appropriate that he be invited to write the Foreword to this collection of my essays, for it was Christopher who urged me to go forward and, among other things, fulfill my promise to address the work of those other two outstanding Marxist historians, Victor Kiernan and George Rudé, which, unfortunately, I did not have the opportunity to include in *The British Marxist Historians.* I would just add that I will always remember the special pleasures and insights garnered from our exchanges, most especially those afforded by our pub-lunches in Oxford but, also, those arising out of conversations and arguments held in the kitchen of the Kaye home on the occasion of the extremely successful visit in 1985 to the University of Wisconsin-Green Bay by Christopher and Bridget Hill inaugurating our annual Historical Perspectives Lectures Series.

Really, there are so many colleagues and friends who have participated— whether they have liked it or not—in the development of the ideas, observations and assertions to be found in the chapters which follow. Along with the critical support and commentary of Bridget and Christopher Hill, Heather and Victor Kiernan, Doreen and George Rudé, Rodney Hilton and

Jean Birrell, and Dorothy and Edward Thompson, I want to highlight the invaluable discussions and arguments had with Ellen Meiksins Wood, Henry Giroux, Daniel and Jeanne Singer, Ron Baba, Carl Chinn, Chris Dyer, Joyce Salisbury, Bill Langen, Jerry Lembcke, Tony Galt, Craig Lockard, Hugh Miller, Ray Hutchison, Jerry Rodesch, Stephanie Cataldo, Susan Jackson, Dave Jowett, Karen Walch and Ron Sexton. In this vein, I should restate also my appreciation of the original and continuing encouragement of my work in this area provided by Anthony Giddens and William Sewell, Jr. Of course, responsibility for what I have come to say and contend is mine.

I would also like to thank the publishers, Routledge, in particular, Cecelia Cancellaro, the most enthusiastic editor for which one could hope, for inviting me to organize and prepare this collection of my writings. At the same time, I must acknowledge and thank the several publishers and journal editorial boards (indicated at the outset of each chapter's notes) who have given their permission to use in this collection the articles and essays which previously appeared in their publications. And in this literary vein I should also record once again my appreciation of the staff of the UWGB Cofrin Library, especially Jennifer Tillis, whose aid and assistance have been indispensable to my work.

As ever, the most important contributions have been made by my family, my daughters, Rhiannon and Fiona, who give me so much joy and the sense of continuity so crucial to critical historical study and thought—especially, perhaps, for those of us who would like to see some dramatic *changes* made in our own social orders!—and my foremost colleague, comrade, and companion, Lorna. Thanks and credit are imperative, but words alone are never sufficient. The book itself is dedicated to my sister, Phyllis, and my "brothers," Ron Baba and Henry Giroux, each of whom has made special contributions to its development *and* to my own personal and intellectual formation and progress.

Harvey J. Kaye
Green Bay, Wisconsin
January 1992

INTRODUCTION

What Archimedes said of the mechanical powers, may be applied to Reason and
Liberty: *"Had we,"* said he, *"a place to stand upon, we might raise the world."*
—Tom Paine, *The Rights of Man*

In these bicentennial years of the French Revolution and, indeed, the Age
of Revolution, Europe and the world are once again being radically transformed. In 1989 we saw the retreat from empire initiated from above by
Mikhail Gorbachev—actions originally and fundamentally "determined"
from below and, in time, carried out by the peoples of Eastern Europe themselves. Now we are witness to the further collapse of the Soviet Union and
that of the Soviet State itself. Communism is evidently banished, having long
ago been exhausted as a model for socialist development, and in its wake is
the apparent triumph of capitalism and, possibly (though this is said with
decreasing optimism), the development—better, the making—of democratic
polities.

At the same time, for almost a generation now we in the West have been
experiencing what can be called the "crisis of social democracy," that is, the
breakup of the postwar settlements or consensuses constructed around
Keynesianism and the welfare state in both their European social-democratic
and American liberal forms. And, concurrently, there has been the formation
and ascendance to political power of the New Right, most spectacularly in
Britain and the United States under the leadership of Margaret Thatcher's
Conservatives and Ronald Reagan's Republicans, respectively. Empowered
by "class wars from above," and exploiting a host of popular anxieties engendered by the world economic recession and restructurings of the 1970s *and*
a variety of international and domestic political troubles, the New Right co-
alitions of conservatives and neo-conservatives have been not only hostile and
antagonistic towards social democracy and liberalism, but eager to undo the
social and democratic rights and powers secured in the 1960s and early 1970s
by labor and the new social movements of racial and ethnic minorities and
women (among others).[1]

In light of the collapse of Communism and the debilitation of social democracy, not to mention the disasters and tragedies of "Third-World revolutionary regimes," it would appear that "socialism," however conceived, is dead, or nearly so, and just waiting to be carted off for burial in the graveyard of history. In fact, the obituaries have been written and are being communicated not only by conservatives and the corporate media, but by more reasonable and once-sympathetic European and American liberals as well.[2]

Such a scripting of history is, however, not acceptable either as a rendition of past and present, or as an assessment of contemporary and future possibilities. As an argument about past and present it equates not simply the Soviet Revolution but, mistakenly and crudely, the ensuing development of Soviet Communism with the historic struggle for, and vision of, socialism. For those of us who have always comprehended the making of socialism as entailing the extension, deepening and continuous refinement of the ideals and practices of *liberty, equality,* and *democracy,* the formation and history of the Soviet State and Empire under the banner of socialism was, to say the least, a gross and tragic corruption of that struggle and the aspirations it carries with it. (Nor should we forget the perverseness of German Fascism—the most reactionary and horrific face of European capitalism—calling itself "National Socialism.")

In this same vein (but, obviously, referring to a *dramatically* different experience), the making of socialism cannot be reduced or limited to the passage and pursuit of the policies and programs of the social-democratic and liberal consensuses instituted in the course and aftermath of the Depression of the 1930s and the Second World War. However much their (varied) establishment represented a real and significant victory of working people over the political economy and culture of capital (and however much their defense remains imperative to the reinvigoration of a radical-democratic and socialist politics), it must be remembered that the creation of the Keynesian welfare states of Western Europe and North America involved merely—or, if you prefer, mostly—the reform and regulation *of* capitalism and, indeed, was conceived of as a means of rescuing capitalism from one of its own periodic crises.[3]

The narratives being broadcast celebrating the demise of socialism as a historical force and alternative not only misconstrue past and present, they also misrepresent and obfuscate the possibilities for democratic-socialist politics today and tomorrow. Without at all underestimating the depth and extent of the crisis of socialism and the significance of the electoral victories and ambitions of the conservative allies of corporate capital (and the devastation they have wrought!), we must not fail to recognize that the New Rights' triumphs are far from secured. While there is no denying their command of our national political agendas for more than a decade, they have *not* succeeded in translating their antipathy for social democracy and liberalism into new conservative consensuses. In other words, their hegemonic aspirations have yet to be fully realized. The material experience of New Right political economies and the oppressiveness and divisiveness of their political and cultural campaigns evidently have undermined the public commitment of working people to social-democratic and liberal politics and parties; however, it appears that the Tories and Republicans still have been unable to completely dissuade working people of their social-democratic and liberal values and ideals. The contemporary state of British and American political life and discourse is best described, perhaps, as one of "cynicism," a widespread sense that political and social action and struggle do not *and* would not make a meaningful difference. Thus, it is arguable that what we find is not so much commitment to the world as it is, as pragmatic acceptance of and accommodation to it.[4]

Clearly, if there is to be a renewal of what used to be called "progressive" politics, then socialists and radical democrats must pursue both critical study of the experience of Soviet Communism and, most importantly, a broad and critical re-examination of the ideas and political practices of the Western Left in all its varieties. And in the process of doing so we must be sure to attend to the full array of questions: necessities and priorities; strategies and tactics, including the imperatives and possibilities of coalition-building; projected plans and programs; and aspirations and visions. Moreover, we should not fail to consider the experience and "accomplishments" of the Right—persistently combating and contesting their campaigns but, also, learning and, where morally and politically appropriate, even making certain of their initiatives our own (with the necessary revisions, naturally).[5]

Of course, there is always the danger that in our eagerness to address "the world as it is and is fast becoming" and our desire to be perceived as "modern," "up to date," and "in tune with contemporary developments"—or, unfortunately, as too many on the Left have been proclaiming, "*post*modern"— we will blind ourselves to the *continuities* between past and present, the persistence of those structures and relations of exploitation and oppression which determine people's lives and must necessarily be confronted if we are to make social orders ever more libertarian, egalitarian, and democratic. And it is for this reason that many of us will and must continue to insist—contra the claims of the "end-of-history" Right and the "postmodern" Left—that Marxism, with its concern for the experience of working people and the oppressed and their varied struggles against the powers that be and the reduction of human experience to the imperatives of capital, has much to contribute to the renewal and reinvigoration of socialist and radical-democratic politics. Thus, the British historian of international affairs, Fred Halliday, has correctly observed that the end of the Cold War and collapse of Soviet Communism liberate Marxism to return to its "point of origin," that is, "the critique of, and challenge to, capitalist political economy." The foremost question to be considered, he says, is "whether, and how far, there does exist an alternative to the predominant model of capitalism and, if so, what social agencies can be mobilized democratically to create and maintain it."[6]

Ever essential to this endeavor are the labors of critical Marxist historians. However much radical-democratic and socialist politics are in need of re-appraisal and revaluation and must be made to address the world as it is, their revitalization will depend not only on formulating plans, policies, and programs alternative to, and more attractive than, those currently being offered *and* on mobilizing and organizing working people and the oppressed more effectively than has been the case at least for the past generation, but *as well*— if not originally—on the cultivation of democratic and socialist historical memory, consciousness, and imagination. Indeed, in the face of widespread popular despair, cynicism, and fatalism, this particular project would seem to be all the more imperative and urgent. To be clear about it: The necessity of critical historical study and thought is not that they are capable of informing us as to what specifically is to be done now, today, in the present circumstances, or that they can provide us with assurances, guarantees, or promises about the future—for they can accomplish neither. (Contrary to the claims and accusations advanced by so many conservative and liberal historians and intellectuals, it is they in their insistence on the inevitability of capitalism, "economic man," and a market economy who are the determinists, *not* Marxists.) Rather, the necessity of critical historical study and thought is, first, that they will enable us to challenge the use and abuse and renditions of past and present promoted by the powers that be in support of the world as it is—or, even worse, as they would have it be—and, second, that they will reveal and remind us—again, contra the claims of the powerful—that, however tragic the dialectic which is history, the making of freer, more equal and democratic polities and social orders *is possible*. Moreover, in addition to countering the narratives of the governors and, hopefully, inspiring within and among us a knowledge, awareness and understanding of history as tragedy *and* possibility, the critical pursuit of the dialogue between past and present is crucial to that essentially pedagogical process of informing our deliberations and agencies with the experiences, struggles, aspirations, and visions of those who preceded us. Drawing upon the poetic words of E. P. Thompson, we might well understand this as the *historical* "education of desire."[7]

In *The British Marxist Historians*, I attempted to show that the labors and ideas of that remarkable postwar generation of historical scholars represented one of the most significant intellectual traditions of the twentieth century. Examining and exploring the works in particular of Maurice Dobb, Rodney Hilton, Christopher Hill, Eric Hobsbawm, and E. P. Thompson, I contended that through their writings they not only had made important contributions to their respective fields of historical study, but also primary contributions: to the development of *social* historiography and, especially, to the approach to the past which has come to be known as history from below or "the bottom up"; to our theoretical and historical understandings of class, class struggle and class formation; *and*—by way of their own recovery of the experience and agency of "the lower orders"—to our knowledge and comprehension of the making of modern Britain and the world. Also, in conclusion to that book, I argued that through their individual and collective endeavors the British Marxist historians had contributed to and helped shape the formation of contemporary democratic and socialist historical consciousness.[8]

The essays brought together in the present volume record my continuing exploration of the British Marxist historical tradition and of Marxism and the writing of history more generally. However, written in the spreading and all-the-more evident shadows of the political victories of the American and British New Rights and the disintegration of the social-democratic and liberal consensuses, and in the midst of the scholarly and extra-academic debates about the "crisis of history" (to be discussed in later chapters), *The Education of Desire,* in addition to being a further collection of historiographical studies, addresses even more explicitly the problematic of the making of democratic and socialist historical memory, consciousness, and imagination, the intellectual and political implications of the scholarly and pedagogical practices of historians, *and* the imperative that Marxist and other critical historians conceive of themselves not merely as scholars but as critical intellectuals, indeed, as historical *critics,* a posture demanding increased attention to and *engagement with* both working people's experiences and concerns and public culture and discourse.

Chapter 1, "Political Theory and History," was originally written as part of *The British Marxist Historians* but, due to reasons of space and editorial dissent, was published separately. Motivated by a perception of a continuing, if not growing, antidemocratic elitism on the part of the intellectual Left, and a concern that its incorporation of the political and cultural insights and ideas of Antonio Gramsci was overemphasizing the concept of "hegemony" without due attention to its counterpart experience, "contradictory consciousness" (and all which it implied) this essay offers an argument for a particular understanding of history making and radical-democratic politics and social change, focusing on the tasks and responsibilities of intellectuals. Reviewing both Gramsci's political thought and the histories of the struggles of the English common people by Hilton, Hill, and Thompson in particular, it stresses that the making of socialist democracy requires a *democratic* socialist practice which recognizes the possibilities within working people themselves and the necessity of both articulating and educating their anxieties and aspirations—never forgetting that in the process "even the educators must be educated."

Chapters 2 and 3 were first prepared as my introductions to the collected essays of George Rudé, *The Face of the Crowd,* and of Victor Kiernan, *History, Classes and Nation-States* and *Poets, Politics and the People,* representing (partial) fulfillment of the promise which I made in the preface to *The British Marxist Historians* to examine and treat their works as I had those of their historian comrades.[9] Along with providing surveys and exegeses of their equally remarkable scholarly accomplishments, both chapters extend my inquiries on the questions of social and class struggle, historical thinking, and the role of intellectuals past and present in shaping both. As I hope I have made clear, Rudé and Kiernan, in their respective ways, have been central participants in the creation and development of the British Marxist tradition, and yet each has offered distinct and original perspectives and reflections on British, European and international history.

Chapter 4, "E. P. Thompson, the British Marxist Historical Tradition and the Contemporary Crisis," speaks even more directly to the development and pursuit of critical history and "historical criticism." Drawing on the observations and propositions of the American political theorist, Michael Walzer, regarding the practice of interpretation and "connected criticism,"[10] it considers Edward Thompson's engagements, histories and, especially, his historically-informed critiques and arguments directed at both his "comrades" on the Left and his "antagonists" on the Right, as a "model" for the practice of historical criticism for both Britons and Americans.

Chapters 5 and 6, "Our Island Story Retold" and "Capitalism and Democracy in America," were written in the wake of the British and American elections of 1987 and 1988 and the defeats, respectively, of Labour and the Democrats by conservative parties dominated by cadres of the New Right. Treating the works of A. L. Morton and Leo Huberman, specifically (and respectively) their texts, *A People's History of England* and *We, the People,* which offered sweeping histories of British and American development from their "beginnings" to the interwar period of the 1930s, I discuss what might still be garnered from them as we deliberate and attempt to respond to the crisis of history, the debilitation of the social-democratic and liberal consensuses, and the use and abuse of the past by the Right and, also, as we possibly seek to articulate new, ever more critical and democratic "grand narratives" of our national experiences.

Chapter 7, "John Berger and the Question of History," is somewhat different than the preceding pieces for, in contrast to the other figures whose works are considered here, Berger is not actually a historian but an art critic, novelist, and essayist. Nevertheless, tracing both the continuities and the changes in his thought, and showing the intimate connections among the many and varied products of his intellectual and creative career, I believe this essay reveals that the most persistent and pervasive themes in Berger's writings are those of historical memory and consciousness, and the possibility of historically informing and educating contemporary imagination and desire.

Although in contrast to my earlier readings of his work, I now find myself expressing certain serious reservations about his project—probably reflecting as much changes in my own intellectual and political sensibilities as in his— I would continue to urge attention to Berger's writings by all of us who dream of an alternative to the world as it is ("intellectuals" in particular), both for the wonder and, also, for the sympathies and sensualities to be found there.

Finally, Chapter 8, "Past and Present," is a set of three notes in response to the related contemporary crises of history and socialism. The first offers a retrospective look at the arguments advanced by the English historian, J. H. Plumb, in *The Death of the Past* (1969) in the light of the historiographical and political developments of the past generation. The second records my interpretation of recent proclamations that we have arrived at the "end of history" and, in reaction to the challenges such proclamations throw down, emphatically restates the critical vision of historical study and practice which inspired and drew so many of us to the discipline in the late 1960s and early 1970s. The third presents my thoughts on the supposed "death of Marxism" and, against such claims, insists upon the necessity of continuing to ask the classical and fundamental Marxist historical questions about exploitation, oppression, and struggle, and of wielding the "powers of the past" in support of the making of greater freedom, equality, and democracy.

I would close this Introduction with an observation made by the young Karl Marx in a letter of 1843. In words which begin to answer the problematic articulated at the outset of these paragraphs by Tom Paine, his fellow radical democrat, Marx wrote:

> It will then be clear that the world has long possessed the dream of a thing of which it needs only to possess the consciousness in order to really possess it. It will be clear that the problem is not some great gap between the thoughts of the past and those of the future but the completion of the thoughts of the past.

1

POLITICAL THEORY AND HISTORY: ANTONIO GRAMSCI AND THE BRITISH MARXIST HISTORIANS

It would I think be easy to show that, since past and future are part of the same
time-span, interest in the past and interest in the future are interconnected.
—E. H. Carr, *What is History?*[1]

There is no denying the contributions of the British Marxist historians to
their respective fields of historical scholarship and, collectively, both to the
development of the perspective known as "history from the bottom up," and
to the development of Marxism as *historical* materialism.[2] Nor has it failed to
be acknowledged that the British Marxist historians' recovery of the past has
been consequential in a political sense, that is, to the making of a democratic
and socialist historical consciousness. However, it has not been adequately
recognized that the British Marxist historians—especially Rodney Hilton,
Christopher Hill, and E. P. Thompson, and including to some extent Eric
Hobsbawm, Victor Kiernan, and George Rudé—have also been contributing to democratic and socialist political theory. By this, I have in mind not
merely the fact that Eric Hobsbawm has written political essays in which he
treats contemporary issues in historical perspective, and that E. P. Thompson
has long been engaged in confronting the growing threat to civil liberties
and the "rights of the free-born Briton" and, too, the threat of nuclear holocaust.[3] Additionally, I mean that these historians by way of their historical
writings on the subject of *class formation* have been affirming, or advancing,
a particular approach to democratic and socialist politics—specifically, that
approach originally articulated by the Italian Marxist, Antonio Gramsci.

The intention of this chapter is to elucidate the political theory of the
Marxist historians in relation to the thought of Gramsci. The essay is divided
into two parts. In the first part I will consider the respective understandings
of class formation and the derived political theories proposed by Marx,
Lenin, and (especially) Gramsci. Also, I will note Gramsci's commitment to,
and interest in, historical study and thinking. Then, in the second part I will
show how the historians, in their writings on English social history, have
provided grounding and support for Gramsci's conception of class formation
and associated political theory—that is, for his concepts of "hegemony" and

"contradictory consciousness," and his argument on the role of intellectuals in class formation and political action.

Gramsci: Politics, Consciousness, and History

> Economic conditions had first transformed the mass of the people of the country
> into workers. The combination of capital has created for this mass a common
> situation, common interests. This mass is thus already a class as against capital, but
> not yet for itself. In the struggle, of which we have noted only a few phases, this
> mass becomes united, and constitutes itself as a class for itself.
> —Karl Marx, *The Poverty of Philosophy*[4]

The subject of class formation "in the full sense"—that is, the problem of class consciousness, or, as it has classically been referred to in Marxist studies, the making of a "class in itself" into "a class for itself"—is both a historical and a political problem. Not only are there the questions regarding class formation historically (i.e., in the past), but also, especially for Marxists, the questions of *how to develop* and/or further the development of working- (and/or peasant-) class consciousness.

When Marx offered the model of "class in itself/class for itself" it was his understanding that the process of class formation was a natural and spontaneous development, occurring concomitantly with the development of capitalist industry. That is, not only would the proletariat grow in size with the growth and expansion of industrial capitalism but, also, through time and in the process of struggle, the formation of the working class as a historical actor would proceed apace, characterized by the emergence of class consciousness and political organization, which Marx equated with *revolutionary* consciousness and struggle. While Marx did not posit any specific form which working-class struggle and, ultimately, revolution would take, he did insist that such conflicts and revolutions would be processes of workers' *self-emancipation*. In fact, not only did Marx and Engels emphasize in *The Communist Manifesto* (1848) that "the emancipation of the working class must be the act of the working class itself," but, moreover, they stated that the Communists "do not set up any sectarian principles of their own, by which to shape and mould the proletarian movement." Indeed, they added that "The theoretical conclusions of the Communists are in no way based on ideas or principles that have been invented, or discovered, by this or that would be universal reformer. They merely express in general terms, actual relations springing from an existing class struggle, from a historical movement going on under our very eyes."[5] And, though he indicated no timetable for the revolutionary changes he both anticipated and worked towards, it is unlikely that he expected the capitalist mode of production to have remained paramount in the late twentieth century. Nor would his conception, or vision, of the outcome of "socialist revolution" have been fulfilled by the tragic and brutal history of the Soviet Union.[6]

Since Marx's time a variety of theories have been offered to explain the persistence of capitalism. Along with the explanations of capitalism's longevity, there have been both implicit and explicit recommendations, or strategies, as to how to respond to the historically-changing circumstances and possibilities, specifically regarding how to overcome the inertia which had apparently set in on the process of working-class formation and radicalization. Such strategies have usually involved, but not been limited to, theorizing the necessary relationship between the working class, sometimes referred to as "the masses," and its "leaders," most often envisioned in the form of a party and its intellectuals.[7] Of course, such discussions should not be surprising since Marx and Engles themselves were active in such an organization, for which they wrote *The Communist Manifesto.*[8] But whereas later theorists in the Marxist tradition have tended to proffer, with reference to "the party" or other strategic alternatives, substitutionist theories (wherein some organization, or other social group, "stands in" for the seemingly inert working class), Marx understood the party to be a support for the working class in "its" struggles, *not* an alternative or surrogate for it.

Such a "substitutionist" conception of the task of the party was, however, developed by Lenin in the historically-specific context of turn-of-the-century Czarist Russia.[9] In fact, Lenin considerably reformulated the party's role and the relationship between it and the working class, arguing—against Marx, and against the Marxism of the Second Socialist International—that "socialist consciousness" could *not* develop autonomously or spontaneously amongst the workers. Rather, as he wrote, "The history of all countries shows that the working class, exclusively by its own effort, is able to develop only trade-union consciousness." Moreover, Lenin asserted that whereas workers could at best formulate demands only for the reform of capitalism, "The theory of socialism . . . grew out of the philosophic, historical, and economic theories elaborated by educated representatives of the propertied classes, by intellectuals."[10] Thus, Bolshevism, or Marxism-*Leninism,* is a theory of substitutionism: the working class can only develop "so far" on its own, its "true" consciousness and "real" interests (i.e., "scientific understanding") must be supplied by others.

The Leninist conception of class formation (in the full sense) was furthered by—at the same time that it provided much of the theoretical legitimation for—Communist Party orthodoxy and Soviet authoritarianism. And, in Western Marxism, Georg Lukács' ideal-type model of proletarian consciousness—against which any real working-class consciousness was adjudged "false consciousness"—further contributed to the elitism and arrogance of "Marxist" intellectuals and party activists.[11] Together, the Leninist and Lukácsian models of class formation and consciousness have predominated in Marxist thought.

In the past few decades there also have appeared the otherwise seemingly quite different theories of the Frankfurt School and structuralist-Marxism. Their explanations for capitalist persistence emphasize variations of "ideological domination" wherein the working class is effectively incorporated, and class resistance and opposition to industrial capitalism are neutralized. As a consequence, the political strategies derived, for example, from both Herbert Marcuse's "one dimensional man" and Louis Althusser's "ideological state apparatuses" are also substitutionist—marginal social groups in the former case, "the party" in the latter.[12]

It is not that there have been no other Marxist conceptions of class formation and consciousness available (for example, there are the writings of Rosa Luxemburg, who had herself warned of the dangers of Bolshevism).[13] But, as Eric Hobsbawm wrote quite accurately in 1974, "Antonio Gramsci, probably the most original communist thinker produced in the West, has been virtually inaccessible to non-Italians, and not very accessible even to Italians."[14] In the years since, however, Gramsci has come to be acknowledged as one of the great political theorists of this century, and his work is not only now readily accessible in Italian (and French) but also increasingly in English, along with biographies, analyses, and criticisms of his thought by Marxists and non-Marxists.[15]

Clearly influenced in his thought by the Italian Hegelian philosopher, Benedetto Croce, and the Italian Marxist, Antonio Labriola, Gramsci (1891–1937) was also influenced by Lenin.[16] However, while Gramsci truly admired Lenin and the example of the Soviet Revolution, he did not merely adapt "Leninism" to the Italian context. Rather, he produced significant and original thought which effectively broke with Lenin on a variety of important and politically-consequential issues.[17] We find in Gramsci's thought a return to Marx's understanding of the inherent creativity of the working-class-in-struggle, but without the assumption that the working class, simply "on its own," can necessarily bring about the changes and developments leading to socialism. At the same time, influenced by Lenin, Gramsci insists on the importance of intellectuals and a "leadership" role for a strongly organized party, but, significantly, and quite the contrary to Lenin, he does not (mistakenly) "privilege" either intellectuals or the party with being either the originators of socialism or the bearers of "true" consciousness and/or "real" interests.

To appreciate Gramsci's argument we need to consider his theory of hegemony and contradictory consciousness. He developed this theory in the course of confronting the historical problem that in Western Europe socialist revolutions had either failed to occur, as in England and France, or were aborted, as in Germany and Italy, though it appeared that all the politico-economic developments necessary for such revolutions existed. It was his assertion that in the West, unlike Russia, ruling-class domination was more extensive and deeper, being both politico-economic *and* politico-cultural, i.e., exercised both through the state and what he referred to as "civil society." Thus, while class struggle had not ceased, for periods of time it was effectively limited, or contained, by the establishment of hegemony, or better, a hegemonic process. Hegemony can be understood as a process in which the lower classes both conform and consent to the given social order—the degree of consent being the essential variable—but not necessarily just on the ruling class' terms. Gramsci himself defines it as "spontaneous consent given by the great masses of the population to the general direction imposed on social life by the dominant fundamental group, consent 'historically' caused by the prestige (and, therefore, by the trust) accruing to the dominant group because of its position and function in the world of production"; adding, elsewhere, that "The fact of hegemony undoubtedly presupposes that account be taken of the interests . . . of the groups over which hegemony is to be exercised, . . . that the leading group make sacrifices."[18]

To be clear about this, Gramsci's "hegemony" is not to be equated with the idea of a "common culture" as in Parsons's consensus theory; nor with the idea of a "dominant ideology being internalized and thus becoming the ideology of the dominated"; nor with the derivative Leninist and Lukácsian concepts of "inadequate" consciousness and "false" consciousness.[19] Again, neither does it refer to the cessation of class antagonism, tension, or conflict. Rather, I would contend, it refers to an *order of struggle,* that is, an order which is constantly being disputed and negotiated, but does not break down into (or through to) revolutionary conflict, nor entail the continuous use of physical force or coercion by the state (or similar authority) to maintain the social order. As the American historian, Eugene Genovese, put it: "Hegemony implies class struggles and has no meaning apart from them. . . . It has nothing in common with consensus history and represents its antithesis—a way of defining the historical content of class struggle during times of apparent social quiescence."[20]

At the same time, by hegemony Gramsci does not mean that consciousness is unaffected. Rather, he offers the concept of "contradictory consciousness," which, as Joseph Femia notes, starts from the fact that there may often be "incompatibility between a man's conscious thought and the unconscious values implicit in his action."[21] Gramsci asks: "is it not frequently the case that there is a contradiction between one's intellectual choice and one's mode of conduct?"; leading into the question: "which therefore would be the real conception of the world: that logically affirmed as an intellectual choice? or that which emerges from the real activity of each man, which is implicit in his mode of action?"[22] Moreover (possessing important implications for political action), Gramsci asserts:

the contrast between thought and action cannot but be the expression of profounder contrasts of a social historical order. It signifies that the social group in question may indeed have its own conception of the world, even if only embryonic; a conception which manifests itself in action, but occasionally and in flashes—when, that is, the group is acting as an organic totality. But this same group has for reasons of submission and intellectual subordination, adopted a conception which is not its own but is borrowed from another group.

Thus, contradictory consciousness and its consequences are described:

The active man-in-the-mass has a practical activity, but has no clear theoretical consciousness of his practical activity, which nonetheless involves understanding the world insofar as it transforms it. His theoretical consciousness can indeed be historically in opposition to his activity. One might almost say that he has two theoretical consciousnesses (or one contradictory consciousness): one which is implicit in his activity and which in reality unites him with all his fellow-workers in the practical transformation of the real world; and one, superficially explicit or verbal, which he has inherited from the past and uncritically absorbed. But this verbal conception is not without consequences. It holds together a specific social group, it influences moral conduct and the direction of will, with varying efficacy but often powerfully enough to produce a situation in which the contradictory state of consciousness does not permit of any action, any decision or any choice, and produces a condition of moral and political passivity.[23]

The task for socialist intellectuals in these terms becomes *not* one of supplying "true" consciousness or "real" interests *to* workers, but rather of making manifest or, better, explicit that which exists latently, or implicitly in experience, activity *and* consciousness. Gramsci proffers: "First . . . it must be a criticism of 'common sense,' basing itself initially, however, on common sense in order to demonstrate that 'everyone' is a philosopher and that it is not a question of introducing from scratch a scientific form of thought into everyone's individual life, but of renovating and making 'critical' an already existing activity." Nor is this a one-sided process, for as Gramsci continues: "It must then be a criticism of the philosophy of the intellectuals out of which the history of philosophy developed and which, insofar as it is a phenomenon of individuals . . . can be considered as marking the 'high points' of the progress made by common sense, or at least the common sense of the more educated strata of society but through them also of the people."[24] In other words, the relationship is dialectical, and the making of critical consciousness develops out of that dialectic. Furthermore, the "socialist future" is not constructed merely in the studies of philosophers or social scientists, but in "embryonic" form in the activities, practices, consciousness, and struggles of working people, which socialist intellectuals are to develop dialogically into a program of action and an alternative and oppositional hegemony.[25]

I would contend that though Gramsci by no means resolves all the problems of radical political action, his historical and political vision provides one means by which authoritarianism and a bureaucratic state might be avoided in favor of a democratic socialism. In his conception of revolutionary change, the development of an alternative social order begins *prior* to the *climactic* political act, the "overthrow" of the capitalist state. Moreover, socialist intellectuals and "the party," however essential their "leadership" roles, are themselves understood as dependent, not just on the existence of the working class, but on workers' experiences, practices, values, and "ideas."

Arguably, Gramsci's commitment to history was a crucial determinant of the originality in his political thought. Indeed, no Marxist or, for that matter, any other political theorist placed more importance, more emphasis, on historical study and thought as the foundation, the grounding, for thinking and deliberation about human affairs than did Gramsci. A student of linguistics at the University of Turin (1911–14) and, thereafter, a journalist and socialist and communist political activist before his arrest and imprisonment by Mussolini's Fascist regime (1926–37), Gramsci was not himself a historian "of the archives." Nevertheless, his writings consistently express a direct interest in the past *and* in both its relation to the present and its implications for the making of the future. Over and over again his criticism of the ideas and arguments of other writers and intellectuals, both Right and Left, both those he despised and those he respected, had to do with their inadequate attention to history and the resulting ahistorical or, in many instances, antihistorical character of their formulations and propositions. This was unacceptable. For Gramsci the very "nature of man is history." In all areas, and at all levels of analysis, historical investigation and consideration are imperative: "It is not enough to know the *ensemble* of relations as they exist at any given time as a given system. They must be known genetically, in the movement of their formation. For each individual is the synthesis not only of existing relations, but of the history of these relations. He is a precis of all the past."[26]

A truly historical approach to past and present, Gramsci insisted, would provide the basis for a critical perspective on the contemporary world. It would serve to demonstrate, and remind of, the *historicity* of human experience; that is, it would not only register that the way things are is not the way they have always been, but, also, contribute to the demystification of the present order and the rule of capital by revealing the forgotten and obscured or suppressed *social* origins of the structures, relations, and practices perceived and assumed to be natural—or divinely ordained—and, therefore, inevitable. In these terms, Gramsci challenged the practices and pronouncements of philosophers: "Philosophy cannot be separated from the history of philosophy, nor can culture be separated from the history of culture. . . . one cannot be a philosopher . . . without having a consciousness of its historicity"; and, also, those of economists: "The critique of political economy starts from the concept of the historical character of the 'determined market' and of its 'automatism,' whereas pure economists conceive of these elements as 'eternal' and 'natural.' " Thus, however much he appreciated Croce's contributions, and garnered insights from his philosophy which he was to turn against the crude and economistic Marxists of the Second International, Gramsci found the Hegelian's "speculative history" and "historicism" insufficiently *historical*. And, in another direction, Gramsci did not hesitate to criticize (at length) and reject the work of the Soviet Marxist Nikolai Bukharin, *The Theory of Historical Materialism: A Popular Manual of Marxist Sociology* (1921), as "dogma": "It has been forgotten that in the case of a very common expression [historical materialism] one should put the accent on the first term—'historical'—and not on the second, which is of metaphysical origin. The philosophy of praxis is absolute 'historicism.' " Against Croceans, vulgar Marxists, and, of course, "Nietzschean charlatans" he would state simply: "The problem is precisely that of seeing things historically."[27]

Confronting his imprisonment and realizing the impossibility of his continued participation in the *making* of history, Gramsci determined that he would take up all-the-more-energetically the study and writing of history. Clearly arising from the need to maintain his intellectual spirit and mental health, though seemingly overambitious in view of his circumstances, he wrote to his family in 1927 from a jail in Milan that he planned to pursue four major scholarly projects. The first of these was to do "research on the history of Italian intellectuals" and to connect it to a related project on which he had already written, "the Southern Question," that is, the development and underdevelopment of Southern Italy and "the importance of B. Croce."[28]

Even if he did not "write history" as the activity is commonly understood, Gramsci's *Prison Notebooks* and *Letters from Prison* are monuments of erudition and classics of historical thought and reflection, most especially regarding Italian and European politics and culture. And, as he himself said of Marx, it is arguable that Gramsci can be seen at his best in his most concrete studies. Moreover, although (obviously) kept from the archives and restricted as to the "library" he was able to accumulate, Gramsci's notebooks not only bear witness to his historical imagination, but proffer valuable historiographical suggestions and attest to the contributions he might have been able to make to the discipline. For example, more than three decades before the late sixties explosion of social history, Gramsci was calling for both a *socialization* and a *democratization* of the study of the past. First, he proposed a more "sociological" approach to political and cultural history:

> From our point of view, studying the history and the logic of the various philosophers' philosophies is not enough. At least as a methodological guideline, attention should be drawn to the other parts of the history of philosophy; to the conceptions of the world held by the great masses, to those of the most restricted ruling or intellectual groups, and finally to the links between these various cultural complexes and the philosophy of the philosophers.[29]

"Democratization" refers, first, to Gramsci's demand for the writing of the "history of the subaltern classes"—the experience, struggles, and aspirations of workers and peasants and their contributions to the making of history. In this vein we should recall the beautiful words Gramsci wrote to his son not long before his death in 1937:

> I think you must like history as I did when I was your age, because it deals with living men, and everything that concerns men, as many men as possible, all the men in the world in so far as they unite together in society, and work and struggle and make a bid for a better life, all that can't fail to please you more than anything else. Isn't that right?[30]

He fully appreciated the difficulties involved in commencing such studies, the nature and authorship of the historical records and the very paucity of them. For these reasons he urged the creation of appropriate archives, the initiation of monographic studies, and the exercise of sympathetic but critical objectivity when pursuing such research.

Yet, as he made clear, a more democratic historical practice also had to involve expanding historical pedagogy. Knowledge of past and present was not to be pursued to broaden the horizons and/or better inform the traditionally educated elites, nor merely to sensitize socialist intellectuals to the persistent and manifold forms of lower class movement and agency. Historical knowledge—both that of "high" culture and politics and that produced by the "new history" he was urging—were to be a part of the education of working people.

> If it is true that universal history is a chain made up of the efforts man has exerted to free himself from privilege, prejudice and idolatry, then it is hard to understand why the proletariat, which seeks to add another link to that chain, should not know how and why

and by whom it was preceded, or what advantage it might derive from this knowledge.[31]

It seems most appropriate that the increasing recognition of Gramsci's work in English-speaking countries has been due to the efforts of historians in particular, the British Marxist historians included—if not especially.[32]

The Historians: The People, Conflict, and Ideas

> Sometimes those who were defeated have made as great a contribution to the
> ultimate result as have the victors.
> —E. H. Carr, *What is History?*[33]

The British Marxist historians have come to be recognized as a "school of history" (in a fashion similar to the *Annales* historians in France).[34] This is only appropriate, for they share common historical and theoretical problematics. Their common *historical* problematic has been the transition from feudalism to capitalism, the contemporary framework for which was provided by Maurice Dobb in *Studies in the Development of Capitalism*. Its publication instigated the now-famous "transition debate" of the late 1940s and 1950s, which continues even today by way of the work of Immanuel Wallerstein, Robert Brenner, and Perry Anderson (among others).[35]

The *theoretical* problematic of the British Marxist historians was well indicated in the transition debate. Against economistic and culturalist approaches, they argued that the transition had to be understood in terms of the historically-specific class conflicts and struggles of late medieval and early modern England. Moreover, as Hilton argued most forcefully, the central conflict was between feudal lords and peasants, not lords and urban merchants or petty capitalists. Essentially, the central hypothesis which has guided the work of the British Marxist historians is the proposition offered by Marx in *The Communist Manifesto* that "The history of all hitherto existing societies is the history of class struggle." Thus, the approach to historical study of Dobb, et al., might best be termed *class-struggle analysis,* and in this way they have developed Marxism as a *theory of class determination.*

Very much a part of their class-struggle analysis of history, the British Marxist historians have also made important contributions to the development of the historical perspective known as "history from below," or with particular reference to their own writings, history "from the bottom up." They have taken seriously the historical experiences, actions, and struggles of the lower classes, recovering the past which was *made* by them but was not *written* by them: Hilton and Hobsbawm on peasants; Hill, Rudé, and Thompson on the "common people"; and Hobsbawm and Thompson on the working class.[36]

Though they never established a school or research institute, as did the

Annales historians in France, the British Marxist historians did work together from 1946 to 1956 as members of the Communist Party Historians' Group.[37] However, along with so many others, Hilton, Hill, and Thompson left the Party in 1956–57 in reaction to the Soviet invasion of Hungary. (Hobsbawm stayed in and has remained a Party member to this day.) Nevertheless, together these historians founded and were central figures in the development of the journal, *Past & Present,* which is today considered one of the leading journals of social history.

A relationship between the work of the historians and Gramsci's thought has been referred to by various writers[38] and acknowledged by the historians themselves. For example, in one of the first articles on Gramsci in English, Christopher Hill referred to Gramsci as the "greatest Marxist thinker in Western Europe. Above all he is a fresh and stimulating thinker."[39] Hill discusses several aspects of Gramsci's thought, but focuses on Gramsci's original ideas regarding the relationship between intellectuals and the working classes. He then concludes with a reference to Gramsci's concern for historical education and consciousness. Also (as I will discuss at greater length in chapter 3), Victor Kiernan has written similarly appreciative, though much more fully developed, essays on Gramsci. These deal with Gramsci's unique development of Marxism; the relevance of his writings to international studies and the problem of development and underdevelopment; and the nature of Gramsci's vision of socialism. (Indeed, I would argue that the last of these, "The Socialism of Antonio Gramsci," is the most beautifully written introduction to, and appreciation of, Gramsci as socialist humanist available.)[40]

Eric Hobsbawm, often referred to as the premier Marxist historian today for his work in such areas as labor and working-class history, peasant studies, and modern world history, has also been much involved with Gramsci's writings and ideas. In two essays written in the 1970s, Hobsbawm argues that Gramsci "pioneered a Marxist theory of politics."[41] Also of interest is Hobsbawm's recollection that his now-classic book, *Primitive Rebels,* was much influenced by a reading of Gramsci on "non-political protest movements."[42] Finally, it should be noted that Hobsbawm has made use of the concept of "hegemony" in his discussion of European social order in *The Age of Capital, 1848–1875,* the second part of his three volume history of the nineteenth century. In brief, he describes the period as involving

the massive advance of the world economy of industrial capitalism, of the social order it represented, of the ideas and beliefs which seemed to legitimatise and ratify it: in reason, science, progress and liberalism. It is the era of the triumphant bourgeois, though the European bourgeoisie still hesitated to commit itself to public political rule. To this—and perhaps only to this—extent the age of revolution was not dead. The middle classes of Europe were frightened and remained frightened of the people: "democracy" was still believed to be the certain and rapid prelude to "socialism."[43]

(Before proceeding, it should be noted that Eric Hobsbawm has said that "frankly, if Gramsci had not invented this particular term [hegemony] . . . we would have written much the same, except we would have called it something else").[44]

E. P. Thompson's writings, too, include discussions of Gramsci's thought. First, his often-cited exchange with Perry Anderson (and Tom Nairn)[45] in the mid-1960s involved argument over the way(s)in which "hegemony" might be used in historical and social analysis. In his essay, "Origins of the Present Crisis," Anderson sought to sketch out a framework for a "totalising history . . . of modern British society" focusing on "the global evolution of the class structure." Essentially, Anderson argues that Britain's crisis and the crisis of the labor movement can be traced back to the English Revolution of the seventeenth century in which, according to him, the "economic structure" was transformed, but not the "social structure or superstructure," and which, due to its religious and "pre-Enlightenment" character, left no significant ideological legacy. Furthermore, Anderson argues, the intact social structure meant the continued domination of the (feudal) landed aristocracy which, for a variety of historical reasons, was later able to merge, as the senior partner, with the rising industrial bourgeoisie, and thus continue to shape British life. Because the proletariat's most heroic struggles against capitalism occurred before the "adequate" development of socialist (i.e., Marxist) theory, "it evolved separately but subordinate, within the apparently unshakeable structure of British capitalism." Thus, "a supine bourgeoisie produced a supine proletariat."[46] Anderson describes this historical development in terms of what he contends is Gramsci's conception of hegemony, but (without going into detail) his understanding of hegemony is only vaguely Gramscian. That is, he presents the hegemonic process as *total*—both politically and culturally—and fails to recognize that it is a process of continuous conflict and struggle.

Thompson's reply to Anderson, "The Peculiarities of the English," is both historical and theoretical in form. But his criticisms of Anderson's use of "hegemony" is a mostly semantic dispute. He does not directly challenge Anderson's version of what a hegemonic process entails. Later, however, in the course of developing an alternative interpretation of eighteenth-century English society to that which conceives it as a period of consensus and stability, Thompson does present a picture of gentry–common people relations which clearly makes use of a well-developed Gramscian concept of hegemony.[47] That is, by hegemony, Thompson does *not* mean consensus: "Hegemony does not entail [at least not in the eighteenth century, he says] any acceptance by the poor of the gentry's paternalism upon the gentry's own terms or in their approved self-image." Rather, he means, as stated earlier, an "order of struggle." In eighteenth-century England, Thompson asserts, there was a robust plebeian culture greatly distanced from the patrician culture and its conception of social order—sometimes resisting or even opposing it, sometimes accommodated to it—but, nevertheless, operating within its limits. The maintenance of the hegemonic order, then, was no simple process, especially following on the upheavals and changes of the seventeenth century.[48]

Perhaps most interesting of the works of the British Marxist historians in relation to Gramsci's ideas, however, are those writings of Hilton, Hill, and Thompson in which they take up most directly the problem of class formation: specifically, Hilton's discussion of the Peasant Rising of 1381; Hill's work, especially on the "middle sort" among the common people of seventeenth-century England, but also that on the "lower orders"; and Thompson's *The Making of the English Working Class*.[49]

Rodney Hilton is the British Marxist who has most actively pursued the study of medieval history and the feudal mode of production, focusing in particular on the historical experience of the English peasantry. His many writings have made important contributions to the reconceptualization of feudalism, not as a stable and static social order, but as one of contradiction, struggle and movement. Along with Marc Bloch, M. M. Postan, and George Duby, Hilton has revealed the class-structured character of medieval life and the ideological nature of viewing medieval social order in terms of estates or orders.[50] But he has gone on to show that feudal Europe was not only a class-divided society but one of class-struggle. Moreover, based on his analysis of lord–peasant relations as class struggles, and his conscious pursuit and development of history from the bottom up, Hilton has actively and effectively confronted the "enduring myth of the passive peasantry."[51]

This confrontation is evidenced in all of his writings, but most especially in his book, *Bond Men Made Free: Medieval Peasant Movements and the English Rising of 1381*.[52] The significance of Hilton's work is not just that he has indicated the historical and geographical extensiveness of the occurrence of medieval peasant movements to the feudal social structure as opposed to being the product of crises. But rather, what has been significant in Hilton's work is that he shows that peasant movements as *class struggles* were consequential to medieval social change and development and, in their aims, both purposeful in the historically specific terms of the Middle Ages and significant as contributions to later historical periods and generations' struggles. Of course, to argue that they were consequential is not to assert that they were successful; but neither should the contrary assumption be made—as it so often has been—that because they were not necessarily successful they were, therefore, inconsequential. Furthermore, to argue that medieval peasant movements were consequential is not to imply that they were all of equal extent (in time or space), intensity, and importance. They varied historically in (dialectical) relation to the changing feudal society.

In *Bond Men Made Free*, Hilton examines the English Rising of 1381 in comparison to Continental peasant movements such as the Jacquerie of 1358, the Tuchin movement of the 1360s in France, and the fifteenth century wars of the *remensas* in Catalonia. Here he takes up the problem of class formation directly in his discussion and analysis of the *class consciousness* which emerged among the peasants in the midst of these peasant struggles. He observes that the continental peasant movements evidenced the existence of "negative class consciousness," a "bitter hatred of the landowning nobility, sometimes even of all the rich or well-to-do." But in the English Rising of 1381 (often called the Peasant's Revolt) there emerged a "positive class consciousness," that is, there developed a recognition of the "mutual interests of peasants and other basic producers."[53]

Chief among the demands put forth by the rebels at Mile End and Smithfield in June 1381 was the abolition of serfdom. But there was also a demand made for the elimination of all peasant obligations to landowners, both monetary and personal. Moreover, there were not only immediate demands. The movement also seems to have possessed a "long-term programme of political action" involving a conception of an alternative society and how to achieve it. As Hilton presents it, the peasants and their allies envisioned a "popular monarchy." In such a state, there would be no hierarchy or social classes standing between the people and their king. In other words, there would be no feudal ruling class owning lands and controlling law and administration. In fact, Hilton notes, some of the rebels had in mind to establish county regional monarchies rather than a single monarchy with a king distant from the people. The making of laws and the administration of justice were somehow to be taken care of by the people. The church was to be reorganized in a similar fashion. There was to be "a people's church whose basic unit would be the parish, again with no intermediate hierarchy between Christians and the single bishop or archbishop who, as head of the church, was the ecclesiastical equivalent of the people's king." Thus, the rebels sought freedom and equality (at least in political terms). Though some things were to be held in common, they appear to have imagined "a regime of family ownership of peasant holdings and artisan workshops, with the large scale landed property of the church and the aristocracy divided among the peasants."[54]

The rising failed to bring about the popular and egalitarian monarchy, but it was consequential. Though it did not succeed in ending landlordism, it seems to have been the rising which forced an end to the post–black death feudal reaction. Moreover, it contributed, along with the struggles which continued after it, to the decline of the feudal-seigneurial regime in England and, thereby, "help[ed] the development of agrarian capitalism. And from this, in turn, industrial capitalism sprang."[55]

Perhaps the most radical assertion which Hilton makes regarding the historical significance of the struggles of the medieval English peasantry concerns their contribution to later generations' struggles. If *equality* and *liberty,* or *freedom,* are at the core of the modern concept of individualism, then it is not to the bourgeoisie that we ought to attribute its origins. "The assertion of freedom against feudal subordination was not, as is often supposed, a specific contribution of the bourgeoisie," but rather, Hilton contends, it was the contribution "of the peasantry of the feudal era."[56] That is, "one of the most important if intangible legacies of medieval peasants to the modern world is the concept of the freeman, owing no obligation, not even deference to an overlord."[57]

Hilton's assertion of the development of a positive class consciousness among the peasants and artisans of late fourteenth-century England is a major act of historical reappropriation. It has not been uncommon for historians and others to view the aspirations of the movement as 'sermon-induced, hallucinatory, fantasies'. For example, as Norman Cohn writes of the 1381 Rising: ". . . fanatical *prophetae* mixed with disoriented and desperate masses on the very margin of society."[58] Hilton rejects such an interpretation. Seeming to confirm Gramsci's argument on the role of intellectuals—though in this case in a medieval social context—Hilton argues that the importance of John Ball and his fellow clerics was that they "seem to have re-inforced the peasant demands for freedom of status and tenure by a broader articulation of contemporary feelings." The *prophetae*—"poor priests, chaplains and parish clerks"—were, as Hilton states, the "medieval equivalent of the radical intelligentsia." Furthermore, he argues: "What is remarkable is the way that their vision of a society of free and equal men and women fused with the ancient peasant demand for freedom of status and tenure, in the formulation of a programme which, though entirely incapable of realisation, given the historical forces at work in the late middle ages, did challenge root and branch the ideas of the ruling class."[59]

Christopher Hill's domain has been seventeenth-century history, most centrally the English Revolution. Though quite varied, Hill's writings can be comprehended in terms of two major theses. The first is that the English Revolution was a "bourgeois revolution," and the second is that there was a "democratic revolution in the revolution" which occasionally threatened but never succeeded in happening. The former, which succeeded, "established the sacred rights of property (abolition of feudal tenures, no arbitrary taxation), gave political power to the propertied (sovereignty of Parliament and common law, abolition of prerogative courts), and removed all impediments to the triumph of the ideology of the men of property—the protestant ethic"; the latter, which did not, "might have established communal property, a far wider democracy in political and legal institutions, might have disestablished the state church and rejected the protestant ethic."[60]

Hill's numerous writings on the English Revolution as bourgeois revolution are often focused on what he terms the "middle" or "industrious sort of
people." This group, or middle class, was beneath the large landowning and
mercantile families, and above the "lower orders," or propertyless, who depended on wage labor and/or charity for their survival. It consisted of "most
merchants, richer artisans, the independent peasantry (yeomanry) and well-
to-do tenant farmers."[61] Hill pursues studies of the middle sort of people in
particular because it was this class (though not alone) that turned the Civil
War into a revolution. They did not start the Civil War, nor consciously will
that it would result in a social order conducive to the further development of
capitalism, but they turned that struggle into the English Revolution.

In these writings on the middle sort of people we can see the historical
perception and elaboration of Gramsci's assertion that "A human mass does
not 'distinguish' itself, does not become independent in its own right without, in the widest sense, organizing itself; and there is no organization without intellectuals."[62] Hill discusses this process as it developed in sixteenth-
and seventeenth-century England both in religion and secular intellectual
practices. In what is arguably his best book, *Society and Puritanism in Pre-
Revolutionary England,* Hill treats the body of doctrines and practices that
was labelled Puritanism and its appeal to the middle, or industrious, sort of
people. Especially significant in this context was the concern of the Puritan
middle sort over the appointment of preachers and lecturers in the local
churches, for this involved confrontation over a central institution (and its
practices) of ruling-class hegemony. As Hill explains:

> In the sixteenth and seventeenth centuries the Church had a mo-
> nopoly of thought-control and opinion-forming. It controlled edu-
> cation; it censored books. Until 1640 the publication of home news
> was prohibited; privately circulated newsletters were available to the
> rich, but were beyond the means of the poor. So in the absence of
> other media of communication, sermons were for the majority of
> Englishmen their main source of political information and political
> ideas. Men come to church for news. . . . The pulpit fulfilled indeed
> quite different functions from those which are expected of it today.
> In addition to disseminating news, sermons had replaced the con-
> fessional as a source of guidance on moral and economic conduct.
> Even an orthodox clergy man like Robert Sanderson used the pul-
> pit to denounce monopolies and the corruptions and excessive fees
> of the law courts. Nor should we forget the illiteracy of a large
> proportion of the population. For all except a favoured few the
> words of the parson, even when they were not accepted as gospel,
> necessarily formed the starting-point for discussion.[63]

In other words, "control of the pulpit was a question of political power"—which Charles I well expressed in words to his son, "People are governed by the pulpit more than the sword in times of peace."[64] The Puritan middle sort sought to appoint their own ministers—by election of the congregation!—and, thereby, also spread the gospel to the "dark corners of the land."[65] Thus, Hill observes, there was

> rivalry for control of the pulpit, as men came increasingly to want different doctrines preached. But attitudes towards preaching as such also came to diverge. The approach of the Puritans was simple. They wanted more preaching, as much more as possible, so as to carry the Gospel into all corners of the land, even the darkest, and to raise the educational and disciplinary level of all members of all congregations. Since salvation came through the Word, it could not be preached too much. "There is not a sermon which is heard, but it sets us nearer heaven or hell," said Preston confidently. Government and hierarchy saw things differently. They appreciated very clearly the explosive, anarchic possibilities of unlimited preaching: their emphasis was on control from above.[66]

We might say—in Gramscian terms—that the Puritans were involved in "counter-hegemonic" practices.

On the secular side of class formation and the ideas which appealed to the middle sort of people in this period, Hill's major study is *Intellectual Origins of the English Revolution*. In the introduction to the book he boldly states that "Whilst the intellectuals despaired and anatomised, whilst doctors prescribed elephant tusks as a remedy for melancholy, our merchants and artisans, confident in their ability to handle things, busy . . . modernising the institutions of their society, were in search of an ideology." Hill considers the development of the new ideas in, and new conceptions of, science, history and the law, and their contributions to the making of the English Revolution. He does so by focusing on the pivotal figures of the period in those areas: Francis Bacon, Walter Raleigh, and Edward Coke. Thus, for example, regarding Bacon's work, Hill argues that his essential contribution was to synthesize and systematize the practice and thought which had been developing during the sixteenth century in scientific and medical studies, with the very active support of the middle sort of people, especially in London around such alternative centers as Gresham College ("alternative," that is, to the conservative Oxbridge universities). Bacon emphasized the empirical and experimental approach to knowledge and, thereby, "elevated to a coherent intellectual system what had hitherto been only the partially spoken assumptions of practical men." In fact, "what he strengthened was a body of ideas which had pushed its way up from below." In this way, he "caught the optimism of the merchants and craftsmen, confident in their new-found ability to control their environment [after 1640 especially], including the social and political environment; and their contempt for the old scholasticism." Similarly, Raleigh, in respect to history and historical consciousness, and Coke, in his assertion of the primacy of common law and its elevation to the level of a national myth, synthesized and articulated ideas and perspectives which appealed and gave "confidence" to the middle sort of people: "All three provided ideas for the men who hitherto had existed only to be ruled, but who in the sixteen-forties would help to take over the government. Together with the Puritan sense of destiny and emphasis on self-help, they prepared men for revolution."[67]

Hill's writings on the English Revolution as a defeated democratic revolution have also involved discussions of the middle sort of people, but have increasingly focused on the "lower orders" of the common people and the radical religious groups. Not only has he written of the Levellers, who sought political democracy, but of the Diggers, who called for economic democracy (if not socialism or communism), and of the Seekers, Ranters, Muggletonians, etc., whose "politics" stressed cultural revolution. He stresses that they have too often been marginalized by historians who have been more interested in narrowly political or religious aspects of the seventeenth century. Hill has sought to show that the ideas articulated, fought for, and/or *practiced* by those groups were politically and culturally meaningful and consequential in seventeenth-century terms and that they contributed decisively to the making of modern history.[68]

Of special importance in this context are Hill's studies of the class-differential interpretation of ideas in seventeenth-century England, which demonstrate that culture and ideas, or ideologies, are not so one-dimensional as we have often thought, nor the common people, or lower classes as simple. As he puts it in *The World Turned Upside Down:*

> Something analogous [to the English Revolution] occurred during the French Revolution. Middle-class revolutionaries proclaimed the Rights of Man, and seem to have been genuinely taken aback when the Fourth Estate claimed that they too were men. The distinction between active and passive citizens fulfills the same function as that between godly and ungodly . . . both justification by faith and the Rights of Man suffer from the same inescapable contradiction: in order to give the not-yet privileged confidence to fight against the old-type of inequality it is necessary to appeal to that in them which unites them against the privileged: their common humanity, the equality before God of those who believe themselves to be elect.[69]

The work which Hill has gone on to pursue deals with the question of what happened to the radicals and their ideas following the revolutionary decades. His analysis of the revolutionary decades has already shown that, given the opportunity, lower-class expressions of grievances and visions of alternative social orders can be most articulate. Thus, it is quite possible that before 1640 and after 1660 the same sentiments are there but expressed in different ways, and in different places. The theoretical conclusion is that "we should not exclude the possibility that a class-dominated society may contain an egalitarian society struggling to get out; nor assume that the hegemony of one set of values excludes the possibility that other values exist, at a lower social level, or in the interstices, geographical or social, of an apparently homogeneous society."[70]

Edward Thompson has also explored the class-differential interpretation of ideas and the articulation of the practices, values, and ideas of the "common people" by "intellectuals" in his celebrated work, *The Making of the English Working Class*.[71] The book is a study of the formation of the working class in England from 1790 through to the early 1830s and the coming to consciousness of that class, culminating in Chartism—the first working-class political party.[72] In what has become the manifesto for historical studies from the bottom up, Thompson states one of his intentions in writing the book:

> I am seeking to rescue the poor stockinger, the Luddite cropper, the "obsolete" hand-loom weaver, the "utopian" artisan, and even the deluded follower of Joanna Southcott, from the enormous condescension of posterity. Their crafts and traditions may have been backward-looking. Their communitarian ideals may have been fantasies. Their insurrectionary conspiracies may have been foolhardy. But they lived through these times of acute social disturbance, and we did not. Their aspirations were valid in terms of their own experience; and if they were casualties of history, they remain, condemned in their own lives, as casualties.[73]

At the same time, Thompson makes known what he opposes. He expresses hostility towards other historians, economists and sociologists regarding their treatment of the problems of class and class formation. That is, he criticizes the tendency of so many social scientists to treat class as merely a structure or category and the related tendency of economic and social historians "to obscure the *agency* of working people [and] the degree to which they contributed by conscious efforts, to the making of history."[74] He also points out the "political" character of the work, for he states that he has written it in opposition to the Old Left assumption that the working class has a real existence—objectively defined—from which one can "deduce the class-consciousness which 'it' ought to have (but seldom does) if 'it' was properly aware of its own position and interests," and the proposition which follows, that a "party, sect, or theorist," is needed who can furnish the consciousness "not as it is, but as it ought to be." And he also writes in opposition to the New Left view of the working class as "irretrievably co-opted, economically and/or ideologically, by capital," which produces its own variation of substitutionism, i.e., intellectuals and/or students standing in for class-conscious workers. In both cases, Thompson argues, what is lacking is a sense of history and a proper understanding of class struggle.[75]

Thompson's research for *The Making of the English Working Class* produced a quite different conception of class struggle and formation, especially regarding the role of intellectuals. Like Hilton and Hill, Thompson presents a historical interpretation which is most supportive of Gramsci's thought. We can see this in his analysis of the tradition of the "free-born Englishman" and the historic role of Tom Paine. In the late eighteenth century, he explains, this tradition involved, in spite of the continuing limitations placed on "freedom of the press, of public meeting, of trade union . . . [and] political organization, and of election," a birthright of liberties: "Freedom from absolutism . . . freedom from arbitrary arrest, trial by jury, equality before the law, the freedom of the home from arbitrary entrance and search, some limited liberty of thought, of speech, and of conscience." As a result of their being persistently asserted, contested, and reasserted, they became part of a moral consensus which, Thompson says, should not be underestimated. He discusses this moral consensus as if it were a map of a liberated territory. Its boundaries denote the area in which the English people were unwilling to tolerate interference or transgression by the authorities. He states that the worldview of the common people was not necessarily democratic, in any positive sense, but it was "anti-absolutist." They saw themselves as individualists, with few affirmative rights, yet nevertheless secured by the laws against the intrusion of arbitrary power.[76]

It was Tom Paine who best articulated this tradition, and he did so in a new and radically significant fashion. Yet, Thompson contends, the significance of the ideas set forth in *The Rights of Man* (Paine's extremely popular reply to Edmund Burke's *Reflections on the Revolution in France*) was not so much in their originality, which was limited, but in their articulation and reshaping of the ideas, attitudes, and assumptions of the existing "ideology" of the "free-born Englishman." Paine provided a "new rhetoric of radical egalitarianism, which touched the deepest responses of the 'free-born Englishman' and which penetrated the sub-political attitudes of the urban working people." The arguments of *Rights of Man* broke through the categories and conventions of constitutionalism which had structured the moral consensus and set forth far wider economic claims that were so necessary for the emergence of a labor movement.[77]

Later, Thompson shows how this radical tradition of the 1790s had to go underground in the repression of the early years of the nineteenth century but was nourished in complex and (sometimes) contradictory ways in Luddism (machine breaking) and Methodism. Moreover, he details how this tradition articulated by Paine was continually developed and propagated by "artisan-intellectuals" and thus re-emerged in the 1820s as a central idea of the developing working-class consciousness and culture.[78] The conclusion one is led to by *The Making of the English Working Class* is that the consciousness of the English working class was formed in the process of class struggle and through the creation of a dialectical relationship between working people and "intellectuals." And, furthermore, one is led to conclude that the political expression of that consciousness, in Chartism, whether or not it was specifically "socialist," cannot be reduced to "trade union" consciousness.[79]

Finally, we should note George Rudé's work of synthesis, *Ideology and Popular Protest* (to be discussed more fully in the next chapter).[80] In the book— based in great part on the work of Hilton, Hill, Hobsbawm, and Thompson, as well as his own studies of eighteenth and early nineteenth-century England and France—Rudé has presented a "Gramscian" analysis of rebellion and revolution in "pre-industrial" Europe and the Americas. Essentially, Rudé argues that such political struggles have depended on, in addition to "historical circumstances and experience," the "intersection" of the "inherent ideas of the people" and the "derived ideas of the intellectuals," themselves historically related.[81]

In the light of the past . . .

> A historically-minded generation is one which looks back, not indeed for the
> solutions which cannot be found in the past, but for those critical insights which are
> necessary both to the understanding of its existing situation and to the realization of
> the values which it holds.
> —E. H. Carr, *The New Society*[82]

The historical writings of the British Marxist historians—Hilton, Hill, and Thompson—relate the struggles of fourteenth-century peasants and their allies, seventeenth-century common people, and artisans and laborers of the early industrial revolution, to remake their respective Englands according to their historically-specific understandings of liberty, equality, and community. We have seen that these historians have thereby provided historical confirmation of the theory of class formation and the derived political theory offered by Antonio Gramsci. However, this should not be construed as an argument that the British Marxist historians are therefore specifically "strategists" of socialist politics.

As I contend in *The British Marxist Historians*,[83] it is true that these historians have been practicing a particular political strategy; that is, by their historical writings they have been contributing to the making of a democratic and socialist historical consciousness. But, as the above statement by E. H. Carr warns, historical knowledge cannot tell us what to do *now, specifically*— for at best, knowledge of the past is a counsel, not a scientific proof. It has also probably been observed that the popular struggles of which the historians have written did not succeed in "turning the world upside down," and Antonio Gramsci died in a Fascist prison.[84] To put it mildly, these are grounds for serious reservations.

And yet, in the midst of the contemporary crisis and reappraisal of socialism—in which Soviet regimes have testified to the horrors and dangers of socialism without democracy, and capitalist states bear witness to the persistence of democracy without socialism but, also, to the persistent threat of fascism—the works of the historians and the critical reflections of Gramsci do speak to us. They tell us that in spite of the oppression, alienation, and exploitation of feudalism, capitalism, and (so-called) socialism, the subordinated are not reduced to the level suggested in the works of such diverse figures as Lenin, Marcuse, and Althusser. In other words, people are not dupes and, thus, the task of radical-democratic and socialist intellectuals is not to bring "true" consciousness or a "scientifically-correct understanding" to working people, but rather to assist in the process of making more coherent and articulate that which exists in "embryonic fashion."

I admit that this may seem populist, idealist, romantic, and even utopian. But historical experience increasingly confirms my beliefs that, first, it is preferable to live in a democracy without socialism than a socialism without democracy, and second, that the necessary *making of socialist democracy* requires a *democratic* socialist practice.

2

GEORGE RUDÉ,
ALL HISTORY MUST BE
STUDIED AFRESH

George Rudé has been referred to as the "exiled doyen of our social historians."[1] "Exiled" denotes the fact that he spent almost his entire university
teaching career not in Britain, but in Australia and Canada. "Doyen" addresses his original contributions to the field of social history over four decades and the influence which they have had on the development of the discipline. The contributions include: his pioneering researches into the history
and sociology of the "pre-industrial crowd," which resulted in such innovative and renowned works as *The Crowd in the French Revolution, Wilkes and
Liberty, The Crowd in History, 1730–1848,* and *Paris and London in the Eighteenth Century;*[2] his masterful syntheses of eighteenth-century history, like
Revolutionary Europe, 1783–1815 and *Europe in the Eighteenth Century;*[3] and,
through these and other books such as *Captain Swing* (co-authored with Eric
Hobsbawm), *Protest and Punishment,* and *Criminal and Victim,*[4] his fundamental initiatives and regularly renewed efforts in the development of the
approach to the study of the past known as "history from below" or "the
bottom up."[5] Moreover, regarding the making of history from below, not
only did Rudé's work on the experience and struggles of the common people
of eighteenth-century France and England serve as a model for social historians, but, as will be explained later, it provided an important link between
two of the great historical traditions of this century, the "British Marxist
historians" and the social historians of the French Revolution.

This chapter offers an introduction to Rudé's work as a Marxist social historian. In all, he has written fourteen books, edited two others, and authored
numerous articles, essays, and reviews.[6] These many writings are quite varied
(as partially indicated by the aforementioned titles); nevertheless, in spite of
the many historical subjects pursued, there are certain historical and theoretical concerns which have persisted through the course of Rudé's scholarly
career. Thus, rather than attempt to survey his work in geographic, chrono-

logical, or subject-specific terms, the present essay will consider it in terms of the three themes which have characterized and shaped it: identities, ideologies, and histories.[7] "Identities" refers to Rudé's pursuit of "the faces in the crowd," which can be seen as the central problematic not only of his early explorations of the so-called "mob" of the eighteenth century, but equally of his studies of the English agricultural labourers' struggles of the early 1830s and his later writings on crime, protest, and punishment in the first half of the nineteenth century. "Ideologies" refers to his persistent endeavor to "put mind back into history," originating in his early writings as attempts to answer the question of the "motivation" of the eighteenth-century crowd, but later shifting to a concern for the "ideology of popular protest." And "histories" treats his continuing interest in making sense of the "movement" of history in terms of both comprehending historical periods like "revolutionary Europe" and the "transitional," "pre-industrial" eighteenth century, and understanding the role of human action in such periods, as in his book, *Robespierre;*[8] and it also refers to his own critical thinking about historical practice and its relations to both "politics" and "theory." Thus, following a brief biographical sketch, this chapter is organized in terms of those three themes.

George Rudé

George Frederick Elliot Rudé[9] was born on February 8, 1910 in Oslo, Norway. His father, Jens, was an engineer and "inventor," and his mother, Amy, was the daughter of an English banker. They lived in Norway until 1919 when they moved to England. His father's work as an inventor produced little money, but they did have a small income provided by his mother's family inheritance. Nevertheless, Rudé's education consisted of prep school in Kent, public school at Shrewsbury on a scholarship, and a degree in modern languages at Trinity College, Cambridge. Upon graduating in 1931 he took up a post as a modern languages master at Stow.

Rudé's upbringing and political education must be described as "conservative"; he was not a part of the generation of Cambridge Communists centered around Trinity in the 1930s.[10] However, in 1932, on a six-week vacation trip to the Soviet Union with a friend, Rudé was so impressed with what he found there that he returned to England a "committed communist and anti-fascist." During the next few years he immersed himself in the Marxist classics and in 1935 he joined the British Communist Party. He left Stow soon after and moved to London, intending to work in industry as an organizer for the Party; and though he did work actively with the Party through the 1930s, he did not end up in industry but, once again, in schoolteaching at St. Paul's in London. It was also in these years that he met Doreen de la Hoyde, to whom he has been married ever since.

During the Second World War, Rudé worked full-time for the London fire service and also remained extremely active with the Party. At the same time he began to study part-time for a first degree in history at the University of London. He has said that his interest in history was kindled by his readings of Marx and Lenin. His commitment to historical studies continued to intensify and grow, and upon receiving the B.A. he went on to complete a Ph.D. at London with a dissertation titled "The Parisian Wage-earning Population and the Insurrectionary Movements of 1789–1791" (1950). These were difficult times for George and Doreen Rudé, for he had lost his teaching post in 1949 for politically-related reasons, and the chill of the Cold War kept him out of university posts. Nevertheless, he persevered in his researches, first in Paris and later in London, and was eventually able to secure a full-time history post at a comprehensive school in north London.

Although financially difficult, these years were formative both for Rudé's scholarship and for the contributions he was to make to social historiography. Indeed, it is arguable that these were *the* formative years in the making—or *re*making—of social history, and Rudé himself was a central participant in two of the "groups" fomenting this "from the bottom up." On one side of the English Channel were the British Marxist historians, Hilton et al., who, during the years 1946–56 were joined together in the Communist Party Historians' Group, of which Rudé was a most active member; on the other side of the Channel were the "students" of the French Revolution, working under the direction, or influence, of Georges Lefebvre.

As I have argued, each of the British Marxist historians was to make outstanding individual contributions to his or her respective domain of historical study, but, also, as a group, they were to make important collective contributions to the discipline of social history and historical-social theory more generally. Framed historically by the question of the "transition from feudalism to capitalism" and theoretically by the grand hypothesis offered by Marx and Engels in *The Communist Manifesto* that "The history of all hitherto existing society is the history of class struggles," their studies—from the medieval to the modern—have been among the most important in the development both of history from below and of Marxism as a theory of class determination.[11]

Rudé's work has clearly been bound up with these initiatives and developments, but a few points should be noted here which will be considered further in the course of this essay. First, although *class-struggle analysis* has been a central feature of Rudé's readings and renditions of the historical record, it appears that he has been less willing than his fellow British Marxist historians to read "class" experience and formation in his subjects than they have in theirs. Second, although Rudé's view of the eighteenth century—in both England and France—is shaped by the question of the transition from feudalism to capitalism, and he has himself addressed it,[12] his own work indicates reservations about extant formulations of that process and more often has been rendered in terms of the ensuing process of industrialization. Yet, if Rudé's writings evidence a certain reticence about both class and the transition question, they do not regarding the need to re-examine the past *from below,* and in this effort he has been a foremost protagonist.

It is also noteworthy that Rudé himself made a unique and significant contribution to the historical explorations and deliberations carried out by the Historians' Group. Organized into "period sections," the Group's two major sections were those focusing on the sixteenth through seventeenth centuries, and the nineteenth century; however, there was a serious gap in the Group's coverage between the period of the English Revolution and that of the Industrial Revolution. As Eric Hobsbawm recalls, "[the eighteenth century was] a no man's land between the Group's two most flourishing sections, we simply had nobody who knew much about it, until George Rudé, a lone explorer, ventured into the period of John Wilkes."[13]

Although in my own work I have stressed and celebrated the contributions of the British Marxist historians to the making of history from below, Rudé's own experience reminds us that they were not alone in this effort. Pursuing his research on popular insurrections in Paris during the French Revolution brought Rudé into contact with Georges Lefebvre, who took a special interest in his work, and, also, with Albert Soboul and Richard Cobb. Soboul, Cobb, and Rudé became close friends and through shared archival adventures and labors contributed immensely to each other's scholarship (indeed, Lefebvre referred to them as the "three musketeers").[14] Their "mentor," Lefebvre, was, of course, the great historian of the French Revolution whose work on the peasantry and urban protests dramatically revised the form and content of the historiography of the Revolution of 1789,[15] and laid the bases for the writings by Soboul on the Parisian *sans-culottes,*[16] by Cobb on the "revolutionary armies" and *sans-culottes* in the provinces,[17] and by Rudé on the "revolutionary crowds." Thus, scholarly and personal connections were established between the British Marxist historians and these social historians of the French Revolution which must surely have contributed to the development of both social history and history from below. (In fact, as Rudé regularly acknowledges in prefatory remarks to his major works, it was Lefebvre who originally proffered the term "history from below.")[18]

Out of his researches in the 1950s, Rudé published a series of important articles on eighteenth-century protests in Paris and London, one of which, "The Gordon Riots: A Study of the Rioters and their Victims" (1956), was awarded the prestigious Alexander Prize.[19] However, he was still unable to secure a post at a British university. When, finally, he was offered such a position in 1960, it was not in Britain but at the University of Adelaide in Australia. Thus, at the age of fifty, he commenced his university teaching career *and* his "exile" from England. His emigration to Australia also occasioned his departure from the Communist Party (for, although he did not actually resign his British membership, neither did he join the Australian Party).[20] From 1960 to 1987, Rudé held professorships at the universities of Adelaide and Flinders in Australia and, for seventeen of those years, at Sir George Williams University in Montreal which, in the 1970s, was part of a merger creating Concordia University. Also, he has held visiting professorships at Columbia University in New York, Stirling University in Scotland (which offered him its foundations chair of history that, had he chosen to accept it, would have ended his "exile" in 1967), the University of Tokyo, and the College of William and Mary in Virginia.

Rudé has been recognized as an outstanding lecturer and teacher, talents cultivated, no doubt, in his many years as a schoolteacher. His former students in Australia have honored him by establishing the "George Rudé Seminar" held every two years in that country; and, in Montreal, Rudé was the founding director of the Inter-University Centre for European Studies/ Centre Interuniversitaire d'Etudes Europeenes, an enterprise established to foster historical and interdisciplinary exchanges between the English and French branches of Canadian scholarship. Finally, it should be noted that Rudé, having reached the age of sixty-five, was actually a half-time professor at Concordia University from 1975 to 1987, spending the rest of each year in England, in Sussex; and, as we know, he continued to produce works of primary importance, like *Ideology and Popular Protest*.[21] His last book, *The French Revolution*, was published in late 1988. A study of the Revolution "after 200 years," the book received welcoming and critically appreciative reviews.[22]

Identities: "The Faces in the Crowd"

In *Europe in the Eighteenth Century* (1972), Rudé observed that "whatever image the eighteenth century has projected, it has never been that of an age of the common man."[23] Indeed, that we have now begun to comprehend that century in terms of the experience of the "common people" is due in good part to his own original research and writings on the crowds of revolutionary Paris and Hanoverian London. What he succeeded in doing was to reveal, as Asa Briggs phrased it, "the faces in the crowd" and to thereby challenge the long-standing assumptions held and assertions made about it by writers on both the Right and Left. More specifically, his accomplishment was to restore to the eighteenth-century crowd—as an historically-specific mode of popular collective behavior—its historical and political identity. Essentially, Rudé recognized that merely because the "menu peuple" of France and "lower orders" of England were excluded from their respective national political communities, did not mean that they were therefore without social and political interests, grievances, ideas, and aspirations—*or* the means of expressing them.

Rudé's original writings on "the faces in the crowd" include the articles published in the 1950s that were later collected in *Paris and London in the Eighteenth Century,* but his most significant primary works were *The Crowd in the French Revolution* and *Wilkes and Liberty.* Framed by narratives of the "larger" struggles, to which they were so central, these books offer analyses of the actions, social compositions, leaderships, motivations, and legacies of the crowds of Paris and London, respectively. From his very first studies of the French Revolution, Rudé confronted the traditional conservative view, originally presented by Edmund Burke in his *Reflections on the Revolution in France* (1790), that the crowd was peopled by "the swinish multitude," an image later surpassed in color by the French historian, Hippolyte Taine, when he described its participants as "dregs of society," "bandits," "thieves," "savages," "beggars," and "prostitutes." [24] Yet Rudé also had to deal with the picture advanced by the more liberal and "democratic" historians; for example, discussing the work of Jules Michelet, an upholder of the Republican tradition, he notes how Michelet conjured up the revolutionary crowd as "the embodiment of all the popular and Republican virtues," equating it with the spirit of "le peuple." [25]

The problem, Rudé observes, is that conservatives and "Republicans" alike had projected their own political aspirations, fantasies and/or fears onto the crowd without having asked the basic historical questions. He attributes this practice not so much to scholarly laziness or lethargy but to the fact that regardless of the antagonistic character of their views, they had been arrived at from a shared vantage point: *"from above*—that is, from the elevation of the committee room of the Committee of Public Safety, of the rostrum of the National Assembly or Jacobin Club, or of the columns of the revolutionary press." [26] When Rudé later extended his researches to Hanoverian London, he found a distinct but similar set of notions prevailing as to the composition and character of the crowd. For example, Horace Walpole's original assessment of the Gordon rioters as being "chiefly apprentices, convicts, and all kinds of desperadoes" was echoed almost a century and a half later in the work of the historian, Dorothy George, upon which Rudé himself has often relied for historical detail of eighteenth-century London. Dr. George, Rudé states, "too readily assumed that the 'mobs' that rioted were . . . drawn from 'criminal elements,' the slum population, or from 'the inhabitants of the dangerous districts . . . who were always ready for pillage.'" [27]

His initial excursions into the archives of, first, revolutionary Paris and, later, Hanoverian London convinced Rudé that it was necessary to push further with his re-examinations of their respective crowds and to start by asking the primary questions: "What? Who? How? and Why?" especially "*Who*" and

"*Why*"; indeed, as Rudé himself has admitted, "Who?" became his particular obsession in response to the continually "vague or prejudiced generalizations of historians."[28] In *The Crowd in History, 1730–1848,* a "synthetic" work written following the publication of his original studies of the eighteenth-century crowd, he proffered six questions to serve as guides for the study of the crowd in the "pre-industrial age":

> 1) What actually happened, both as to the event itself, and as to its origins and aftermath? . . . 2) How large was the crowd concerned, how did it act, who (if any) were its promoters, who composed it, and who led it? . . . 3) Who were the target or the victims of the crowd's activities? . . . 4) More specifically, what were the aims, motives, and ideas underlying these activities? . . . 5) How effective were the forces of law and order? . . . 6) Finally, what were the consequences of the event, and what has been its historical significance?[29]

Yet, as Rudé forewarns, to pose such questions is one thing, to be able to answer them is another, for it depends on the availability of suitable records, by which he means not only the historian's traditional sources—"memoirs, correspondence, pamphlets, provincial and national newspapers, parliamentary reports and proceedings, the minutes and reports of local government and political organizations, and the previous findings of historians, chroniclers and antiquarians"—but, also, "police, prison, hospital, and judicial records; Home Office papers . . . tax rolls; poll books and petitions; notarial records; inventories; parish registers of births, deaths and marriages; public assistance records; tables of prices and wages; censuses; local directories and club membership lists; and lists of freeholders, jurymen, churchwardens and justices of the peace." The necessity of the latter records is both pragmatic *and* political in nature. It is a practical issue because the traditional sources are not likely to provide the answers to the crucial questions "Who" and "Why," nor, for that matter, sufficient data to address the others adequately. It is a political issue because what the former sources are most likely to provide us with is the perspective "from above," since they are the records of the ruling and upper classes—"government, the official political opposition, the aristocracy, or the more prosperous middle class"; the participants in crowd actions like riots "rarely leave records of their own in the form of memoirs, pamphlets, or letters."[30]

He does not fully pursue the logic of his argument here, but it is clear from his own work and remarks elsewhere that even the latter sources (police, prison, hospital, and judicial records . . .) must be approached most critically *and* from the bottom up, for they, too, have been by and/or for the governors. As the historical sociologist, Barrington Moore, Jr., once put it: since "in any society the dominant groups are the ones with the most to hide about the way society works," to maximize objectivity and write critical history, "For all students of human society, sympathy with the victims of historical processes and skepticism about the victors' claims provide essential safeguards against being taken in by the dominant mythology. A scholar who tries to be objective needs those feelings as part of his ordinary equipment."[31] In "The Changing Face of the Crowd," Rudé reflects on his eighteenth-century studies and, revealing no surprises, speaks of his own particular sympathies: "I did not approach my subject without commitment. . . . This does not mean I have ever felt *politically* involved with the wage-earners, craftsmen or rioters with whom I have largely been concerned, but that I have always felt a bond of sympathy with them, whether their activities have been peaceful or rebellious."[32]

What answers did his questions garner in the "police records of the Archives Nationales and the Paris Prefecture de Police" and the various "London and metropolitan records . . . [especially] judicial records"? In contrast to Taine's picture of the revolutionary crowd as having been made up of "dregs, criminals and bandits," Rudé found that "For all their diversity of scope, organization and design" there was "a certain uniformity of pattern in the social composition of these movements: . . . they were drawn in their overwhelming majority from the Parisian *sans-culottes*—from the workshop masters, craftsmen, wage-earners, shopkeepers, and petty traders of the capital."[33] Similarly, Rudé's labors in London revealed that neither could the Hanoverian crowd be so readily "fobbed off" as a "mob" recruited from amongst "slum dwellers" and/or "criminal elements." Fully acknowledging—as he also does in *The Crowd in the French Revolution*—that there were occupational and gender variations in the composition of the crowd depending on the "occasion" of its mobilization in strike, riot, or demonstration he states that it was, in fact, generally composed of "wager-earners, (journeymen, apprentices, labourers, and 'servants') . . . craftsmen, shopkeepers, and tradesmen."[34] At the same time, it should be noted that although his dramatically redrawn historical pictures of the Parisian and London crowds are filled with "working" people, Rudé is insistent—against various socialist renditions of the *sans-culottes* and lower orders—that these were not specifically "working-class" movements and, in fact, that there did not even yet exist specifically *class* formations in these pre-industrial social orders.[35] (This argument will be considered again in the last section of the present chapter, in relation to his discussion of the transitional character of the eighteenth century and his understanding of class in that period.)

Uncovering the faces in the crowd was only a first step towards restoring its historical and political identity and those of its participants. The issues of the direction and purpose of crowd actions remained, for it might be argued that the composition of the crowd, or "mob," was not so significant if its participants were merely bribed and/or driven by a desire for loot, both of which also raised the specter of hired gangs and conspiracies. But the question of leadership and motivation were also addressed by Rudé. Regarding the former he did find that the crowds of both capital cities were more often led by those from "without" than from "within" and, moreover, that such leaders were usually from higher social strata,[36] which could be read as supportive of the conservative view that the crowds were "mindless mobs" directed from above for purposes not all their own except in the most immediate sense of the assuagement of hunger (e.g., bread riots) or the expectation of lucre. *Or,* on the contrary, it might be taken as supportive of the liberal and republican position that, for example, in the French Revolution the crowd—*"the people"* enjoined with its revolutionary bourgeois leaders—was indeed the embodiment of the "republican spirit." In other words, "who" the leadership was is inadequate on its own; of crucial importance are the degree of "autonomy" of the crowd and the "motivation" of its participants.

The next section of this chapter will survey Rudé's persistent interest in the motivation and ideology of popular protest, and also note further his understanding of the legacies of such protest, but it should be stated here that his findings contradicted the contentions of both conservatives and liberals. That is, they reject both the view that the crowd was simply and "mindlessly" motivated by hunger and/or greed, and that which reduces the crowd—in the name of "good *or* evil"—to having been merely an extension of the aspirations or conspiracies of its leaders. It is true, as will be shown, that Rudé's discussions of the "social psychology" of the crowd provide a good deal of weight to material motivation—perhaps occasionally too mechanically, as in his analyses of the revolutionary crowd's responsiveness to changes in the price of bread—and, also, that they do attribute the "political" development of the Parisian *menu peuple* and London "lower orders" in great part to the efforts of their "upper-class" leaders in what might be viewed as a "Leninist" fashion. However, he never treats the crowd and its participants in a one-dimensional way, for even his earliest studies reveal that the lower orders, too, had interests and aspirations which sometimes coincided with those from above and, yet, at other times, did not.

The Crowd in History, 1730–1848 appeared in 1964. Limited to France and England, it drew on Rudé's previous studies and, at the same time, extended his explorations into the nineteenth century. The book also represented both a self-conscious effort on his part to respond somewhat to his critics and to develop a "historical model" of the pre-industrial crowd addressed not only to historians but, as well, to sociologists, who, Rudé found, had not advanced much beyond their historian colleagues on the subject. At the outset he offers a brief summary description of the pre-industrial crowd which, appearing in the "transitional period" before the full development of an industrial social order, was marked by historically antecedent modes of popular protest, and yet was already beginning to evidence characteristics of industrial protest.

> In our transitional period the typical form of social protest is the food riot, not the strike of the future or the millenial movement or the peasant *jacquerie* of the past. Those engaging in popular disturbances are sometimes peasants (as in the past), but more often a mixed population of what in England were "lower orders" and in France *menu peuple* . . . ; they appear frequently in itinerant bands, "captained" or "generaled" by men whose personality, style of dress or speech, and momentary assumption of authority mark them out as leaders; they are fired as much by memories of customary rights or a nostalgia for past utopias as by present grievances or hopes of material improvement; and they dispense a rough-and-ready kind of "natural justice" by breaking windows, wrecking machinery, storming markets, burning their enemies of the moment in effigy, firing hayricks, and pulling down houses, farms, fences, mills or pubs, but rarely by taking lives.[37]

In conclusion to the work, Rudé wonders if "all the vigour, heroism and violence . . . led to any positive results? . . . [That is,] what did the crowd achieve?" Though he exempts certain episodes from his generic assessment, his answer is that "In terms of immediate gains, it must be admitted that it achieved comparatively little." However, this does not mean that "the crowd"—as the most aggressive mode of popular protest and struggle—was historically inconsequential. Indeed, Rudé contends, both the crowds of the *menu peuple* and those of the "lower orders" contributed in dramatic ways to the making of eighteenth-century history. For example, on the crowds mobilized for "Wilkes and Liberty!" he writes: "The Wilkite disturbances in London not only achieved a remarkable series of personal victories for Wilkes himself but contributed substantially to the growth of a mass radical movement in England."[38] And, in a 1970 lecture on "The French Revolution and Participation," he says of the significance of the *sans-culottes'* initiatives that

> They certainly helped to push the Revolution leftwards; without their intervention the Jacobins could never have come into power; there would have been no "democratic dictatorship of the Year II"; and it is doubtful if the monarch would have been overthrown. . . . They also won important concessions for themselves though they proved to be short-lived: the Maximum Laws, for example, with a ceiling placed on food prices; and the right to vote and to sit in local government.[39]

Moreover, the legacies of the Hanoverian crowds—especially those of "Wilkes and Liberty!"—and the revolutionary crowds of Paris can be recognized, Rudé declares, in the Chartist movement of the 1830s and 40s, and in the revolutionary struggles of 1830 and 1848, respectively.

The Crowd in History not only offered a summary of his crowd studies, it also pointed ahead to his primary researches of the next twenty years, first on "Captain Swing," and then on crime, protest, and punishment during the Industrial Revolution. Although distinct in period and subject, these later writings continued to evidence Rudé's commitment to restoring the historical and political identities of the "lower orders."

Before proceeding, a problem regarding Rudé's crowd studies which is most evident in *The Crowd in History* should be registered. Although Rudé is eager to present the period 1730–1848 as transitional, in order, no doubt, to formulate it in historically specific terms, he does not actually explore the relations between the developing modes of popular protest and "contention"[40] and the changing relations of production and "class" experience. The historical sociologist, Charles Tilly, noted this to some extent in his critically appreciative review of *The Crowd in History* when he wrote that Rudé's analysis does not adequately take up "underlying social changes."[41] This point will be returned to in the final section, for it relates to Rudé's apparent reservations about treating the eighteenth century in terms of class and the transition to capitalism. However, this was not to be a problem with his next book, *Captain Swing*, either because its subject, the English agricultural laborers' rising of 1830, occurred later in time and, thus, the structures of class were "clearer," or, possibly, because the work was co-authored with Eric Hobsbawm who, as something of an economic historian, had already written directly on the question of the transition and was much more attuned to the political economy of class.

Bringing together in one project Hobsbawm's critical perceptions and knowledge of the development of capitalism, industrialization, "primitive rebellions," and "machine breakers,"[42] and Rudé's intimate acquaintance with the "pre-industrial crowd" and passion and skills for archival labor and analysis, *Captain Swing* is a truly outstanding piece of historical scholarship. The particular skills of each historian are evident in the division of labor in the book: the introductory, background, developmental, and concluding chapters are by Hobsbawm; the chapters providing the details and "anatomy" of the rising are by Rudé (so also are the chapters on "Repression and Aftermath").[43] Nevertheless, as a collaborative work we find in the very opening lines a primary concern for the identities of the agricultural laborers which seems so characteristic of Rudé.

"Hodge"; "the secret people," "brother to the ox." Their own inarticulateness, our own ignorance, are symbolized by the very titles of the few books which have attempted to recreate the world of the English farm-labourer of the nineteenth century. *Who were they?* . . . Except for their gravestones and their children, they left nothing identifiable behind them for the marvelous surface of the British landscape, the work of their ploughs, spades and shears and the beasts they looked after, bears no signature or mark such as the masons left on cathedrals.

We know little about them, because they are remote from us in time. Their articulate contemporaries knew little more, partly because as townsmen they were ignorant about the country and cared nothing for it, partly because as rulers they were not allowed to enter the self-contained world of the subaltern orders, or because as rural middle class they despised it. . . . The task of this book is therefore the difficult one, which nowadays—and rightly—tempts many social historians, of reconstructing the mental world of an anonymous and undocumented body of people in order to understand their movements, themselves only sketchily documented.[44]

Captain Swing is, of course, a study of the subject originally treated by the Hammonds in *The Village Labourer*.[45] Hobsbawm and Rudé wrote their own book, they said, not only because there was more to tell about the rising, but because there were "new *questions* to ask about the events: about their causes and motives, about their mode of social and political behaviour, the social composition of those who took part in them, their significance and consequences." They explain that, before 1830, the agricultural workers were no longer peasants but the social order in which they lived was still "traditional, hierarchical, paternalist, and in many respects still resistant to the full logic of the market." This was not a static situation, however, and in the decades leading up to 1830 this rural society experienced major changes brought about by "the extraordinary agricultural boom (and subsequent, though temporary, recessions)." The changes involved the alienation of the laborers' lands and the transformation of their hiring contracts, that is, the actual or further proletarianization of the labor force. Moreover, the reduction of the relationship between farmer and laborer to the "cash-nexus" stripped the laborer of "those modest customary rights as a man (though a subordinate one) to which he felt himself to have a claim." And yet, the agricultural workers were "proletarian only in the most general economic sense," for the nature of their labor and the social order in which they lived and starved inhibited the development of "those ideas and methods of collective self-defense which the townsmen were able to discover."

Nevertheless, (finally) instigated by the economic crisis of 1828–30 and stimulated by the French and Belgian Revolutions of 1830 and the contemporary British crisis, the agricultural workers expressed their demands by a variety of means: "arson, threatening letters, inflammatory handbills and posters . . . and [most significantly] the destruction of different types of machinery." Their demands—"to attain a minimum living wage and to end rural unemployment"—appear merely economic or "(though not formally) trade unionist." However, while the rising was never revolutionary (nor was there ever a call for land reform), Hobsbawm and Rudé's analysis shows that "there was a wider objective: the defence of the customary rights of the rural poor as free-born Englishmen, and the restoration of the stable social order which had—at least it seemed in retrospect—guaranteed them." [46]

As Fred Krantz observes: "Rudé's hand is clearly present in the sections noted as primarily worked up by him," and his "method and technique" enable them to advance a "provisional profile of the village disposed to riot" based on village size, social structure, land tenure and type of agriculture predominating, propensity to religious "independence" and proximity to "local communications centers, markets and fairs." Indeed, Krantz claims, comprehended in terms of national and local historical developments and particularities, Hobsbawm and Rudé essentially provide a "fully three-dimensional, empirically-grounded, analytic 'model.'" [47]

The chapter on "Who Was Swing?" is also impressive in its survey of the evidence on incendiaries, letter-writers, machine-breakers and wage-rioters, along with that for their leaders and allies. Observers were quick to recognize—for they often occurred in broad daylight—that wage riots, marches, ransomings, and machine-breaking were "perpetrated" by local laborers, but against contemporary opinion—for these were not "daylight" actions— Hobsbawm and Rudé's examination of the evidence shows that incendiaries and letter-writers too were locals. The "movement's" leaders and allies were often craftsmen and (even) farmers, the reasons for, and significance of which are discussed. In general, Rudé and Hobsbawm find that "The rioters were generally young men or men of early-middle age. . . . overwhelmingly they were in their twenties or thirties" and, moreover, "the proportion of married men among the rioters was also high." In fact, the evidence "suggests a relatively high degree of stability and 'respectability' among the rioters as a whole." The conclusion to the chapter states:

> By and large, the labourers of 1830 fully deserved the good reputations that their employers gave them. They were not criminals: comparatively few had even the mildest form of prison record behind them. But they believed in "natural right"—the right to work and earn a living wage—and refused to accept that machines, which robbed them of this right, should receive the protection of the law. On occasion, they invoked the authority of the justice, or government—and even of the King and God himself—to justify their views and actions. For like most "primitive rebels," and like Sir John

Hampden 200 years before, they were firmly convinced that justice—and even the law—was on their side.[48]

Captain Swing not only offered a reinterpretation of the origins of the agricultural workers' movement, as well as its practices and aims, it also offered a new view of its consequences. Hobsbawm and Rudé contend that the myths and ignorance about the movement being a failure were due in good part to the urban bias of the historians of social movements. For example, against the traditional view they reveal that "agrarian unrest continued well into the 1850s, and social incendiaries can be traced down to about 1860." Nevertheless, they acknowledge that the rising was a failure in that it neither succeeded in restoring the old social order, nor—except for a brief period—did it do much to improve the workers' standard of living. And yet in one important respect the agricultural workers' movement succeeded: "The threshing machines did not return on the old scale. Of all the machine-breaking movements of the nineteenth century that of the helpless and unorganized farm-labourers proved to be the most effective. The real name of King Ludd was Swing."[49]

The laborers may have believed that the law was on their side. The judges who tried those caught believed otherwise. As Hobsbawm and Rudé note: "In all 1,976 prisoners were tried . . . 252 were sentenced to death (of these 233 were commuted, mainly to transportation, some to prison) . . . 505 were transported (of these 481 sailed). . . . From no other protest movement of the kind—from neither Luddites, nor Chartists, nor trade unionists—was such a bitter price exacted."[50] The chapters in *Captain Swing* on "Repression" and those transported to "Australia" inspired Rudé's next two primary studies: resident in Australia and then Canada, Rudé wrote *Protest and Punishment: The Story of the Social and Political Protesters Transported to Australia, 1788–1868* (which includes work on "protest and punishment" in Canada); and later, having returned to England in semiretirement, *Criminal and Victim: Crime and Society in Early Nineteenth-Century England*. These two books are classic Rudéan works. Fred Krantz describes Rudé's writing style as "pointillist" and, I would add, none is perhaps more so than these, for Rudé's principal mode of presentation of his findings in both books is to lay out numerous cases, episodes, or micro-tales of crime, protest, and punishment in order to introduce us directly to the faces in the crowd and the experiences which instigated their appearance in the courts or inclusion among those transported to Australia. In essence, in these works Rudé seeks to redeem those whose "crimes" were "protests" from the mass of those whose crimes were not. As he states at the outset of *Protest and Punishment*, in general we know a good deal about transportation and those who were transported from the writings of other historians; however, we do not know enough about those "whose crime was to have rebelled or protested against the social conditions or institutions of the country from which they came."[51]

The problem, Rudé explains, is "How do we make a distinction? How do we separate one type of convict—the protesting convict—from the rest? . . . How do we distinguish between 'protest' crime and crime in general?" Law-and-order conservatives, he complains see all protest as a "crime against established society"; liberal writers have tended to comprehend all crimes as a form of protest; and yet others have proposed more "realistic" models, like Engels who tried to distinguish between crimes against property and others. Rudé also notes, appreciatively but critically, the model advanced by Edward Thompson and his colleagues at the Centre for Social History at Warwick University in the early 1970s, which distinguished between "*social* crime" and crime in general (a distinction which Hobsbawm and Rudé themselves offered in *Captain Swing*). For Rudé, however, these are all inadequate. Instead, he proposes "protest crimes," "marginal crimes," and "crimes in general," and he proceeds to explain his reasoning and method of reading the "cases." In brief, in comparison to the notion of "social" crime which may, nevertheless, be a "private act that has little to do with protest,"

> Protest . . . is also a *collective* act though it may not always be carried out in the company of others. Such acts are fairly easy to recognize in the case of trade-union militants, machine-breakers, food-rioters, demolishers of turn-pikes, fences or workhouses, administers or receivers of unlawful oaths, treasonable or seditious persons, armed rebels and city rioters—all those, in fact, who generally protest within the context of a "popular movement." . . . But there are others: those whose activities belong to the shadowy realm between crime and protest where it is often no easy matter to tell the two apart. I refer to such types of law-breaking as rural incendiarism, poaching and smuggling, cattle-maiming, assaults on peace officers, and the sending of anonymous letters. These types of *marginal* protest . . . have to be judged, as it were, on their merits and treated with care and discrimination.[52]

Protest and Punishment is not merely a study of the British-Australian "experience" but includes those who were transported from Ireland and Canada as well. Reviewing the records of those who were transported, Rudé arrives at a total of 3,600 "protest criminals," that is "about one in forty-five of all transported convicts." Treating their experiences "from both ends: both in the Australian context and in that of the countries and counties in which the protests were made," Rudé reminds us that "Behind these figures are the faces of the men and women. . . ."[53] And his two concluding chapters are, again, characteristically Rudéan: "Who were the Convicts?" and "Who were the Protesters?" In the former he considers the historically changing view of the convicts from that of being "scum" to "heroes," and back again; and in the latter he compares the characteristics—age, literacy, martial status, and criminal record—of the protesters in particular with the convicts in general. In the end he expresses concern that these protesters not be lost in the mass of those who were transported, and that the protesters who were transported be accorded the respect that is owed them: "the names of two dozen of such men, at most, appear in the *Australian Dictionary of Biography* and a few more in the *DNB;* so these will not be forgotten. . . . But there are others no less worthy to be remembered. . . . They, too, no longer deserve to be hidden in the shadows with all the other unsung heroes. Let them be allowed to emerge and bask a little in the approval that posterity has too long refused them."[54]

In *Criminal and Victim,* Rudé's primary questions are "Who robbed whom?" and "Who were the victims as well as their assailants?" in England during the first half of the nineteenth century. To answer them he focuses on Sussex, Gloucestershire, and Middlesex because the first was rural, the second varied demographically and economically, and the last was urban and commercial. In a somewhat more developed fashion Rudé specifies the different "types" of crime: "(1) *acquisitive* crime, or crimes committed strictly in pursuit of material gain; (2) *survival* crime, in which the criminal's main concern has been to feed or clothe or shelter himself and his family at a time of unemployment or trade decline; and (3) *protest* crime, or crimes committed in attempting to redress injustice or social ills."[55]

Roughly summarized, Rudé's survey of the records of the three counties demonstrates that criminals were in the great majority of the laboring and working classes, and victims were "of the 'middling' or upper classes: most often shopkeepers, merchants, or householders and (in the rural counties) farmers, with a fair 'sprinkling of gentry. . . .'" This leads him to ask two specifically "class" questions. First: "Does this tendency of criminals to belong to different, if not opposing, classes in this confrontation mean that through crime and the combating of crime, they are engaged in a form of class war?" His answer to this is that although the innovations and changes of the time in England's criminal law and justice system were "a direct expression of a new class system and therefore an expression of class rule" and, also, their implementation and operation were characterized by "class bias," the prevalence of "acquisitive" crimes and "survival" crimes—as opposed to "protest" crimes—deny the description "class war."[56] The second question posed is: "Can one rightly speak of the existence of a 'criminal class,' or of 'criminal classes'?" Allowing for the existence of a "minority of hardened criminals and isolated gangs of 'professionals,'" he responds that these "were not in sufficient numbers to constitute a 'criminal class,'" and the words he finds most appropriate to refer to accounts which suggest otherwise is "fantasies."[57]

Ideologies: *"Putting Mind Back into History"*

We have seen that along with confronting the long-accepted views of eighteenth-century Paris and London, Rudé also had to deal with the concomitant views of the direction and purpose of the crowds' actions. In "The Motives of Popular Insurrection" (1953) he notes that to Taine and many other historians "the revolutionary crowd is a conscienceless rabble, quite incapable of political thought, driven to rebel by the prospect of easy loot or by monetary inducements,"[58] and, similarly, in "The London 'Mob'" (1959) he notes that "While conceding that 'mobs' might be prompted by hunger, they [contemporaries] were even more ready to believe that the desire for loot or drink acted as the major factor in such disturbances; any sort of political awareness, however rudimentary, was not seriously considered. The 'mobbish sort' being notoriously venal, bribery [with its accompanying charge of 'conspiracy'] by interested parties was deemed a sufficient stimulus to touch off riot or rebellion."[59] As was indicated in the previous section, although the leaders of the crowds were most often from "without" and "above" those who composed them, the *menu peuple* and "lower orders," Rudé's research revealed that the persistent conservative presumption as to the motivation of the Paris and London crowds were not substantiated by the evidence. Still, there remained the issue of the autonomy of the crowd and its participants: What were the motivations of the "common people" who took part in crowd actions? Were they their own or simply those of their higher strata leaders?

In his crowd studies of the 1950s and early 1960s, Rudé repeatedly declares that along with recovering the "faces in the crowd" he is interested in the "motives" of those who took part in riots, demonstrations, and rebellions, and in exploring the "social psychology" of the eighteenth-century crowd. In this he was seeking to open up historical study to social science thinking; the study of collective behavior has often been pursued—then, and now—in social-psychological terms, and the study of motivation in particular has been associated with the discipline of social psychology. Thus, we find Rudé in his crowd studies using language like "the deeper urges and impulses of the 'mob'" and "entering into the minds of its participants."[60] Yet he was not only being influenced by contemporary social science practice, he was also following the lead of his mentor, Lefebvre, who had been extremely interested in developing *historical* social psychology and, as Rudé says, provided models for such in works like *The Great Fear of 1789: Rural Panic in Revolutionary France*.[61] In Lefebvre's own words: "Social history can therefore not be limited to describing the external aspects of antagonistic classes. It must also come to understand the mental outlook of each class."[62]

Rudé's own approach to the study of motives in his crowd writings is materialist. Pointing out that crowd actions and popular movements antedated the specifically *political* struggles of the "revolutionary bourgeoisie" and "middle sort" of Paris and London, respectively, Rudé, early in his work, examined the possible links between economic hardship and popular disturbance (following, here, the lead of the French historian, C-E. Labrousse), and he found that popular protest was apparently quite responsive to price and wage fluctuations. This, he contended, illustrated that the motives of the crowds and their participants were not *simply* reflections of the aspirations of their "upper-class" leaders.[63]

Later, in his book-length studies of the eighteenth-century crowd, he continues to assert that the "most constant motive of popular insurrection during the Revolution, as in the eighteenth century as a whole, was the compelling need of the *menu peuple* for the possession of cheap and plentiful bread and other essentials" (*The Crowd in the French Revolution*), and "Far more tangible [than other factors] is the evidence of a concordance between the movement of food-prices and certain phases of the 'Wilkes and Liberty' movement in the metropolis" (*Wilkes and Liberty*).[64]

On their own, such arguments seem to reduce the causes of crowd actions to economic determinism and, although Rudé recognized that this was a problem with Labrousse's work, his own analyses are, as I have stated, occasionally too mechanical. But Rudé does not treat the crowd one-dimensionally. His studies characteristically go on to consider the other, less immediately material, motives which inspired crowd actions and popular protests. Indeed, both *The Crowd in the French Revolution* and *Wilkes and Liberty* are ultimately narratives of the political education and development of the crowds of Paris and London. As Rudé presents it, the political education of the revolutionary and Wilkite crowds involved the subscription or "absorption" of the ideas of the revolutionary bourgeoisie and politically-active "middle sort" by the *menu peuple* and "lower orders," respectively.

In a chapter of *The Crowd in the French Revolution* titled "The Generation of Revolutionary Activity," Rudé discusses the various ways in which the revolutionary slogans and ideas of "the rights of man" and "sovereignty of the people" were transmitted from bourgeois leaders to the *menu peuple*. For a start, although literacy was not common among the *sans-culottes* of Paris (and even less so in the villages), many could read. Those who could would read aloud at meetings of workers and others from the journals and pamphlets being produced by political writers which were often addressed directly to them. More significant and systematic was the "indoctrination of the *sans-culottes* with the ideas of the advanced political groups," which occurred by way of their "enrollment in the National Guard and, above all, in the clubs and societies and Sectional Committees." Finally, also important in "spreading ideas and moulding opinions," were the discussion and debates which transpired in "public meeting-places, workshops, wine-shops, markets, and food-shops."[65]

The revolutionary slogans and ideas, Rudé regularly reminds us, were not those of the *sans-culottes* themselves; and his use of such words as "indoctrination" to refer to the communication of those ideas by the revolutionary bourgeoisie to the *menu peuple* clearly evidences a Leninist conception of political education: the *sans-culottes* were on their own incapable of anything more than *economic* motivation ("trade union consciousness"); movement beyond that required the leadership and *political* ideas developed by bourgeois intellectuals. However, Rudé does evidence certain reservations about this formulation of the relationship. That is, the *sans-culottes* subscribed to the revolutionary ideas "because they appeared to correspond to their own interest in the fight to destroy the old regime and to safeguard the Republic," *but* they comprehended those ideas in their own terms—it was a process of "absorption" *and* "adaptation." Moreover, Rudé continues, because their own experience and interests were other than those of the revolutionary bourgeoisie, in time their different understandings of the "rights of man" and "sovereignty of the people" strained the "alliance." Also, in a footnote, Rudé does acknowledge that the *menu peuple* likely had political ideas of their own, though he adds that "These can, however, have played no part in stimulating participation in revolutionary movements, except in that of 4–5 September 1793."[66]

More important were the efforts of the *menu-peuple* to protect or restore their "traditional rights." In fact, Rudé proffers, against the views of both the conservatives *and* the writers and historians of the Republican tradition, that the crowds and their *sans-culottes* participants were hardly the "passive instruments" of their revolutionary bourgeois leaders, for had they been they would have been "imbued with a desire for 'total renovation'"—they would have actually sought to "turn the world upside down." Rather, he finds: "At every important stage of the Revolution the *sans-culottes* intervened, not to renovate society or to remodel it after a new pattern, but to reclaim traditional rights and to uphold standards which they believed to be imperilled by the innovations of ministers, capitalists, speculators, 'agricultural improvers' or city authorities."[67]

Thus, Rudé's Leninism is indicated by his apparent equation of *material* motivation with the *menu peuple* and the origination of "ideas" with the revolutionary bourgeois leadership, and yet we also see that his materialist conception of the necessarily "class-differential" comprehension of those ideas leads beyond a crude or simplistic Leninism.

In the same fashion that popular movements were already in motion prior to the French Revolution they were, too, in Hanoverian London prior to the campaigns for "Wilkes and Liberty!" Indeed, Rudé points out that eighteenth-century London was actually more turbulent than Paris up until the Revolution and, furthermore, that the "lower orders," or "inferior sorts of people," of London were actually characterized by a greater political awareness than the Parisian *menu peuple*. This, Rudé explains, was due in great part to the legacy of seventeenth-century struggles, but also because the London "middle sort" were closer to the "lower orders" than were their French counterparts to the *sans-culottes* and thus they were "more appropriate educators." [68] Although, in general, popular movements were imbued with a sense of the seventeenth-century revolutionary tradition, the "*economically-motivated*" food riots and industrial disputes of Hanoverian London were not "political" movements, Rudé insists. The Wilkite movement, however, which Rudé sees as paralleling but not actually merging with the "industrial" struggles, had dramatic effects on the political development of the London crowd and the political education of the "lower orders." [69]

The question of motivation is considered at several levels in the book, *Wilkes and Liberty*. Again, Rudé grants that there was a significant relationship between the "material" motivation of the "inferior sort"—"rising food prices . . . wage demands and industrial disputes"—and the Wilkite movements, but, as he says, the former does not sufficiently explain the latter: "Beyond that, we must look to a complex of political, social and economic factors, in which the underlying social changes of the age, the political crisis of 1761, the traditional devotion to 'Revolution principles,' and Wilkes's own astuteness, experiences and personality all played their part." [70] Especially, we should note his discussion of Wilkes's "appeal" to the common people—both "middle" and "lower sort"—in his campaigns for press freedom and political liberties. First, Wilkes's experience represented, or personified, the political experience and growing sense of injustice which had been accumulating: "Small wonder, then, that among such citizens and gentry, alarmed at the whole trend of events since the accession of George III, there should be many to whom Wilkes, who had been persecuted more relentlessly than any other by the new administration and returned blow for blow and insolence for insolence, might appear as an object of sympathy, respect or even of veneration." [71] Moreover, Wilkes's "image" was greatly enhanced by his own skillful and persistent espousal of the principles of liberty and freedom which harkened back to the "Revolution Principles" and successfully harnessed and mobilized the common people's understandings of "the rights of the freeborn Englishman."

Wilkite crowd actions were, then, more "political" in character than those linked specifically to the price of bread or to wage and industrial disputes, but, like the economically—and socially—motivated popular movements, that for "Wilkes and Liberty" was also a "defensive" struggle asserting the "*traditional* rights" of Englishmen against seemingly "new" oppressions. In other words, Rudé does not exaggerate the political development of the crowd and its participants: "It took time, of course, before such movements of the 'inferior set of people' became impregnated with a more solid body of political ideas and principles and before the notion of 'liberty' . . . began to clothe itself in the more tangible garbs of demands for annual Parliaments or an extension of the franchise—demands already voiced by tradesmen and freeholders [the "middle sort"] but not as yet by the smaller craftsmen, journeymen, and urban wage-earners." This further political development of the "lower orders" he attributes in good part to ideas from "without" and "above," in particular to the French Revolution and the writings of the English democrats.[72]

Rudé does not fail to acknowledge the violence of crowd actions—in the case of "Wilkes and Liberty" as much as in the others. But, as he indicates, the very culture of Hanoverian London was violent, and "the violence of the poor was, in part at least, but a reflection of the violence of their rulers and social betters."[73] In fact, he declares, in contrast to the violence of the upper strata, that of crowd actions was characteristically against property not lives!

Indeed, Rudé's research reveals that even in the most "reactionary" of crowd actions, that of the Gordon Riots which were directed against Roman Catholics, the violence was not directed against the Roman Catholic community as a whole, but rather against the propertied and wealthy. There was a distinctly "class" bias to the events. Rudé does not claim that religion was a cloak to the real motives, but he does call for a recognition of the "social protest" dimension of the riots.[74]

In his laudatory review of *Wilkes and Liberty* in *The Guardian* (9 February 1962), A. J. P. Taylor wrote that Rudé had "put mind back into history and restored the dignity of man." This was well-deserved praise for his crowd studies—both for *Wilkes and Liberty* and, I would add, *The Crowd in the French Revolution*. Yet, as I have shown, Rudé's study of motives suffered from a kind of elitism in that it tended, first, to attribute material motivation to the lower orders and the original possession of ideas to the higher, and second, to portray the views of the former as merely defensive and "backward looking" and those of the latter as "forward looking." Thus, the political education of the lower orders is seen as depending on the propagation among them of the "progressive" ideas of the revolutionary bourgeoisie or middle sort. Rudé himself was to move towards this very conclusion. Writing in the introduction to *Ideology and Popular Protest* (1980), he looked back and described how his treatment of the question "Why?" changed from focusing on the problem of "motivation" to focusing on "ideas or beliefs."

> [C]oncern with motivation led me to attempt to distinguish between the long and the short term and to draw a dividing line between "socio-economic" and "political" factors and to attempt to explain how the two became related and merged in such movements as that of the *sans-culottes* in the French Revolution or of the Londoners that shouted for Wilkes and burned down Roman Catholic chapels and schools in the riots of the 1760s to 1780.

But, as I have come to realize, the study of *motives*—even when some attention is paid to such elusive concepts as N. J. Smelser's "generalized beliefs"—is an unsatisfactory one in itself, as it tends to present the problem in a piecemeal fashion and fails to do justice to the full range of ideas or beliefs that underlie social and political action, whether of old-style rulers, "rising" bourgeois or of "inferior" social groups.[75]

The change in Rudé's approach to the question "Why?" can be described as a shift from a concern with motives in the social-psychological sense—though it should be made clear that Rudé's work never fell into "psychologism"—to an interest in the social history of ideas or "ideologies." This was signalled somewhat in *The Crowd in History* and *Captain Swing*, and thus it might have been due to his having extended his scholarly efforts into the nineteenth century, for in these later years the "emergent" ideas of the eighteenth century were adapted, revised, *and* more clearly articulated in the course of social change and the making of the more specifically working-class movements. It was also due no doubt both to the changes taking place in the historical discipline to which he had himself contributed so much and to those occurring on the Left. In the late 1960s and early 1970s, social history and "history from below" began to move to the forefront of the historical profession; at the same time—and to some extent fomenting the former development—the New Left's rebellion against the orthodoxy and economism of the Old Left had fostered a new interest in ideas and cultural questions *and* the discovery and recovery of a "Western Marxist" tradition including George Lukács, the theorists of the Frankfurt School, and Antonio Gramsci.[76]

The British Marxist historians themselves seem to bridge the Old and New Lefts. At one end of the group are the "senior" figures like Christopher Hill, Eric Hobsbawm, Victor Kiernan, and George Rudé, and, at the other, the (younger) E. P. Thompson, who was a central figure in the break with the Communist Party *and* the formation of the original British New Left. However, *as a group* the British Marxist historians were extremely influential in the development of the "new" history which emerged concurrently with the New Left, and their own writings evidence strong sympathies with its aspirations. Rudé's work on the crowd was quite central to all this, but he was not himself of the New Left. Consider his remark in the article, "Marxism and History," where he quotes Engels regarding the necessity of "authority and centralization" and how it ought to be kept in mind by "young 'revolutionaries' of our own time."[77] Nevertheless, Rudé's work did not remain stuck in its already-noted Leninist mold; indeed, his own writings of the 1970s and 1980s were to be greatly influenced both by the studies of his fellow British Marxist historians and the younger historians who had themselves been inspired by his scholarship and by the contemporary theoretical and historical interest in the ideas of the Italian Marxist, Antonio Gramsci.[78]

In several essays written around 1970, Rudé expresses his new commitment "to trace the origins and course of the ideas that 'grip the masses' (to use Marx's phrase) and play so important a part in both the 'peaks' and 'troughs' of a popular movement," and in this same period he begins to formulate his new model for the study and comprehension of the ideology of popular protest.[79] It is this model that he proceeds to develop in historical terms in a series of marvelous articles published during the next ten years which provided the basis for his book, *Ideology and Popular Protest* (in my mind, his best work for pedagogical purposes!).[80]

The central question which Rudé addresses in this work is "Where did the ideas bound up with popular protest come from?" Though he does not express it in these words, it is evident that he was no longer satisfied with the "Leninist" model which had previously shaped his thinking—a model, as I have implied, which was reinforced by his concern for the social psychology of motivation—for he had come to see that he had underestimated the ideas and beliefs *of* the "lower orders" in the formation of the "ideology of popular protest." However, as he tells it, his survey of the prevailing models to consider the ideas of popular struggle was not immediately rewarding. The Marxist tradition had attended overwhelmingly to the class structure and struggles of industrial capitalist society and had generally neglected the study of pre-capitalist social formations. Moreover, following the orthodox view derived from both Lenin and Lukács, the Marxist tradition had comprehended the development of class consciousness in the ahistorical and dichotomous terms of "false" and "true" consciousness.[81] Non-Marxist writers had more to say about pre-capitalist social orders and cultures, but they regularly failed to perceive the "class"-differential and political nature of culture and ideas as is true, for example, in the *Annales'* concept of "mentalities."[82]

Yet there was an exception in the Marxist tradition, as Rudé discovered. In the writings of Antonio Gramsci, especially those of the *Prison Notebooks,*[83] Rudé found a Marxist thinker whose efforts and experience as a socialist and communist activist in post–First World War Italy had led him to conceive of the problem of *class formation* in terms of the *making* of class consciousness and to consider the place of ideology in both the struggle for domination *and* the struggles against it. Moreover, due to the particular circumstances which Gramsci confronted, he had concerned himself with the consciousness of both the industrial working class *and* the "popular classes"—that is, peasants and artisans—with whom the working class would have to form an alliance in order to challenge effectively the "ruling bloc" of bourgeoisie and southern landowners (supported by the Catholic Church). Along with his absolute commitment to studying and thinking through these problems *historically,* and his attention to more than the so-called "fundamental classes" of bourgeois and worker, Gramsci's primary contribution has been his development of the theory of "hegemony and contradictory consciousness." "Hegemony" describes a historical situation in which the ongoing process of class struggle has been channelled, or contained, and seemingly "pacified" by the ruling class not merely through force and coercion, or the threat of such, but by ideological domination, suasion, compromise, and even incorporation of selected "oppositional" ideas and aspirations.

"Contradictory consciousness" refers to the historically-evidenced fact that although the process of hegemony effectively contains class struggle, inhibiting the eruption of "class war," it cannot be "total," reducing the consciousness of the subordinated classes to "one-dimensionality" or "normative acceptance" of the social order, for the "material" experience of exploitation and oppression continues to shape consciousness and "inspire" antagonisms. Also, Gramsci directs attention to "those less-structured forms of thought that circulate among the common people, often contradictory and confused and compounded of folklore, myth, and day-to-day popular experience."[84] Nevertheless, "contradictory" consciousness and "false" consciousness are not the same: in contrast to "false" consciousness, which is usually understood as awaiting the intervention from *without* and *above* of socialist intellectuals with *their* "ideas," Gramsci's contention is that within "contradictory" consciousness there exists the potential—indeed, bases—for class consciousness, the role of the socialist intellectual being in this case that of *developing* socialist consciousness in a dialectical relationship with the working class. For Gramsci, the working class and socialist intellectuals must establish an "organic" relationship.[85]

Rudé thus provided a Gramscian model, or theory, for the study of popular protest in pre-industrial societies—that is, societies in which we would not expect to find the specifically "class" formations and associated politics and ideologies characteristic of industrial capitalism.

> *Popular* ideology in [pre-industrial society] is not a purely internal affair and the sole property of a single class or group. . . . It is most often a mixture, a fusion of two elements, of which only one is the peculiar property of the "popular" classes and the other is superimposed by a process of transmission and adoption from outside. Of these, the first is what I call the "inherent," traditional element—a sort of "mother's milk" ideology, based on direct experience, oral tradition, or folk-memory and not learned by listening to sermons or speeches or reading books. In this fusion the second element is the stock of ideas and beliefs that one "derived" or borrowed from others, often taking the form of a more structured system of ideas, political or religious, such as the Rights of Man, Popular Sover-

eignty, *Laissez-faire* and the Sacred Rights of Property, Nationalism, Socialism, or the various versions of justification by Faith.

He makes sure to explain that there is "no Wall of Babylon" separating these two kinds of ideology. Indeed, Rudé explains, there is usually "a considerable overlap between them . . . Among the 'inherent' beliefs of one generation, and forming part of its basic culture are many beliefs that were originally derived from outside by an earlier one."[86]

Rudé construes the "historical" perspectives offered by "inherent" and "derived" ideologies in the same fashion that he previously did the aspirations of the "lower orders" and "middle sort"; characteristically, inherent ideology is "backward-looking" and derived ideology is "forward-looking." Inherent ideology can engender a range of acts and struggles like "strikes, food riots, peasant rebellions, and even a state of awareness of the need for radical change"; moreover, significant "popular achievements" have been possible from struggles informed merely by inherent ideology. However, Rudé declares, for such struggles to posit reform rather than restoration and to move from resistance and rebellion to revolution requires the inherent ideology being supplemented by derived ideology—though he notes that this *too* may be conservative or reactionary and "backward-looking" as in the "Church and King" movements of French peasants in the Vendée after 1793. The actual process of merger between inherent and derived ideologies to form "popular" ideology, he observes, occurred "in stages and at different levels of sophistication." Insisting on the historicity of such processes he adds that "whether the resultant mixture took on a militant and revolutionary or a conservative and counter-revolutionary form depended less on the nature of the recipients or of the 'inherent' beliefs from which they started than on the nature of the 'derived' beliefs compounded by the circumstances then prevailing and what E. P. Thompson has called the 'sharp jostle of experience.'" The "determining" force granted to the "derived" ideas should not be construed as the persistence of Leninism in Rudé's thought, for although there are certain residues, it is clear that popular ideology *is* conceived of as a "merger" even having original elements. Moreover, Rudé adds, "all 'derived' ideas in the course of transmission and adoption suffer a transformation or 'sea-change': its nature will depend on the social needs or the political aims of the classes that are ready to absorb them."[87]

His articles and the book, *Ideology and Popular Protest,* are not merely "theoretical" but predominantly "historical" in content. Drawing in particular on the historical studies of his fellow British Marxist historians and those of a younger generation of (predominantly American) social historians, as well as on his own scholarship on eighteenth- and nineteenth-century England and France, Rudé focused on the ideology of popular protest characteristic of the transition from feudalism to capitalism. Thus, in the book there are chapters on: peasants in medieval Europe, under absolutism, and in Latin America; the English, American and French Revolutions (1789, 1830, and 1848); and England in the eighteenth- and nineteenth-century Industrial Revolution, along with a "Postscript" on industrial Britain. As indicated in the previous section, Rudé's crowd studies never failed to raise the question of the "legacy" of popular protest. In these writings on the ideology of popular protest he poses it most directly: "What happens to popular ideology once the rebellion or revolution is suppressed? Does it disappear so that it has to start all over again?" His reply—which is elaborated upon in the course of his book—is:

> No, obviously not. . . . After the defeat of the English Levellers at Burford in 1649, of the Parisian *sans-culottes* in 1795, or for that matter the French *ouvriers* in June 1848 . . . the reaction might be real enough, as it was under the Cromwellian Protectorate and Restoration in England and the Napoleonic Empire and restoration in France. But what is also true is that the popular revolutionary tradition, having led an underground existence out of sight of the authorities, survived and re-emerged in new forms and under new historical conditions when the "people"—the recipients of the previous set of "derived" ideas—had also suffered a "sea-change."[88]

Histories: "All History Must be Studied Afresh"

Rudé has not only been the author of a remarkable set of primary works, but along with the previously-considered *The Crowd in History* and *Ideology and Popular Protest,* he is the author of several masterful historical syntheses and a variety of critical writings on historiography, the most important of the latter being his book, *Debate on Europe, 1815–1850.*[89] This section will look at Rudé's efforts to provide syntheses of the eighteenth- and early nineteenth-century periods, the classical narratives of which his own original scholarship contributed so much to undermining. Although now subject to historical revision, I hope to show that these studies, along with Rudé's primary work, have themselves been influential in inspiring potentially more successful syntheses or narratives. First, however, we should note Rudé's own thinking about the writing of history.

Perhaps because so much of his work as a "pioneer" has entailed confrontations with the narratives and myths propagated by liberal and, especially, conservative writers about the eighteenth and nineteenth centuries, Rudé has regularly been invited to offer his reflections on the practice of history and other historians. His writings in this area are characteristically critical, but, at the same time, always appreciative of *good* historical study, whether from the

Left or Right. His thoughts are well articulated in articles such as "Marxism and History," "Interpretations of the French Revolution," and "The Study of Revolutions,"[90] among others, but are best represented in *Debate on Europe,* which Hugh Stretton describes as "both a novel history of ideas, and a model of the self-knowledge and understanding of the sources of historical disagreement which every working historian ought to have, and all too few do have."[91] The book provides a critical survey of historians' views and studies from contemporary times to the present (1970) of events and developments in European political, economic, cultural, and social history from the end of the Napoleonic Wars to the revolts of 1848. The introduction to the book is a marvelously crisp consideration of the variables or factors shaping historians' thoughts as they pursue, in the words of E. H. Carr, "the dialogue with the past" which is history and the intertwined debate with other historians past and present. In the light of the determining force of national, class, and generational origins, differential access and inclination to different kinds of evidence, and social, political, and religious views upon the interpretive act, Rudé insists that "there can be no single received or universal truth in [history] writing and that the 'varieties of history' (to use Fritz Stern's expression) must be largely attributed to factors such as these." Moreover, we are reminded that however good the history, it is subject to revision because "although the past does not change the present does" and, therefore, the dialogue between past and present is transformed as our experience conjures up new questions, concerns, and sympathies which we introduce into it. Yet, he adds, there are writers whose works, for various possible reasons, continue to speak to historical scholars even after generations, citing in particular the writings of Tocqueville, Marx, and Engels.[92]

Not surprisingly, as a Marxist Rudé stresses the significance of "sociopolitical values" which divide scholars, and he explains that in the course of the book he will be distinguishing historians in terms of three "camps," which he labels "Tory" or "conservative," "Whig" or "liberal," and "socialist" or "Marxist." (Giving each of these a broad definition, Rudé acknowledges that such labels are "of course, generalizations, which never exactly fit" and, thus, there are variations and degrees to which they do.) The question of values is so important, he contends, because values "affect not only the sort of books [historians] write and the judgments they make, but also the records they consult, the questions they ask and the methods they use to prepare and to present their answers." He finds—optimistically, perhaps—that the advent of the "new" social history has seemed to reduce the "polemic" for so long characteristic of historical thinking about the period 1815–50. However, he says, this does not mean that historical practice is any more "value-free" than previously, referring us, for example, to the heated debate underway at the time between liberals and Marxists on the consequences of the Industrial Revolution to working-class standards of living. And yet, he notes at several points in the text that the application of new methods and theoretical insights, along with the "opening up" of new archives, has allowed for real progress in the historical study of certain features of the past.[93] (The issues arising out of the years 1815–50 which have been a part of historical debate and are included in Rudé's survey are, of course, too numerous to indicate. But it should be stated that a reading of Rudé's discussion of the connections between the emergence of particular historical concerns and contemporary social issues—for example, the renewed historical interest in "nationalism" in the post–Second World War period instigated, it would appear, by the resurgence of Afro-Asian struggles for independence—forces one to reflect on the relationship between present-day historical writings and current affairs and concerns.)[94]

Rudé has always been a promoter of the idea that historians should make use of the methods and insights of the social sciences and, as we have seen, he himself drew upon such from sociology and social psychology. After almost thirty years, his "borrowings" from social sciences seem less radical now that historians have enmeshed themselves in everything from econometrics to semiotics. Yet, whereas Rudé sought to "socialize" history without writing out "political" history, the same cannot be said of all the currents of "interdisciplinary" history which have emerged during the past generation. Furthermore, it should be registered that in contrast to a number of contemporary scholars who are inclined to merge history with the social sciences, Rudé has insisted on the essential autonomy of the historical discipline.[95] Indeed—perhaps even contradicting what I have said above—although he has always been ready and eager for a dialogue and exchange with the social sciences, Rudé has often been dissatisfied with the results (as we have noted).

More significant than generically-constituted social-science thought has been the influence of Marx and Engels on his historical scholarship. In "The Changing Face of the Crowd" he commences his personal reflections by declaring what he believes his work owes to a reading of the founders of historical materialism.

> What I learned from Marx was not only that history tends to progress through a conflict of social classes . . . but that it has a discoverable pattern and moves forward (not backwards, in circles, or in inexplicable jerks) broadly from a lower to a higher phase of development. I learned also that the lives and actions of the common people are the very stuff of history, and though "material" rather than the institutional and ideological factors are primary, that ideas themselves become a "material force" when they pass into active consciousness of men. Moreover, I have also learned from Engels that, whatever the excellence of historical "systems" . . . "all history must be studied afresh."

For Rudé, then, a Marxist historian is one who sees history in terms of "class struggle" not "a narrow economic determinism," and he believes "conflict is both a normal and salutary means of achieving progress." He has brought this to bear both in his primary work and in his "synthetic" writings on eighteenth- and nineteenth-century Europe including, in the latter instances, his books: *Revolutionary Europe, 1783–1815* (1964); *Robespierre* (1975); *Hanoverian London, 1714–1803* (1971); *Europe in the Eighteenth Century* (1972), and *The French Revolution* (1988). *Revolutionary Europe*—the first, and probably the most important considering the more than one hundred thousand students and others (not including readers of the translated editions) who have been introduced to the period through its pages!—is a splendidly written text examining the French Revolution and its consequences in European perspective, and providing narrative and analysis along with clear discussions of the many issues which have fascinated historians ever since the fall of the Bastille. The particular "grand narrative" which Rudé offers is expressive of his own scholarship but also incorporates that advanced by his French colleagues, Lefebvre and Soboul, which they had developed out of both the Republican and Marxist traditions. In their works the Revolution is conceived of as a "merger of two distinct movements—the bourgeois and the popular."[96]

This class-structured rendition of the Revolution is also the underlying narrative for *Robespierre,* a book which Rudé refers to as a "political portrait" rather than a personal biography. Robespierre is portrayed extremely sympathetically by Rudé and one necessarily imagines that Rudé's thoughts—as those of an admirer of the Soviet Revolution—are related to his perceptions of Lenin; an idea which is confirmed in the last pages of the volume, where Rudé directly compares and contrasts the leading figure of Jacobinism with that of the great Bolshevik revolutionary. In particular, Rudé's picture of Robespierre is that of a "revolutionary political democrat" persistently asserting the "sovereignty of the people," but, tragically, having to deal with the inherent contradictions of the revolutionary alliance between Jacobins and *sans-culottes* and, for Robespierre, "the Revolution" was paramount in importance. Rudé also finds that although Robespierre was not a "socialist" he was, as Lefebvre had argued, a "social democrat" of sorts (though it should be pointed out that Rudé's definition of a socialist is rather orthodox, for it requires "State ownership").[97] At the end of the book, Rudé offers a historical assessment of the place of the Revolution in history and, within it, Robespierre's particular contribution.

> The French Revolution was one of the great landmarks in modern history. No other single event did so much to destroy the aristocratic society and absolutist institutions of Old Europe and to lay the groundwork for the new societies—both bourgeois and social-

ist—that on every continent, have risen from their ashes since. To this transformation Robespierre made a signal contribution: not only as the Revolution's outstanding leader at every stage of its most vigorous and creative years; but also as the first great champion of democracy and people's rights. And this, essentially, is what establishes his claim to greatness.[98]

The subtitle of Rudé's book, *Europe in the Eighteenth Century: Aristocracy and the Bourgeois Challenge,* clearly signals his view of the class structuring of the period. Introducing the volume, he refers to the "numerous pitfalls" one faces in writing the history of that "pre-revolutionary" century. Such difficulties include the danger of reducing all that transpired to being merely a "preface" to the "Age of Revolution" (to use Eric Hobsbawm's term) and, also, the question of British "exceptionalism." Moreover, he observes, there is the general historiographical problem of "how to stress movement—which is the very stuff of history—as well as the conditions, 'structure,' and 'continuity.'" Admitting to have emphasized "internal conflicts" Rudé forewarns his readers "that a great deal of attention has been paid to social classes, to the institutions and ideas they generate and to the tensions and conflicts that arise between them. These in turn are presented as an important element in the historical process."[99] The book provides a comprehensive portrait of eighteenth-century Europe from population and social structure, to politics, government and ideas, to the struggles which shaped them.

Naturally, Rudé seeks to incorporate "history from below" and the popular classes into his narrative and analysis—though he was constrained by the paucity of such historical scholarship at the time. Thus, the conflicts of the eighteenth century upon which he primarily focuses are those between aristocracy and bourgeoisie, but, as he shows, the antagonisms and conflicts between the popular classes and the upper—both bourgeois and aristocrats—were also crucial determinants of the course of events. Indeed, Rudé contends, it was the fear of the middle class about the "inferior sort of people" which effectively inhibited them from mobilizing the common people against the aristocracy, the consequences of which were to the advantage of the Old Regime. (This fear was overcome in the Revolution of 1789!) It must be said that what is actually most interesting about *Europe in the Eighteenth Century* is Rudé's not unsympathetic renderings of the rulers and dominant classes—for example, his discussion of "enlightened despots" and their efforts at reforms which were destined to failure (or, at best, limited success) "so long as the privileged orders were left in possession of their powers . . . to obstruct their operation."[100]

Hanoverian London is an extremely detailed survey of urban life in the capital. Again, in characteristically Rudéan fashion it evidences his concern to integrate the "lower orders" into the historical picture. And yet, as in *Europe in the Eighteenth Century,* it is arguable that the most intriguing aspects of the work are Rudé's descriptions of the circumstances of the "propertied," aristocratic and bourgeois. Few historians have denied the significance of inequalities of wealth and power in eighteenth-century England, but whereas classes and conflicts were not, perhaps, dramatic innovations in European studies, to insist on the centrality of these—especially conflict—in English life was to oppose the traditional view of the century as one of "consensus." Rudé, however, approaching London from the bottom up, and fully conscious of social and political protests from below, insists that "class hostility" and "conflicts" were a central force in the eighteenth century. (I cannot help but remark that as much as Rudé is renowned for his attention to sociopolitical subjects in history, his insights into the class structuring of experience in *Hanoverian London* never fail to encompass culture and everyday life as well. For example, he writes of how "In the first half of the century there was a tidy class division in drinking: the poor drank gin or cheap brandy, 'the middle sort' drank porter or ale, and the wealthier classes drank French or Portuguese wine.")[101]

Although Rudé's synthetic writings are framed by a "class-struggle and structured" mode of analysis, he remains as ambivalent in these works on the eighteenth century as he has been in his primary studies to present the historical experience of the time in *class*-specific terms. His reservations seem to be due to both an orthodox Marxist understanding of class *and* a commitment to comprehending the past in historically-specific terms; that is, he is both unwilling to impose on, and unable to find in, the eighteenth century the model of "class" experience derived from the nineteenth (both in the sense of "in itself" and "for itself"). In this vein, Rudé has himself acknowledged the significance, and even correctness, of certain aspects of the "revisionist challenge" to the view of the French Revolution as a "bourgeois revolution" (a challenge originating with his own major professor at the University of London, Alfred Cobban).[102] For example, he has said that "terms like *aristocracy* and *bourgeoisie* . . . have developed a Marxist connotation from the nineteenth-century attempt to distinguish between major social groups according to their economic background or role. . . . All this is useful, but obviously these modern connotations can be misleading in the context of the French Revolution in which words such as aristocrat or bourgeois tend to take on political connotations, and thus confusion arises among old and new meanings."[103] However, even though Rudé points to a source of the historiographical problem, he has not himself addressed it sufficiently to answer the revisionist critique which, although it has offered no better alternative, has greatly undermined the "bourgeois revolution" thesis. This is problematic: Rudé offers us a class-struggle analysis of the eighteenth-century and French Revolution but, at the same time, he is unable to actually defend the class-based "bourgeois revolution" thesis.

Yet, there has begun to emerge a Marxian effort to transcend the revisionist critique. Rudé's own student, George Comninel, stimulated in good part by insights found in Rudé's own writings, has begun to advance a new reading of the Revolution. In his book, *Rethinking the French Revolution*,[104] Comninel surveys the Marxist versus revisionist debate and shows how the Marxist tradition has consistently failed to consider critically the origins of its "class" model of the Revolution and the grounds upon which it has been based. He points out that Marx himself uncritically drew his version of the French Revolution from nineteenth-century "liberal/Republican" writers, never actually subjecting the origins, developments, and events of the Revolution to a "historical materialist" analysis and, furthermore, that Marxists ever since have subscribed to—and sought to defend—the "bourgeois revolution thesis," thereby reproducing Marx's originally-mistaken assumptions.

What Comninel calls for—and plans himself to pursue in a second volume—is the suspension, if not the disavowal, of the bourgeois revolution thesis in favor of a return to, and re-examination of, the *history* of the Revolution from a truly critical historical materialist perspective, starting out from the historically specific relations of exploitation and appropriation of late eighteenth-century France and the class struggles to which they give rise. In fact, he provides a provisional rendition of such an analysis in the conclusion to *Rethinking the French Revolution* and, in its recognition of the significance of the popular struggles "without whose intervention the bourgeois and liberal-aristocratic revolutionaries could not have realized their goals,"[105] it is evident that Comninel's efforts have been inspired by the scholarship of his mentor (as well as that of Lefebvre and Soboul). What we must now acknowledge is that although Rudé did not himself pursue it, his own works— by asserting and highlighting the centrality of the struggles from below— actually undermined the bourgeois revolution thesis and greatly contributed to the need for a fresh historical materialist analysis and, likely, a dramatically revised narrative of the Revolution! Thus, Comninel's future work promises to be a major contribution to our understanding of eighteenth-century France and the Revolution of 1789, and to the further development of the class-struggle analysis of history,[106] not to mention representing a tribute to the work of Rudé.

Rudé himself provided the foreword to Comninel's book, and his appreciation and enthusiasm for its arguments are clearly expressed. He especially welcomes Comninel's insistence on both the necessity of rigorously applying the "principles of historical materialism" to the eighteenth century and, in the process, the need to reconsider the assumption that the decline of feudalism necessarily engendered the rise of capitalism in any direct or immediate fashion.[107] This, of course, reflects Rudé's own long-standing doubts and difficulties, noted earlier, about how to conceive the eighteenth century in terms of the transition from feudalism to capitalism and the development of industrial capitalism in both France and England. As indicated earlier, Rudé's problem on this score was due in part to his failure to examine or sufficiently consider the politico-economic processes and developments under way in the eighteenth century in England and France. Although the concept of "pre-industrial" society provided an extremely useful means by which to treat contemporary popular protests in England and France, the political economies and class structures of the two countries were quite different. At the same time, Rudé's persistent reference to the period as "transitional" and his insistence that it not be subsumed—in either the English or French case—under the "feudal" past or, too readily, under the "industrial-capitalist" future (because from his studies it was evident that the struggles of the age were historically unique), can be seen as inviting the pursuit of more rigorous politico-economic analysis of both Hanoverian England and pre-revolutionary and revolutionary France. Indeed, his repeated observation that the primary site of contention in the eighteenth century was "at the point of consumption rather than *production*," and that there was not yet a consciousness of class as in the nineteenth century, has remained an important question only now beginning to be properly addressed by social historians of the Marxian persuasion.[108]

This question posed by Rudé brings us to the work of his fellow British Marxist historian, E. P. Thompson (itself an influence on Comninel's ideas about the French Revolution), for it was Thompson who followed Rudé into eighteenth-century England and, in his own way, ran into the same problematic as his pioneering comrade: how to conceive of the popular struggles of the age? Thompson's answer, like Rudé's, was "class struggle without class." But whereas Rudé did not pursue the self-contradictory implications of this phrase, Thompson has, and in so doing he has explicitly reformulated the Marxian model of class formation. That is, Thompson eschewed the static and essentially ahistorical scheme of "class in itself/class for itself"—which Rudé, too, came to abandon in *Ideology and Popular Protest*—and, instead, offered a dynamic model posing the historically prior existence of class struggle/structure out of which "class," in the sense of a class-conscious formation, may potentially develop or, better, *be made*. Thompson himself explains that the possible attribution of "class" to eighteenth-century popular struggles requires, first of all, critical attention to the historically-specific social relations of exploitation and appropriation (which, it must be added, is—thus far at least—more often implied in his writings than explicitly mapped out). Thompson's work points the way towards a historical-materialist class-struggle analysis of eighteenth- and early nineteenth-century England in terms of the process of "primitive accumulation."[109] Having said this, it remains true that the work under way and to be done on the eighteenth century will have been constructed on the foundations laid not only by Thompson who, as I have previously argued, has articulated in the clearest theoretical terms the class-struggle approach of the British Marxist historians, but also by Rudé who first advanced into the eighteenth century to recover the popular struggles of the time, and thereby called up the problematic of "class struggle without class."

George Rudé's writings on eighteenth-century France, England, and Europe, and his studies of the Age of Revolution reaching from Europe to North America and Australia, have influenced historical and social science scholarship around the globe. Although social historians in the 1980s have ventured down topical, methodological, and theoretical paths which he himself would not have pursued, it is arguable that much of the social-history writing of the past generation, in its pursuit of history from below, was enabled by Rudé's own initiatives to mobilize the methodologies and theoretical insights of the social sciences and, too, by his struggles to widen the social horizons of the past.

I have argued that the political project of the British Marxist historians as a group has been to contribute to the making of a democratic and socialist historical consciousness.[110] There can be no doubt that Rudé, too, in spite of his "exile" from England to Australia and North America for so much of his university teaching career and, thus, his geographical distance from his historian comrades, has been actively committed to that effort. Reading of the *sans-culottes*' mobilizations in the Revolution, of the movement for Wilkes and Liberty in Hanoverian London, of the struggles of the agricultural laborers in industrializing England and the transportation of so many of them to Australia, and of the aspirations and ideas of protests around the preindustrial societies of the Atlantic World, one is necessarily reminded of the words offered by Antonio Gramsci to his son, written from a fascist prison in 1937: "I think you must like history, as I liked it when I was your age, because it deals with living men, and everything that concerns men, as many men as possible, all the men in the world in so far as they unite together in society, and work and struggle and make a bid for a better life."[111]

Historical scholarship continues to "progress" and Rudé's writings have, by their very instigation of new work, become subject to critical questioning by a younger generation of social historians.[112] Yet, even if his studies of popular protest and his texts on eighteenth-century history come to be superseded by new researches and interpretations, or transcended by way of dramatic revisions to our grand narratives, Rudé's contributions will remain relevant as examples of pioneering and committed history writing. Moreover, so long as we continue to ask the central historical questions—"Who?" and "Why?"—we will continue to honor his work, for he would be the first to argue along the lines of the founders of historical materialism that "all history must be studied afresh."

3

V. G. KIERNAN:
SEEING THINGS HISTORICALLY

Victor Kiernan is probably best known as a historian of modern imperial-ism, through such works as *The Lords of Human Kind, European Empires from Conquest to Collapse, 1815–1960, Marxism and Imperialism,* and *America: The New Imperialism,* plus two earlier monographs, *British Diplomacy in China, 1880–1885* and *Metcalfe's Mission to Lahore, 1808–1809.*[1] These books are themselves quite varied both in terms of the subjects they treat and the di-mensions of imperialism they consider, extending from diplomatic and mili-tary to social and cultural history; and they are joined by numerous articles and essays in international studies taking up such diverse topics as the South American War of the Pacific, nineteenth-century imperial rivalries in Central Asia, colonial armies in Africa, the historic relationship between Portugal and Britain and the postcolonial development of India and Pakistan.[2]

Yet, however wide-ranging the subjects and geographical areas dealt with in these writings on imperialism and international history, they represent merely one of the themes of modern European and world history that have engaged Kiernan's historical imagination. One might turn to the *Dictionary of Marxist Thought,*[3] of which he is a co-editor, noting the entries for which he is personally responsible: agnosticism, Christianity, empires of Marx's day, Hinduism, historiography, intellectuals, Paul Lafargue, Ferdinand Lasalle, nation, nationalism, religion, revolution, Manabendra Nath Roy, stages of development, and war. But even this list does not give full account of the subjects on which Kiernan has written, for beyond the history of diplomacy and war, politics and the state, revolution and social change, and intellectuals and religions,[4] he is also the author of articles on labor and the working class,[5] and literature, the arts and cultural studies.[6] Finally, he has translated three volumes of South Asian poetry and prose for publication in English.[7]

It is not, however, just the range, diversity and voluminousness of Kier-nan's writings that warrant our attention, though they are truly impressive.

Just as significant is the consistently critical perspective which he has brought to bear on the variety of issues he examines historically. Kiernan is, of course, closely identified with his distinguished friends and comrades, the British Marxist historians. Indeed, Kiernan has always been very much a part of this cohort as an early and active member of the Communist Party Historians' Group in the period 1946–56, and through the formal and informal relationships that were maintained after 1956 when most of them left the Party.[8] The principal formal link has been the journal, *Past & Present* (founded by Hilton, Hill, Hobsbawm and others in 1952), for which Kiernan wrote an article for the inaugural issue, and served on the editorial board from 1973 to 1983.[9] Nevertheless, it is arguable that Kiernan's scholarship stands somewhat apart from that of his fellow British Marxist historians. His writings, for all their variety, are regularly set within the problematic of the transition to capitalism and they are strongly informed by class-struggle analysis; and to the extent that history from below is generally comprehended to mean having "sympathy with the victims of historical processes and skepticism about the victors' claims,"[10] then Kiernan has been working from the bottom up. However, if history from below is understood more specifically to entail both a perspective *and,* as is more often the case, the recovery of the experiences and struggles of the laboring classes historically, then, except for a limited number of his writings,[11] Kiernan has not exactly been working in this historiographical tradition. Rather, he has been the historian of the original group who has concentrated most on what Perry Anderson has appropriately termed "history from above—the study of the intricate machinery of class domination"—though, it should be stated here, always conceived in terms of the relations of conflict and struggle that determine and shape it.[12]

This chapter is offered as an introductory survey of Victor Kiernan's scholarly career as a Marxist historian and thinker. There are too many directions in which he has travelled as a writer for it to be truly comprehensive, but following a brief biographical sketch it will consider his work on Marxism and history, diplomacy and imperialism, classes and nation-states, and British culture and the making of socialism.

V. G. Kiernan

Edward Victor Gordon Kiernan was born on 4 September 1913 in Ashton-on-Mersey, a southern area of Manchester. He describes his parents as lower-middle class and his family generally as "not political in any active sense but mostly well stored with conservative prejudices." His parents were, however, quite religious and Kiernan was brought up an active Congregationalist, which he views as having been an important formative influence contributing to his later socialist commitments and also to his continuing scholarly interest in the place of religion in history.[13]

Kiernan was educated at Manchester Grammar School, which had only recently set up a History Sixth Form—if it had not it would have meant his entering the "Classical Sixth Form"—and thus he notes that his choice of history was more "accidental" than anything else. In 1931 he entered Trinity College, Cambridge to read history and was an outstanding student. A life-long friend (in spite of their contrasting political trajectories since the 1930s), Professor Henry Ferns presents this picture of Kiernan the young scholar at Cambridge:

> A visit to Mr. Kiernan was my first intellectual encounter with Cambridge University. [He] is a man of my own age. I have always thought of him, however, as senior to me. He was my first supervisor and I was *in statu pupillari* for my first term. Although we became good friends and companions, this feeling of Victor's superiority endured, and for good reason. He had achieved a first class with distinction in both parts of the Historical Tripos. In 1936 he was in his third year as a research scholar and in 1937 he was elected a Fellow of Trinity College. A list of his academic distinctions does not alone account for his authority in my mind then. He was immensely learned. He had a good knowledge of Latin, Greek, French . . . and Spanish. He knew some Italian and was acquiring a knowledge of Urdu. . . . He loved music—particularly that of the seventeenth and eighteenth century. He had an intimate knowledge and love of English literature, which, like his taste in music, seemed concentrated on comparatively few artists of the first rank: Shakespeare, Samuel Johnson, and Wordsworth. If his knowledge was limited to men of the past his taste was catholic.[14]

Having graduated in 1934, Kiernan remained at Cambridge for the next four years, first as a research scholar and then as a Fellow of Trinity. Also in 1934, he joined the Communist Party. Cambridge University of this period has provided the material for numerous reminiscences, exposés, historical studies, and fictional representations, and Kiernan was very much a part of the generation of student communists that has been the subject of so many of those writings.[15] Indeed, among his closest friends and comrades were John Cornford and James Klugmann, the leading figures of Cambridge Communism; also Kiernan was quite close to the Canadian, Herbert Norman.[16] By most accounts, these years seem to have been understood by these young leftists as "the worst of times . . . the best of times." The world economic depression and industrial unemployment, the rise and triumph of Fascism in Central Europe and the ever-increasing threat of a second world war (made even more evident by events in Spain), all contributed to the view that the capitalist world was going through its final crisis. Yet for these students there

was also the sense that they were living through the prelude to socialist revolution, which perhaps by their own efforts they might hasten.[17]

Kiernan did not see his political commitments as being in conflict with his
scholarly labors. He has always been of the opinion that his explorations of
the past were, and should be, connected with his political concerns; indeed,
he says that ever since his days at Cambridge he has held the view that "History and politics are two sides of the same coin." Confronting a world characterized by persisting overseas colonial empires, resurgent European imperial aspirations in Africa and Europe itself, and Japanese expansionism in Asia
and the Pacific, Kiernan focused his research on the historical development
of modern colonialism and empire-building. Especially he took up the study
of Britain's relations with Asia, more specifically, Anglo-Chinese relations.
Thus, he was also motivated to make contact with Asian students at Cambridge who were themselves attempting to deal with the questions of British
and European imperialism and colonialism, and his activity for the Party
principally took the form of working with an Indian Marxist study group
organized by his friend, Herbert Norman.

The product of his fellowship research was the book, *British Diplomacy in
China, 1880–1885.* The outcome of his work with Indian students was his
departure from Cambridge and England to take up schoolteaching in India,
first at the Sikh National College and then at Aitchison College in Lahore
(in what is now Pakistan). Spending the Second World War years in India
(1938–46), Kiernan continued to pursue both the study of British imperialism in Asia and political work in contact with the Communist Party of
India. His historical researches led to another shorter monograph in diplomatic history, *Metcalfe's Mission to Lahore, 1808–1809,* and the mix of his political and literary interests brought him into contact with the Indian Progressive Writers' Association which had been formed in London before the
war. Improving his knowledge of literary Urdu and Hindi, Kiernan was stimulated to begin a series of translations eventually published as *Poems from
Iqbal, From Volga to Ganga,* and *Poems by Faiz.*[18] He also wrote a children's
novel, *The March of Time;* poetry, a collection of which was published as *Castanets;* and several stories, two of which appeared in *Longman's Miscellany.*[19]
These years in India were tremendously important in shaping his later work.
Pre-existing interests expanded and deepened: his study of colonialism and
imperialism grew to encompass the issues of nationalism and nation-state
formation, and he has maintained a lifelong fascination and concern for the
politics and culture of the Indian subcontinent. But also, it is arguable that
this period—living in a colonial society in contact with an intelligentsia
which was, at best, ambivalent about the British war effort—must have contributed greatly to the development of his own perspective on imperialism
and colonialism, which is undeniably critical and yet quite sensitive to the
historical contradictions of those experiences (as I will discuss).

Following the war, Kiernan returned to Cambridge University for a two-year period as a fellow of Trinity during which (amongst other studies) he wrote a two hundred thousand word manuscript dealing with the political and social ideas of Shakespeare's drama. Though publishers were interested in the work, he was unable to carry out the necessary revisions because he was too busy preparing courses for his first university teaching post. His work with the Communist Party upon his return to Britain involved both practical political work within the university and in the town, and contributions to the formation and development of the Historians' Group, the activities of which were centered on London. He was extremely active with the Group in its first few years and remained in contact following his move to Scotland and a lectureship. However, as a formal enterprise, the Group all but fell apart in 1956–57, when many of its central figures left the Party in protest of the Soviet invasion of Hungary and the failure of the British Party to break with the Soviets and reform itself.[20] Kiernan was active in the debates of the time, but he did not leave the Party until 1959, hoping for changes that did not take place. Since then he has referred to himself as an "independent Marxist" with "no enemies on the Left." He has joined no other party or political grouping. In 1948 Kiernan had taken up a lectureship at the University of Edinburgh in the History Department, later being promoted to reader and then professor before retiring as professor emeritus in 1977. By all accounts, his teaching responsibilities were as varied as his researches.

Before turning to consider Kiernan's ideas, another feature, or characteristic, of his erudition should be noted. In addition to important studies based on primary research, Kiernan's scholarship includes masterful works of synthesis drawing on both primary and—in some cases, mostly—secondary study.[21] Moreover, he has been recognized as an exceptionally skilful "historical essayist." This has been accomplished through vast and extensive reading, phenomenal note-taking and file-keeping, and especially, as his longtime friend, Eric Hobsbawm, has remarked, his "encyclopaedic knowledge."[22] In light of recent criticisms that the historical profession is failing to write in such a way as to make its studies meaningful to non-scholars, and the associated call to provide a new syntheses, or "grand narratives," out of the innumerable explorations of the past carried out during the last twenty years and more, it may well be that we should attend as much to the form and shape of Kiernan's writings as to their content.[23]

Marxism and the Necessity of History

Kiernan subscribes to the classical or Renaissance ideal of historical practice wherein scholarship is closely bound up with ethico-political discourse. In this view history is not merely "for its own sake"—as some conservatives have recently insinuated even as they practice otherwise—but in the words of E. H. Carr: "To enable man to understand the society of the past, and to increase his mastery over the society of the present, is the dual function of history."[24] Thus, history is a critical pursuit standing in dialectical relation to social and political thought. Kiernan has been quite direct about the necessity of history for perspective and imagination. For example, in the heady days of the late 1960s he wrote:

> The past is not abolished by being disregarded but turned into a dead weight of habit, stultifying the present. It is only by trying to comprehend the past rationally that we can transform it from a shapeless mass into a platform, or draw energy from it like the giant Antaeus from contact with his mother Earth. The maxim that only active involvement in the present can develop the right sense of touch for the past is a true one, but so is the converse, that only familiarity with the past can impart the right touch for the present. We cannot act on things gone by, but they continue to act on us, and past and present combine to make the future.[25]

In the more bracing experience of the 1980s, discussing the ideological inclinations of nineteenth-century historians, he points to the imperative, or at least potential, of history as critique or demystification, quoting the epigram of Paul Valery that "History is the most dangerous product evolved from the chemistry of the intellect."[26] The intimacy of history and politics for Kiernan must not, however, be construed as implying any tolerance for subordinating the study of the past or its findings to political expediency. He has stated his contempt for the abuse and misrepresentation of history in both the East and the West, by both the Right and the Left, because, as he warns, if history is to contribute to the comprehension and the making of *new* history, it will not do to deceive ourselves: "Any falsification of the past must point a wrong way to the future."[27]

Kiernan's own guide to the past has been, of course, Marx: "A Marxist likes to suppose that all he writes, even if not written in terms of art or Hegelian geometry, is—to adapt Boswell—fully impregnated with the Marxian aether. . . . I, at least, always liked to feel while writing that the Grand Old Man was within hailing distance."[28] For Kiernan, as for his fellow British Marxist historians, Marxism is *historical* materialism (the stress is their own!). It is not to be conceived of as a system of logic or philosophy in either the Hegelian or Anglo-Saxon analytical modes. On a variety of occasions he has expressed a particular frustration with the tendency in Marxist studies towards such practice. In fact, he seems to share the general antipathy of historians towards philosophers: "All that philosophers have discovered since the world began could be written on one sheet of paper—or so one is frequently tempted to conclude."[29] Not a philosophical system, neither is Marxism a model to be applied to, or a formal theory to be simply fleshed out with, historical materials. What Marxism is—or at least what Kiernan interprets it to be—is *historical* theory, to be developed further in the course of historical study and revised in its light. This is not to suggest, however, that Kiernan assumes some kind of monopoly license to have been granted to historians: "What is of solid worth in Marxism lies in its theory of history, its theory of politics, or economics, or art, and its promise if not yet performance of a psychology and an ethic." The main thing is that Marxist practitioners of whatever discipline think historically. Thus, in urging serious attention to the related issues of justice and morality, he writes that they should be studies "not in the abstract but in the setting of history."[30]

Kiernan has long been insistent that Marxist thought give priority to history over models and abstractions. Recalling the early years of the Historian's Group, Eric Hobsbawm notes that there was a tendency amongst them to allow their assumptions and expectations to determine their historical answers. To Kiernan, however, Hobsbawm gives the title "our chief doubter," and Christopher Hill, referring to the same experiences, says of him that "He kept us on our toes."[31] It is quite likely that these reminiscences of Kiernan's participation refer in particular to his dissensions in the course of the group's deliberations in 1947 on the subject of the transition to capitalism, treating specifically the questions of the nature of England's mode of production and social structure in the sixteenth and seventeenth centuries, the class character of the state in that period, and thence the degree to which the English Revolution can be understood as a "bourgeois revolution." In short, Kiernan took issue with the thesis, offered in a document prepared for the Group by Hill, that the Tudor polity was a feudal-absolutist landowners' state. He agreed that the Tudor polity was absolutist, but he held that it could not be defined as feudal because whereas absolutism entailed centralized political power and authority, feudalism was a polity characterized by dispersed powers and authorities. Moreover, the agrarian relations of production around which the social order and the state were formed in the sixteenth century were no longer feudal but much more capitalist. Regarding the struggles of the seventeenth century, Kiernan proposed that rather than there having been only one bourgeois revolution there had actually been several from the fifteenth to the seventeenth century. Finally, on the related question of the characterization of the period as either feudal or capitalist, he suggested that "merchant capitalist" seemed most appropriate to this transitional phase; indeed, Kiernan felt that too much was being made of a supposed distinction between mercantile and industrial capitalists, the former conservative and the latter progressive (a position advanced by Maurice Dobb in his book, *Studies in the Development of Capitalism*).[32]

The Group did not accept Kiernan's criticisms.[33] Forty years later, these questions continue to be debated, though our knowledge of the transition process is greatly increased and the concepts used to analyze it are arguably more refined.[34] We find that the historical evidence and current arguments do support aspects of Kiernan's dissent, especially that the development of agrarian capitalism was well under way in the sixteenth century and that the "bourgeois revolution," though culminating in the struggles of the seventeenth century, was in fact a much longer and more complex process.[35] Yet it would appear that he underestimated the degree to which West European absolutism could be a "feudal" state (a position which he revised in his later writings), and I would argue that, though the transitional centuries remain ill-defined, he was also mistaken both in proposing the term "merchant capitalism" to cover the period and in assessing merchant capital as an essentially developmental force in the process.[36] Nevertheless—perhaps even in spite of, or on account of, the rejection of his criticisms of what was to be the Group's "official" position—Kiernan has remained actively interested in the historical problem of the transition, as evidenced in his many writings on both imperialism and nation-state formation (a point to which I shall return).

Amongst his fellow Marxist historians, Kiernan is both one of the most critical and one of the most appreciative of Marx himself (though this may be due to the fact that Kiernan has seemed far more willing than most to reflect aloud about Marx and the development of Marxist thought).[37] In his 1983 Marx Centennial essay, "History," Kiernan surveys and assesses the development of "historical Marxism." He does so by situating Marx, Engels and a variety of later Marxists in their historically-specific circumstances, acknowledging their personal commitments, the particular intellectual legacies available to them, and the specific international and national developments, demands and possibilities that shaped their work. In this fashion he objectively considers the bases upon which Marxist historical practice has evolved, highlighting in these experiences the ideas worth preserving, subject to further exploration and revision, and the problems demanding urgent consideration either because of inadequate attention in the past, or worse, intellectual corruption, or because Clio has only now thrown them up in such a form that we can properly recognize them.[38]

Critical appreciation of Marx and Engels is evident throughout Kiernan's writings. At one moment he points to where they overemphasized the economic factor in order to secure their materialist perspective; at another, to their imperfectly successful attempts to discover the "logic" of history which might thereafter guide them through the thickets of the past; and, at yet another, to those numerous occasions on which Marx allowed his ideas and aspirations for humanity to outrun the historical evidence. At the same time, however, Kiernan maintains that it was probably this very same "passion" which infused Marx's writings with their continuing relevance: "The most formidable intellect cannot work at full stretch on human problems, except passionately, and all original and intense thought must be one-sided; the eye that sees every aspect of the question sees none of them vividly." Kiernan does not hesitate to remind us that "Marx was an amateur historian," but, of course, one whose "mind roamed over world history at large." Regarding his contributions to historical theory he finds Marx a great explorer: "Much as Columbus and those who came after him convinced men once for all that the earth was round, Marx brought recognition of an order and priority of relationships among all human concerns."[39]

Even as he pays homage to Marx, Kiernan notes that it seems unfortunate that an ever-developing body of thought should go "under one man's name." Amongst the things he may well have had in mind were the labors of Marx's comrade and intellectual partner, Engels, for in contrast to the many philosophers who have attributed the reductionisms in Marxism to Engels, Kiernan expresses warm appreciation (again, critical) for his efforts. Fully aware of Engels's simplification of Marx's thought following the latter's death, Kiernan sympathetically attributes this to Engels having the weighty responsibility of drawing together and popularizing his friend's ideas, which necessarily entailed simplifying them. Kiernan's appreciation is, however, not only on account of Engels' support for Marx and Marx's writings, but just as much because of Engels' own commitment to historical study, a product of which was his pioneering work, *The Peasant War in Germany*. In fact, Kiernan reminds us that it was not unusual for Engels to be pushing Marx into being ever more historical in his writing.[40]

Of those who have followed Marx and Engels, Kiernan feels the greatest affection for the Italian, Antonio Gramsci, whom he dubs the "first great standard-bearer of Western Marxism." In two articles, considering Gramsci's *Prison Notebooks* and *Prison Letters*, Kiernan makes clear that his admiration is inspired by the rich political, cultural, and literary content of these writings and the contributions they might make to socialist thought and practice.[41] Above all else, however, Kiernan seems to respond to Gramsci's commitment to history and his view that Marxism must be "completely historical in spirit." Gramsci's imprisonment for over a decade until his death kept him from carrying out any of the historical researches he outlined in the *Notebooks*, but as Kiernan states admiringly: "All Gramsci's speculations took . . . a historical shape, and history was with him the grand interest, embracing all the rest"; indeed, "No one has laid more stress on history as the accompaniment or vehicle of all thinking about human affairs."[42]

Another practice of Gramsci's that Kiernan commends is his willingness to confront other intellectual traditions not merely for the sake of critique and dismissal but with the intention of learning from them and possibly even drawing out elements to be incorporated into Marxism itself. If historical materialism is to continue to develop, it is essential, Kiernan argues, that it be self-conscious and self-critical about its own inadequacies, responsive to new challenges and demands, and receptive to what may possibly be secured from competing theories: "Marxism in other words cannot generate all its intellectual capital out of its own resources."[43] Kiernan himself has been more than willing to be critical of Marxists whose analyses fail on historical grounds, as he is, for example, with Ernst Fischer's book, *The Necessity of Art,* in a review essay entitled "Art and the Necessity of History."[44] In the same spirit, he has shown himself to be warmly disposed towards non-Marxist scholars whose works have contributions to make to Marxist historical enquiry. For example, in a review essay on Braudel's *Capitalism and Material Life, 1400–1800,* he writes:

> There is also a great deal in the book for Marxists to ponder over, asking themselves whether their categories have grown flexible and subtle enough to accommodate all this multitude of facts and ideas. Their understanding of "base and superstructure" would profit from such an exercise. Above all they might comprehend more clearly how and why mankind has mostly been standing still, instead of focusing their studies on the few "big leaps."[45]

Imperialism and Its Contradictions

Written before the Second World War, Kiernan's first book, *British Diplomacy in China, 1880–1885,* is in one sense a traditional work focusing on the efforts and intrigues of diplomats and statesmen to secure and further their respective countries' interests in late nineteenth-century China and East and South East Asia. In another sense, however, it stands as an attempt at innovation for, as Kiernan explains, he was seeking to unravel the manner in which the politics of diplomacy are bound up with, and expressive of, economic forces, and to thereby bring together the two seemingly separate fields of diplomatic and economic history. This is accomplished well, but the book is, nevertheless, marked by a duality. Within the larger work there is a second, shorter one reflecting Kiernan's Marxist-historical concerns, and therein he presents a sociological analysis of China's historic mode of production, social structure and the state, and class conflicts, influenced by the "hydraulic" theories offered by Karl Wittfogel and others.[46] This latter "work" is indicative of the direction in which Kiernan's postwar and later scholarship would go. Although he continued to publish in diplomatic history right into the 1960s, he increasingly came to see diplomatic affairs, in so far as his own researches were concerned, as of mostly antiquarian interest.[47]

The Lords of Human Kind appeared in 1969 and though there are evident links with his diplomatic writings, it represents a real shift, for it is a study in the historical psychology of race. Set within the process of European expansion overseas, the book surveys the attitudes of merchants and traders, diplomats and military men, and missionaries and colonial officers towards those over whom they sought hegemony. Although concerned with the view, or perspective, "from above," Kiernan appreciates that the development of European attitudes cannot be treated in isolation. Thus, in addition to illustrating how Europeans's racial(ist) and ethnocentric perceptions of the "outside world" were conditioned by the particulars of their countries of origin and therein by class, he shows how these views were shaped by the cultures, social structures, and levels of development of the non-European peoples themselves, which were, of course, determinants of those peoples' capacities to resist, or possibly thwart (as in the case of Japan), European advances, encroachments, and conquests.

The Lords of Human Kind is complemented by Kiernan's later book, *European Empires from Conquest to Collapse, 1815–1960,* published in 1982. Whereas the former treats the cultural dimension of imperial expansion, the latter is a historical sociology of Europe's imperial and colonial wars. *European Empires* looks at Europe's armies and technologies of death and their applications to killing in Africa, Asia, and the Pacific, together with considerations of the ideologies and doctrines of colonialism and colonial warfare, the publicity and political consequences at home, and the resistance and rebellions offered by colonial peoples. A reading of this work should cure one of any nostalgia for Europe's colonialist past. Indeed, both *The Lords of Human Kind* and *European Empires* arose out of Kiernan's mutual historical and political concerns. The first book was intended to provide a historical mirror in which Britons might reflect on their attitudes and relations with non-European peoples, which Kiernan saw as all the more urgent as Britain was ever more obviously becoming a multi-ethnic and multiracial society with all the attendant difficulties exacerbated by postimperial political and economic decline.[48] The second book was also for the purpose of historical reflection and to draw attention to the persistence and continuity of the past in the present: "There are, after all, good reasons for prying into the past with the historians' telescope, and trying to see more clearly what happened, instead of being content with legend or fantasy. Of all the reasons for an interest in the colonial wars of modern times the best is that they are still going on, openly or disguised."[49]

Thus, Kiernan has also explored American history in *America: The New Imperialism,* published in 1978. In it he provides an interpretation of American history in which expansion and imperialism are conceived as central to its development. Though not offering an original thesis as to the causes of American imperialism, the book is effectively written, connecting the historically particular modes of the United States's "march westward" and hegemonic advances globally to the changing complex of its regional and class forces and conflicts. Kiernan's observations on American history and politics, in the book and related articles,[50] are often acerbic, yet in the very same texts

he exhibits and expresses a sensitivity to, and appreciation of, the tensions
and contradictions which have characterized American growth and development. At the beginning of the book he writes:

> America's early settlers left an England astir with progressive im-
> pulses, and might have seemed to be building in the wilderness the
> better society that the Levellers tried in vain to build in England.
> But there was always in this new land a duality, a division of the
> soul as deep as the racial cleavage between black and white. Aspi-
> ration towards a new life was never to succumb entirely to what our
> ancestors called "the world, the flesh and the devil." Yet these latter
> temptations remained potent, and imperialist hankerings—running
> all through America's history and at last becoming its most obtru-
> sive feature—have been one consequence.[51]

Published in the wake of the Vietnam War, *America: The New Imperialism*
joined those studies which have sought to demolish that powerful historical
myth of Americans which holds that the United States has never been a "colonial" power: but it is also made quite clear in the course of the historical
narrative, as well as in an earlier article, "Imperialism, American and European," how the development of American imperialism has contrasted historically with that of Europe: "It lost interest overnight in its first flutter with
colonialism, in a volatile fashion impossible to a Europe rancid with heredi-
tary ambitions and vendettas." Nevertheless, foregoing direct colonialism
American empire-building led the way towards *neo*-colonialism.[52]

In line with his pronouncements on Marxism and history, Kiernan's studies in this area have not been pursued for the purpose of elaborating a formal
theory of the causes of imperialism and colonialism, but they have been written in relation to the development of Marxist historical thinking on the subject. In the foreword to *Marxism and Imperialism,* a collection of articles published in 1974, Kiernan remarks that the strength of Marxist and Leninist
thought has been in economic analysis, and "In this preoccupation Marxism
continued Marx's own turning away . . . from a many-sided approach to history and society towards a narrower concentration on their economic structure." This, however, was inadequate. Marxist work on imperialism had become "most vulnerable to criticism through its comparative neglect of other
motive forces, political or psychological." In other words, Marxism had been
reduced and was now being equated too much with economics and economic
determinism. *The Lords of Human Kind, European Empires* and *America: the
New Imperialism* can be read, then, as efforts to "round out" Marxist investi-
gations. Yet, they are more than merely attempts to add politics and culture
to economics. Although Kiernan does not attend adequately to political
economy, his studies do represent, as I have indicated, explorations of the

dialectical relations between class and imperialism, and thus his writings in this area (along with those on nationalism and nation-state formation to be discussed) are very much a part of the British Marxist historians' development of Marxism as a "theory of class determination." As Kiernan suggests: "Modern imperialism has been an accretion of elements, not all of equal weight, that can be traced back through every epoch of history. Perhaps its ultimate causes, with those of war, are to be found less in tangible material wants than in the uneasy tensions of societies distorted by class divisions, with their reflections in distorted ideas in men's minds."[53]

Where he has spoken directly to the theoretical questions, as in "The Marxist Theory of Imperialism and Its Historical Formation," we find it has been in the fashion of his previously noted article, "History." That is, he brings the theory face to face with historical experience, his purpose being to separate out "what may be of permanent value in it from what was ephemeral, or has been discounted by later history."[54]

In the past several years Kiernan has often been invited to consider and address the *consequences* of imperialism and colonialism both for Europeans and for Africans and Asians. His assessments remain critically objective and his observations offer little comfort to either party. For example, however much his own writings attest to the brutality of conquest and oppressiveness of colonialism, he also feels compelled to state in conclusion to *European Empires* that "Even with the aid of machine-guns and high explosives, the total of deaths inflicted on Afro-Asia by Europe must have been trifling compared with the number inflicted on it by its own rulers, in Africa chiefly through wars, in Asia chiefly through crushing revolts."[55] Indeed, since Kiernan has consistently been attentive to the pre-existing modes of class domination amongst *both* the colonizers and the colonized, he has necessarily recognized that "So many lands were under alien or semi-alien rule that the overthrow of thrones might be welcomed as the deliverance which Europeans professed to be bringing."[56] (It need hardly be said that remarks such as these are not intended to absolve Europeans of their colonial histories and atrocities.)

What about the longer-term, the so-called "developmental" consequences of European imperialism and colonialism? This is a question Kiernan himself asks, noting that "Western thinking has usually favoured the view that colonialism, despite much that is shameful in its record, rescued backward or stagnating societies by giving them better government, and transformed them by drawing them out of isolation into the currents of the world market and a world civilisation"; but, of course, as he is fully aware: "Each nation—feeling itself the strongest—has sought to impose its will on others, but to think of itself as their warden or rescuer."[57] His own answer is historical. First, he distinguishes between the early colonialism of Spain and Portugal—when "Europe was still too little developed to have much to bestow"—and the later northwestern European imperialisms following on the Industrial and American and French Revolutions. Then he considers the differing effects of these latter imperialisms on various Asian and African peoples, for clearly the impact of European expansion on, for example, India, China and Japan was dramatically different.[58] Nevertheless, allowing for significant historical and moral reservations, it appears that Kiernan does comprehend European imperialism and colonialism as having been "progressive," at least initially, in the development sense.

It is here that we encounter most directly a central characteristic of Kiernan's conception of history, one that links him closely with Marx and Engels, perhaps more so than any of the other British Marxist historians. I am referring specifically to his sense of history as *tragedy*. He aims us toward it himself with reference to imperialism when he writes: "Conquest and occupation were grievous experiences; whatever beneficial results might ensue, the cure was at best a harsh one, like old-style surgery without anaesthetics. Only in the light of their tragic vision of history could Marx and Engels contemplate conquest as sometimes a chapter of human progress." On another occasion, he observers that there is a "sombre contradiction at the heart of imperialism."[59] That is, if we subscribe to the assumption that economic development—or, "modernization"—is preferable to the persistence of "pre-industrial" social orders, then we are drawn inevitably to the historically "realistic" position that northwestern Europe's intrusions overseas were a required catalyst for change and development because it was the only region dynamic enough to accomplish it. This was Marx's and Engels' view and, thus, they welcomed capitalism's revolutionary momentum; and this is Kiernan's view—up to a point. As he reminds us, though Marx and Engels had a tragic vision of the past, they were optimistic about the future and, indeed, too ready to separate the two, crediting capitalism with too much revolutionary determination and, as a result, they failed to recognize the way in which it would compromise and incorporate pre-capitalist forces to accomplish its ends.

Kiernan, too, sees European imperialism as having been necessary to instigate change and, potentially, development, and yet he also recognizes—more so than Marx and Engels—how the tragedy was compounded. Not only did imperialism have the effect of reinforcing class power at home and abroad—this fact Marx and Engels had sadly realized—but, as Kiernan shows, this often helped to bring about the coalescence of bourgeois and aristocrat in Europe (thereby making a fatally important contribution to war and fascism in the twentieth century) and the buttressing or calling into being of "parasitic ruling groups" in the colonies. Thus, at the same time Kiernan sees imperialism as having been progressive, at least to some extent, he also indicates how, in time, it was inevitably "deforming" to both colonizers and col-

onized. In the end he declares that the real contribution of European imperialism "was made less by imposing its rule on others than by teaching others
how to resist it," [60] referring both to the capitalist modernization from above
of Japan and the ideologies and forces of nationalism and socialism in Asia
and Africa, which, I would add, have generated their own dialectics of hope
and tragedy.

Classes, Nation-States and Force

In "Notes on Marxism in 1968," Kiernan emphasizes that "Marxist history
owes much of its strength to its grasp of the importance of class." This is not
because we should expect to find fully formed class-conscious assemblages in
every epoch; indeed, such moments are rare—modern Western Europe being
exceptional in so many ways. Rather, it is because of the centrality of *class
struggle* in the movement of history. (In this way, Kiernan aligns himself with
his fellow British Marxist historians.) He suggests that there have been,
broadly speaking, only two types of class societies, each characterized by the
role of the ruling class in the process of production. The first type, occurring
twice in history, is where the ruling group organizes production; in its early
form exemplified by the ancient civilizations of the Near East, and in its
modern form by capitalism (and, we should add, the now-collapsing state
socialism). The second type, which has been much more common historically, covers the whole array of "feudal" modes of production in which the
rulers are "parasitic" on production. Even though he provides this generic
model of the latter type, Kiernan insists that the historical varieties of "feudalism" need to be examined much more closely for they are quite distinct
forms of appropriation. He especially urges further investigation of medieval
European feudalism "for it was the incubator of modern capitalism and of
the whole world-civilisation of today." [61]

Kiernan himself has shown greatest interest in the European aristocracy,
originally the feudal ruling class, which he explains (here distinguishing his
work from that of Hilton, et al.) in these lines:

> Even if classes were likely to disappear soon, they would deserve all
> the light that Marxism can throw on them. They will remain em-
> balmed in the common culture, the amalgam of values, to which
> every class like every race by its unique contact with life has a
> unique contribution to make. It is of peculiar importance . . . to
> scrutinise the ruling classes of the past and their cultural record:
> feudal ruling groups still more than capitalist, because they were set
> more apart and above societies they controlled, enjoyed a more
> unique status and privilege and commanded a kind of awe that no

mill-owners however rich can aspire to, so that so far as those so-cieties formed any meaningful whole it was the aristocracies that represented it.[62]

Then, in a brief but intriguing discussion of the characteristics of Europe's feudal ruling classes, he proffers the idea that in spite of their distance and separateness from those over whom they ruled, their experience was both unique *and* metaphoric of human experience as a whole. Following Shake-speare, he finds in the aristocracy in its declining years as a ruling class, "in-carnations of the tragic spirit we all dimly feel in the lives of all of us."

Kiernan's book, *The Duel in European History: A Study in the Aristocratic Ascendancy*,[63] is an exploration of a practice that was charged with political and cultural significance. Originating earlier, the modern duel actually devel-oped in the sixteenth and seventeenth centuries, a period characterized by chronic warfare, lingering into the nineteenth century and carried abroad in the course of European expansion (for example, to the United States). Kier-nan argues that the duel was an "exclusive" class practice, its moral and ide-ological purpose being to secure the nobility's "*esprit de corps.*" Moreover, duelling served to reduce intra–ruling-class conflicts to symbolic propor-tions; that is, since it was confined to individuals, as opposed to whole fam-ilies and their entourages, it required only a limited number of victims. Ac-tually it might be said that duelling reflected the development of aristocratic individualism under the influence of the age of emergent bourgeois individ-ualism. At the same time, duels which pitted noble vs. bourgeois provided a mode of incorporation of bourgeois individuals by the aristocracy.

Kiernan's previous studies of the aristocracy are also framed by the transi-tion from feudalism to capitalism but focus more directly on the political dimension. Twenty years before the current heightened attention to the is-sues of nationalism and state formation, Kiernan was pursuing such ques-tions,[64] doing so in a Marxist fashion which presented the state as class-structured but allowing for it an autonomous role in social change. His most significant writings in this area are his article, "State and Nation in Western Europe," and his book, *State and Society in Europe, 1550–1650.*[65] In these, Kiernan concentrates on the absolutist monarchy and state of the sixteenth and seventeenth centuries. Revising the position he took in the Historians' Group discussions of the 1940s, Kiernan argues that the absolutist monarchy was essentially a feudal polity "existing primarily for the benefit of the landed nobility," which remained the dominant class but was decreasingly a "govern-ing class." Still, he does see difficulties with this formulation: "Absolutism was the highest stage of feudalism much more than the first stage of bour-geois or middle-class hegemony. To speak of the new pattern as "feudal" is, all the same, liable to many confusions; the least misleading designation for it may be 'the aristocratic state.' "[66] Kiernan demonstrates how the absolutist state came to be established out of the very "crisis of feudalism"; i.e., out of the absolute monarchy having secured the seigneurial order by subduing both peasant discontent and noble intra-class conflict, and at the same time limiting the authority of the latter in its own favor. How this was effected varied, of course, across Europe, but it did not represent a " 'freezing' of the status quo." This is evidenced in part, he says, by the fact that the absolute monarchs themselves were quite often "new men," though admittedly establishing themselves on "old foundations."[67]

That absolutism was essentially feudal, or aristocratic, was of crucial significance, for this was a formative state in the making of the modern world, and the absolutist state itself was the political crucible in which the many rich tensions of late medieval society were melted down to varying degrees, reformed and bequeathed to the modern. Thus, however dynamic nascent capitalism was—and was to become—it was originally shaped by aristocratic states and imbued with feudal elements of which it would not so easily rid itself. It is not very difficult to see how these works are related to his writings on imperialism. As Kiernan says, the absolute monarchies did not set out to establish national states but rather "Each aimed at unlimited extension . . . and the more it prospered the more the outcome was a multifarious empire instead of a nation."[68] Nevertheless, inheriting territorial roots from their medieval antecedents, the absolutist polities were the embryonic experiences out of which developed the nation-state, western Europe's major political contribution to the world.

There is to be no mythologizing of the origins of national states for Kiernan. To start with, it is his contention that the State molded the Nation (out of the existing materials of "nationality") more than vice versa, and *State and Society* portrays at length how this process was determined by war and class conflict. Indeed, the absolute monarchies committed so much of their resources to warfare that it has often been assumed that the development of absolutist states was due mostly to "foreign pressures." Kiernan, however, dissents, insisting that the pressures toward inter-monarchical bellicosity were primarily internal in that there was a continuing need to turn "outwards" the intra-class conflicts of the nobility and the class antagonisms between them and the common people.[69] The militarism of the developing absolutist states also provided an outlet for the surplus labor thrown up by the crisis of feudalism; although, as Kiernan shows in "Foreign Mercenaries and Absolute Monarchies," their armies depended most heavily on foreign hirelings. This had several advantages. First, however unwilling the common people were to be exploited in order to pay for the wars, they were less eager to fight in them, so foreign mercenaries were a welcome alternative for monarchs. Secondly, foreign mercenary armies strengthened the monarchs against their nobles. Thirdly, though they were more costly to employ they could be sent home when no longer needed and there was no obligation to the widows and orphans of those who did not return. Fourthly, professional soldiers regularly kept up with the latest technologies of war. Finally—and perhaps most importantly—it was safer politically than arming one's own peasants and, moreover, foreign mercenaries were especially useful in suppressing rebellions, an important feature of government in the sixteenth century.[70]

A legacy of feudalism, the absolutist state thus took on a warlike character which, Kiernan observes sadly, it was to pass on to the modern state. This was of tragic consequence, for however intimate the relationship between Mars and markets has been, there was, he surmises, nothing inherent in the laws of capital that it should seek outlets in arms and conquests.[71] It might be noted in this context that Kiernan's admiration for Engels is in part attributable to the fact that he, more than Marx, was a student of war, to the point of being nicknamed "The General" by Marx's family.[72] Kiernan himself wrote in 1968 that "The fortunes of Marxism must depend a great deal on its ability to illuminate the causes of war both past and present."[73]

Kiernan's articles, "Nationalist Movements and Social Classes" and "Conscription and Society in Europe before the War of 1914–1918,"[74] extend his class-structured analysis of nation-state formation and the place of the military in those experiences. These too reveal how there was nothing natural or organic about nationalism and nation-states, which were in great part "creations from above" (by the state, not a divinity). In the article on conscription, Kiernan notes how compulsory service has appeared throughout history and in each episode reflects much more about the society than simply how it raises up an army. In the case of late nineteenth-century Europe, he argues that conscription to the military served as a mode of educating the masses both to the political and ideological requirements of the nation-state and the regimenting demands of industrial capitalism.

In "Nationalist Movements and Social Classes," Kiernan traces the development of nationalism as a political force from its origins in northwestern Europe—in England first of all, across the continent through the course of the nineteenth century and, by way of selected countries, around the globe in the twentieth, showing how the class bases of nationalist movements varied in the different historically structured contexts. Considering the European pattern, Kiernan links its emergence in the early modern period to the growth of capitalism within the framework of the absolutist state. Undermining traditional social relations, capitalism provided for even more intense class antagonisms requiring both a stronger state apparatus and a renovated set of ideologies. In this context it was the urban middle classes that were most important to the development of nationalism: "Patriotic feeling could bolster their self-esteem and confidence, and by identifying themselves with it they could better aspire to a leading place in a changing pattern of society."[75] Indeed, he notes how the national revolt of the Dutch was something of a "bourgeois revolution" and how the "bourgeois revolutions" of England

and France were imbued with nationalist fervor. Aristocrats, however, found nationalism much less convenient, for it entailed the incorporation of the popular classes into public life; and Kiernan asserts, whereas for peasants and the lower-middle classes the appeal to "national community" was attractive, the urban proletariat originally had different priorities, though in time it too responded as it increasingly had to attend to the activities of the state and its political culture.

The revolutions of 1789 and 1848 had dramatic effects on the history of nationalism as a political force. The significance of the former is that it provided the basis for "nationalist movements of opposition" which might be either conservative or progressive. Later, the struggles of 1848 put fear into the hearts and minds of bourgeois and aristocrat alike and thus, as Kiernan describes, national states were even "more rapidly to be built from above with modern administrative resources," as was most definitely the case in Germany. Thereafter, with the development of socialist and communist parties commanding working-class allegiances, "patriotism" became "the last refuge or reaction, and nationalist labels were favorites with right-wing parties" (for example, Franco's "Nationalist" movement and Hitler's corruptly titled "National" Socialists).[76] Nevertheless, as his comparative-historical narrative illustrates, nationalism remained an ambivalent force in this century, even being married to socialism in the defence of the Soviet Union in the Second World War and in the anticolonial struggles in Africa and Asia.

Along with his work on aristocracy, absolutism and nation-state formation, Kiernan has pursued research and writing on revolutions. In "Revolution" he surveys the social and political struggles from the sixteenth to the nineteenth century, highlighting the bourgeois revolutions of the Netherlands, England, and France. His concern, as we should expect, is with the way class forces and conflicts shaped the course of these upheavals. Though subscribing to the view that social revolts are usually instigated by "intensified pressure from above," and also that "Revolutions more than anything else can only be carried forward by minorities," Kiernan does not discount the role of the popular classes. In resistance and revolt the common people contribute to the movement of history; this is true even in defeat, to the extent that fear of social upheaval determines the actions of states and ruling classes. As to the classification of the Dutch, English, and French Revolutions as "bourgeois" Kiernan's view is that "They were not projected, fought and won by any bourgeoisie, though this class would be their chief heir. Capitalism was as yet embryonic." Indeed, repeating a proposition he advanced in the Historians' Group in 1947, he adds that "Bourgeois revolutions, like 'bourgeois art,' are made for the more or less reluctant bourgeoisie by the radical petty-bourgeoisie." Moreover, the lower-middle classes, laborers and, in the French case, the peasantry, who did most of the fighting, did not have in mind the furthering of capitalist development.[77] Nevertheless, whatever the contradictions and ironies, these revolutions did represent "progress," which is all-the-more apparent when contrasted with the absence or failure of such revolutions.

Appropriate to his tragic vision of history is Kiernan's primary work in this area, *The Revolution of 1854 in Spanish History,* published in 1966.[78] The volume is dedicated to his father, to whom he credits his initial interest in Spain, but there can be no doubt that it has also been determined by the dramatic impact which the Spanish Civil War (1936–39) had on the political formation of Kiernan's generation.[79] As a study of the "Bienio" of 1854–56, the book is Kiernan's effort to unravel the historical origins of twentieth-century Spain and its Civil War: "Brief as it was a great deal of history was concentrated in it; nearly all the persistent problems of modern Spain—political, economic, cultural—asserted themselves forcibly; nearly all the parties of the epoch had their roots in it."[80] Essentially, the tragedy of the Revolution, with its grave consequences for both Spain and Europe, was the failure of the Spanish liberals and, in their wake, Spanish democrats, to mobilize mass discontent or place themselves at the head of the popular struggles that presented themselves, which might have enabled them to renovate Spanish society along the lines of a bourgeois revolution. But, of course, as much of Kiernan's work reminds us, history does not operate according to formulae and we find in the disruption of 1854–56 the first interventions of the Spanish proletariat as a class, which in the shadows cast by the upheavals of 1848 represented too much of a threat to the propertied for them to risk too great a commitment to social transformation.

British Culture and the Making of Socialism

Though very much the member of the original Historians' Group who went on to pursue the study of "who rides whom and how" rather than the story of the common people, Kiernan has always set his work in the context of class relations and struggle. Moreover, he has regularly called for the past to be explored from the bottom up and, as noted earlier, he has himself written several pieces in the genre.[81] The questions which seem to underlie and/or inform these studies and concern him most—in response to which he offers a variety of historical observations—are "What is the relationship between the struggles of the working class and the making of socialism?" *and* "What is the task of intellectuals in those terms?" His observations are as objective as ever and his assessments are far from sanguine. He notes that Marx may have been overly impressed by the 1844 weavers' insurrection in Silesia, to the point of assuming that the proletariat was innately revolutionary. Kiernan disagrees: "There are no revolutionary classes in history, none whose intrinsic nature compels revolt." As for the revolutionary instincts of the working class in particular, Kiernan reminds us that "Workers everywhere have been readier to fight against the establishment of industrial capitalism than for its abolition, once firmly established."[82]

Actually, in several essays we do find Kiernan moving quite close to and, in certain cases, actually intersecting with the initiatives of his fellow Marxist historians to rewrite British history from below and, within it, to affirm the centrality of radical-democratic and socialist struggles. In "Patterns of Protest in English History," Kiernan offers a historical survey of the politics of "direct action" carried out by "the people" against the prevailing powers of the State and its governors. With some apparent pride he notes that "It was in the English-speaking world that direct action as a concept originated and found a name, like so many political things before that have passed into currency everywhere" (referring to particular twentieth-century events in Britain, the United States, and India). Mobilizing the historical studies of his comrades on the Peasant Rising of 1381, the English Revolution of the seventeenth century, the crowds of Hanoverian London, the "making of the English working class" and Chartism, Kiernan writes to undermine further the myth that English liberal and democratic political development was a continuous, progressive, smooth and evolutionary process. He does not deny the element of reality in the progressive model, but he is insistent that the forward motion of change has been motivated by struggles from below.[83] (I would just add that contrary to recent tendencies on the Left to eschew—if not denigrate—this project of reappropriation, it remains a crucial task in the face of Conservative and New Right attacks portraying radical-democratic and socialist politics as alien to British life.)

History from the bottom up—in the specific sense of recovering the history lived and made by the common people or "lower orders"—is also well represented by Kiernan's "The Covenanters: A Problem of Creed and Class," a study of the Scottish peasant, small tenant farmer, and artisan movement of the seventeenth and early eighteenth centuries which fought for the reformation (or restoration) of the Kirk. As Kiernan reveals, the Covenanters were inspired by a popular Calvinism and Scottish nationalism. And yet, although their aspirations were essentially conservative, their struggle was expressive of a democratic spirit—for their vision of the Kirk was a people's church controlled by the people.[84]

Though rather different in subject matter, Kiernan's essays "Wordsworth and the People" and "Socialism, the Prophetic Memory," are also intimately linked to these labors. In fact, the article on Wordsworth originally appeared as a chapter in the book, *Democracy and the Labour Movement,* prepared by the members of the Historians' Group in 1954 both to honor one of their mentors, Dona Torr, and to provide a showcase for their scholarship. The title of the work declares their project, and in the foreword John Saville and his co-editors affectionately record their appreciation of Torr's influence and contributions and enunciate the spirit informing their development of history from the bottom up: "She has taught us historical *passion*. . . . History was not words on a page, not the goings on of kings and prime ministers, not mere events. History was the sweat, blood, tears and triumphs of the common people, our people."[85]

Kiernan introduces Wordsworth as having "devoted the greater part of his life to the study of political and social questions"; indeed, several years later in a review essay in *The New Reasoner,* he wrote that "Wordsworth stands out, with perhaps only Dante, Shakespeare, and Milton beside him, among the greatest of political poets, interpreters that is of the hopes, fears, passions of political life."[86] Specifically, in the article, Kiernan considers Wordsworth's perception of the growing chasm, the alienation separating poet and people and his desire to secure a means by which to span the distance between "himself and the world of men." He notes how Wordsworth, "disgusted with his own sort of people . . . turn[ed] away from the educated classes to the "common people," towards whom history was, as it were, forcing him all through his years as a great poet." Kiernan's assessments of Wordsworth's attempts to connect with and articulate the experiences of the "lower orders" are critical (a point to which I shall return), but even as he chronicles the poet's incapacity to bridge the gap, he does not fail to appreciate his ambitions and sympathies, and to admire the development, however problematic, of a "*democratic* theory of diction."

Written twenty years later, "Socialism, the Prophetic Memory," considers the varied roots of socialist thought and politics, both religious and secular. Though not limited to English or British developments, the essay is most attentive to the English "utopian" heritage (which Kiernan's senior colleague in the Historians' Group, Leslie Morton, had come to make his own).[87] Kiernan first highlights both the fourteenth-century democratic priest, John Ball, and early-modern churchman and visionary, Thomas More. Then, under the heading of "indigenous English socialism," a term borrowed from the Christian socialist, R. H. Tawney, he introduces the nineteenth-century utopian socialists, Robert Owen and William Morris, who confronted the "progress" of the Industrial Revolution with their own visions of alternative social orders. Finally, he offers a set of reflections on the socialist experience of this century. As "the prophetic memory," socialism is here conceived as the ancient but persistent vision of freedom from the tyranny of the monopolization of wealth and power: "From the point of view of socialism, it is a question of depriving a limited number of men of a 'freedom' based on a bloated power over the community's economic life, in order to liberate the growth of countless others, both as individuals and as members of a meaningful community."[88]

Still, however much these writings flow into the narrative stream of the struggle for "the rights of the free-born Briton" they are also classically Kiernanesque. Even in those which are most evidently pursued as history from the bottom up, Kiernan never fails to be objectively critical regarding the limits and inherent contradictions of the popular movements he is considering. For example, in "The Covenanters" he appreciates the historical significance of their efforts—"Most of the resisters came from a downtrodden mass exploited since time out of mind by superiors against whom they had never attempted to rise. For them to rise up now and challenge authority was an immense feat in itself"—and recognizes that their immersion in Calvinist theology was their first "introduction to the world of intellect." Yet he is compelled to observe that their experience and their ideology inhibited the emergence of a struggle to reform the social order:

> In a slippery world, as treacherous as one of their upland bogs, their treaty with God, a perpetual bond never to be broken, was a comforting certainty to which they could hold fast. Neighbourhood sentiment might be strong, but Scots villagers had no such organization of their own as the commune of old Russia, or Vietnam, with fixed rights of cultivation and a traditional leadership. Only an unearthly vision, a pole star invisible to others, could lend them the sense of fraternity they needed. Devotion to their image of the Kirk may be seen as the false consciousness of a class, a coming together in defence of ideals instead of interests. Covenanters had a deep sensation of being wronged and oppressed, but they turned their indignation against an imaginary oppressor, a giant or monster called Erastianism, casting a still more horrid shadow of Popery and Idolatry. Rejection of bishops was an unconscious rejection of the social order.[89]

Such critical assessments are not at all reserved for "pre–working-class" movements as we see in Kiernan's essay, "Labour and the Literate in Nineteenth-Century Britain."[90] Here he pursues a theme not unlike that of "Wordsworth and the People," that is, the perceptions of the "literati" of the laboring classes and, in particular, the experiences of those who sought, in political or cultural terms, a collaborative relationship with them. In sum, Kiernan records that the "intellectuals" who did seek to "surmount the barriers" separating labor and the literate were generally disappointed by their encounters. His own view is that the British working class has rarely ever been interested in turning the world upside down. It is true that Kiernan expresses a certain admiration for the struggles which E. P. Thompson narrates as "the making of the English working class," culminating in the Chartist movement, the first working-class political party: "It is indeed remarkable that out of a mass so 'degraded' and 'demoralized' [as the novelists and social commentators had written] a labour movement of such dimensions and vitality should have arisen."[91] But whereas the Chartists and their forebears are

to be admired, the late Victorian working class has retreated into "labourism": "Whatever their weaknesses, it appears that the first generations of the
proletariat were capable of some vision of a world cleansed and renovated,
and of the mighty put down from their seats. . . . After mid century the
labour movement was stiffening into 'labourism,' content with what im-
provements could be got by trade unions, and relinquishing any design of
transforming society." Moreover, he later adds: "Working-class withdrawal
from the political arena and from the national culture went together";
though he equally admits that workers' self-enclosure in "labourism" not only
insulated them from socialism but from the worst features of ruling-class
ideology as well.[92]

Kiernan's conclusion to "Labour and the Literate" indicates that he sees
socialist politics in almost Leninist fashion: "it would seem that socialist consciousness has always been restricted to a very few, and that the bulk of the
working class (as of every other, it may be) is inert except when activated by
some direct material stimulus." This picture of the late nineteenth-century
working class has been criticized by various labor historians. I would subscribe to their criticisms for although the working class was far from the
socialist consciousness envisioned by Marx and Engels, working people did
evidence a class consciousness which may even have entailed what James
Young has referred to as "socialism from below."[93] The problem, I would
argue—and I believe Kiernan would agree (I will explain why shortly)—has
not been merely working-class "labourism" but at least equally the incapacity
of socialist intellectuals to comprehend and effectively articulate working-
class aspirations.

Along with their objectively critical assessments of popular movements,
these same essays are also clearly Kiernanesque in their attentiveness to the
political and ideological presence and determination of the rulers of the day.
In "Patterns of Protest in English History"—which is as much an examination of resistance from above by Britain's rulers in the name of law, order,
and property as it is of popular protest—Kiernan points out how "direct
action" from below was readily matched by those on high. That is, the State
and its governors have been quick to respond with their own modes of direct
action.[94] However, as Kiernan also shows, with great respect for their ingenuity, when British ruling classes have been incapable of suppressing the challenges to the political and social order in one *direct* action they have not
generally pursued a further escalation of hostilities but have, rather, sought
to disarm or incorporate elements of the opposition and its demands in order
to avoid an even greater crisis. This pattern of limited conflict and struggle
has, he reflects, made English and British history seem "exceptional" in comparison with Continental experience, leading him to the further observation
that "If our own ancien regime ever does come to an end, it may be through
pressure of opinion stiffened by the cumulative effect of numerous small nib-

blings and scratchings. Before this happens, recourse by the other side to direct action, official or unofficial, must be expected in the future as in the past."

In a review of the work of his fellow British Marxist historians, Kiernan has stated that:

> "History from below" . . . may have had all the more attraction because in England the people, or working class, has so signally failed, or rather has not tried, to take control in the present. One consequence has been a relative neglect of study of the dominant classes, their formation, culture, mode of consciousness, self-imaging, which all have their importance, along with external power and wealth.[95]

A prime example of his own pursuit of the actions of the elites or ruling classes in British history is "Evangelicalism and the French Revolution." This essay, first published in the inaugural issue of *Past & Present* in 1952, presents an original contribution to the debates which have taken place around the Halevy thesis that Methodism provided an antidote to political revolution during the course of the social upheavals and dislocations of the Industrial Revolution. To these discussions both Eric Hobsbawm and Edward Thompson were later to offer their own distinct contributions; the former arguing that, contrary to the Halevy thesis, Methodism and Radicalism advanced together, and the latter insisting that "religious revivalism took over at the point where 'political' or temporal aspirations met with defeat."[96] Kiernan, however, in his concern for the agency of those on top, is led to consider the manner in which the upper classes of early nineteenth-century England sought to harness the popular resurgence of religion against the threat of the spread of Jacobinism and atheism which they saw emanating from revolutionary France. He acknowledges at the outset that his examination of evangelicalism is one-sided in nature, stressing its service in "support of order and stability." Moreover, he fully accepts the fact that even as a "conservative" force the revival of religious enthusiasm must be recognized as "something 'popular,' originating from the people, like every genuine religious impulse." Indeed, he states, Wesley himself was more a "liberator" than a "creator" of the movement to which he "gave his name and imprint."

Kiernan thus advances no simple "dominant ideology" thesis, for as he notes: " 'New Birth' teachings embodied, in part and imperfectly, the early efforts of common people to adapt themselves to an altering environment"; and they were in fact received with hostile response by Church and State elites. Yet, he explains, this made them all-the-more effective when taken up by other upper-class voices equally eager to defend the social order: "In religion as in politics, an idea which is to disarm discontents must at some time, in some sense, have seemed both to friend and foe an idea of rebellion. We are only held securely by fetters we have helped to forge ourselves; no-one else can tell the exact fit of our wrists and ankles." Not easily taken up by the Church, it was not until Wilberforce articulated and created a movement which could bring together the "two nations" in such a way as to equalize souls without levelling the classes that evangelicalism was to become an acceptable practice within the established order. Cutting two ways, Methodism was to be an effective ideology of the "rising" middle classes: on the one hand, it was critical of old aristocratic and clerical elites and, on the other, it offered to the working classes and themselves a culture which inspired, but not towards revolution.

Kiernan, then, is no populist. However much he may appreciate their historical accomplishments, and be prepared to admonish writers who underestimate them, he remains persistently objective about popular and working-class movements and, apparently, very much an "elitist" on cultural and political questions. This requires further explanation. Kiernan's position is not that the arts, letters, and political thought of the past were, or are, to be transmitted to, and passively received and preserved by a working class recently admitted to the ranks of the literate and educated. Rather, it is that after a promising start, the post-Chartist *self-enclosure* of the working class in the "culture of labourism" has, at great expense to both the further enrichment of the common culture and the advance of socialism within it, inhibited the working class from "appropriating" and "*developing* the things belonging to the common stock." But, of course, is this not the very same aspiration expressed by Antonio Gramsci in his vision of a truly democratic and socialist education?[97]

Moreover, even as he has been critical of working-class culture and politics (and admiring of the ingenuity and tenacity of the ruling classes), he has been equally critical of the intellectual "class" including, if not especially, those who would seek an alliance with the common people and working class. This can readily be seen in the essays on Wordsworth and "Labour and the Literate," and it is equally characteristic of his many other writings on intellectuals and the "literati."[98] He faults intellectuals both for their theory—finding them no less subject to illusions than the common people themselves, though perhaps of a "higher" order—and for their practice. For example, he recounts how Ernest Jones, the Chartist, called upon writers to join *with* and write *for* the people, but observes that most often they proceeded to "write *about* the working classes . . . as sympathetic critics rather than allies."[99] And, as we know, this was a positive development in comparison with the perennial service of intellectuals as managers of polity and society on behalf of the ruling classes. Then, there has been the equally unfortunate tendency in the face of popular apathy, if not antipathy, to their courtings, for intellectuals to envision themselves standing in for "the people" in the making of socialism, with all the antidemocratic dangers involved. As much as Kiernan might be characterized as an elitist, his conception of socialism is much too democratic to permit him to subscribe to a political strategy in which intellectuals serve as a proxy for the agency of the working class.

Critical of the culture and politics of the common people and censorious of intellectuals' practices, Kiernan's perspective is apparently pessimistic. However, without resorting to Gramsci's favorite aphorism, "Pessimism of the intellect, optimism of the will," I would insist that even if Kiernan's remarks occasionally incline towards cynicism, his own writings contradict both cynicism and any insurmountable pessimism. For a start, along with a certain humor and romanticism—often expressed in rich metaphor and allusion—Kiernan is capable of a most pointed anger, as we encounter in "On Treason." In this essay, originally published in 1987 in the *London Review of Books*, Kiernan defends the commitments of his generation of young communists in the 1930s and the war against fascism, in the face of renewed efforts to blacken that experience through commercial and political exploitation of the "Cambridge spies."[100] Noting past and present "treacheries" of the Right, he vehemently challenges the patriotic rhetoric and political and economic schemes of the Thatcher government. Outraged by the equation of Toryism with the "national interest" he writes: "Morally, the 'treason' of the thirties cannot for a moment be compared with the morass of crooked dealing, profit-gorging, deception, looting of national resources and indifference to national welfare, that make up the world of Thatcherism."

Another aspect of Kiernan's work which takes us beyond a one-dimensional pessimism or fatalism is his insistence on "seeing things historically." The absence of historical consciousness has been debilitating for both the intellectual Left and the working class:

> Socialism and humanism alike stand in need of a rational consciousness of the past, still silently at work in the present. Any country where ordinary folk could be got to think seriously about their past would have a better chance of a brighter future; fortunately for our governors, a serious concern with history is a slow outgrowth of culture, and does not come of its own accord to men and women, few of whom retain much recollection of things done or suffered in even their own bygone years.[101]

Confident about the intimacy of history and politics, Kiernan's own studies clearly have been intended as interventions in contemporary debates. Yet, again, if Marxist thought is to contribute to contemporary political life and discourse it must become ever more responsive to the insights to be garnered from the dialogue between past and present—and, as we have seen, Kiernan himself has not hesitated to point out particular inadequacies in Marxist and socialist thinking which need to be addressed in the engagement with history. In "Socialism, the Prophetic Memory," he writes: "Marxism always disclaimed any necessitarian belief in revolution coming of its own accord, but it was led by its 'scientific' logic into some undervaluing, not of the factor of human will, but of the ideas and ideals, the emotional wants left by religion and many other things of the past, which are needed to create the will to socialism."[102]

Most persistently, perhaps, Kiernan has called for a greater sensitivity to religion and religious experience. Marx and Engels have not infrequently been misrepresented on the question of religion, he notes; but in any case, he says, they gave too much weight to the "wastebasket theory of history" which assumes that historical development would naturally lead to the demise of religion, and "to this day Marxism has scarcely corrected this underestimation, or made sufficient allowance in its general theory for the energy and tenacity of religion . . . one of the determining forces in human history."[103]

As was noted at the outset of the chapter, Kiernan's own upbringing, like that of some of the other British Marxist historians, was in Protestant Nonconformism, and he has never failed to appreciate both its influence in his own movement towards socialism and, in history, its role in dissent and opposition. He wrote in a review of Eric Hobsbawm's *The Age of Revolution* that "However subservient to State and ruling class Protestantism might become, it could never entirely lose its original character of *protest*—against supernatural pretensions of fellow-mortals, against thought-control and the blanketing out of human intelligence, against religion as a boundless, endless opium-dream."[104]

Radical religion, dissent and Nonconformism have been, of course, an important theme in the writings of Christopher Hill and E. P. Thompson, and, as we see in the essays on the Covenanters and evangelicalism, for Kiernan as well. Indeed, in the concluding lines to "The Covenanters" we are presented with one of the most direct calls for intellectuals of the Left to reflect on popular religious experience:

> The Covenanters may be charged with misleading their class. . . .
> Yet if their gospel was too other-worldly to cope with hardships like hunger, the simply bread-and-butter movements of our day have proved equally incapable of lifting men's minds to anything so ideal, so distant, so necessary as socialism. How to reconcile the two visions, pushed so far apart by our society and its maladies, is what Marxists hitherto have been as far as anyone else from discovering.[105]

In fact, Kiernan's own explorations remind us that for all of the subsequent antagonism and conflict between Western socialism and Christianity, socialism itself is an "offspring of Christianity," and thus he can propose in his article on "Religion" in *A Dictionary of Marxist Thought* that "It may indeed be said that, like Marx at the outset of his intellectual life, Marxism has found in the historical scrutiny of religion one of its most stimulating tasks."[106] Kiernan has also felt compelled to disclaim Marxism's long practice of eschewing the discourse of morality, ethics, justice, and rights, though ever insistent that they be studied "not in the abstract but in the setting of history."[107] Thinking no doubt of studies from the bottom up then being conducted by his fellow British Marxist historians, as well as his own, he offered the following argument in "Notes on Marxism in 1968," which Thompson was to elaborate as a central tenet in his critique of Althusserian structuralism a decade later: "Every social struggle or movement of resistance has also been a moral issue, over which individuals took risks for the sake of their fellows. Resistance to oppression has not only speeded technical progress, but has built mankind's moral reserves, its accumulation of moral capital."[108]

Along with religion and morality, Kiernan has long demanded that Marxism be attuned to the arts which, he says, also had "a share in inventing" the idea of socialism. In particular among the arts, he stresses literature, of which he has himself long been an active student, as articles on Shakespeare, Milton, Wordsworth, and Tennyson, and the literary references always to be found in his other writings, illustrate. (Urging me to broaden my intellectual and cultural horizons, he remarked that "A historian without strong literary interests is like a man without a shadow.") Noteworthy in this context is the well-grounded statement by Margot Heinemann, herself a prominent student of Shakespeare and his contemporaries, and also a comrade of the former members of the Historians' Group, that "Much of the most distinguished Marxist literary commentary of recent years has indeed come from people who are primarily or partly historians—among them A. L. Morton, Victor Kiernan, E. P. Thompson, Jack Lindsay, and Christopher Hill."[109] This should not be too surprising since, on the one hand, there is a long record of Marxist historiographical interest in literature commencing with the "old man" himself, as Professor Prawer so comprehensively reveals in *Karl Marx and World Literature* and, on the other, there is an even longer tradition, as Fred Inglis reminds us, wherein "the English intellectual tries to explain his ideas or to interpret those of others by resituating them in his literature."[110] Kiernan's concern, nevertheless, is that Marxists learn to draw upon the creative expressiveness and values and aspirations articulated in literature, most especially, it should be noted, in *poetry*.

In "Wordsworth and the People," Kiernan emphatically declares: "There will not be another great poet who has not learned much from Marx. Marxism also has much to learn, that it has not yet learned, from poetry." In a

historical and biographical fashion the "lesson" to be derived from Wordsworth's experience, as I have shown above, relates to his unfulfilled desire to
transcend the divide between poet and people, reflecting on Kiernan's part,
as Bill Schwarz contends, a central concern of the Historians' Group regarding their own "isolation" from the working class in the 1950s.[111] Indeed,
Thompson later made this question of Wordsworth's experience a subtext of
The Making of the English Working Class, which is revealed in the closing paragraphs of the book when he brings the Romantic poets and radical artisans
together as "parallel" oppositions to the rise of "Acquisitive Man." The tragedy he ponders is that "In the failure of the two traditions to come to a point
of junction, something was lost. How much we cannot be sure, for we are
among the losers."[112] Kiernan himself issued a warning derived from the
personal histories of the Romantic poets: "An artist who does not feel the
People as a force positively on his side may soon come to feel them as something against him."

In a postscript to "Wordsworth and the People" written in 1973, Kiernan
recalls the challenge but acknowledges that the relationship has become ever
more problematic. He then proceeds to highlight the values in Wordsworth's
poetry which should have special resonance today. In particular he refers to
a stress on "individual autonomy" in the midst of nondemocratic and anonymous corporate and collective institutions (capitalist and socialist) and a
preservationist concern for the environment.[113] Also relevant here, Kiernan
has mused in his article on "The Socialism of Antonio Gramsci" that the
English amongst all Europeans are the richest in poetry and history but,
sadly, "the most indifferent to both"; and in "Labour and the Literate" he
signals the tragic element in this state of affairs: "Without memory of yesterday there can indeed be no vision of tomorrow and in this light history is
indispensable to progress."[114]

To comprehend fully the character of Kiernan's pessimism it is essential to
more fully appreciate and understand his tragic vision of history. Without
underestimating the sense of loss and fatality, it should be recognized that his
conception of tragedy is also imbued with an awareness, an expectation, of
historical movement and so it also involves a sense of hope and possibility.
In his own words: "if tragic drama ends on a note of acceptance, of turning
away from past to future, this only epitomizes human experience that
through storms and stresses, the strife of wills and its unguessable outcomes,
new beginnings are at last reached." He finds this tragic vision of history
most brilliantly expressed in the works of Marx and Engels—"Early Marxism
adopted a panoramic vista of the past as tragic as its outlook on the future
was optimistic; later Marxism has not yet found a convincing alternative"—
and, of course, in Shakespeare. In "Notes on Marxism in 1968" he writes:
"the development of a theory of tragedy, and a special theory of Shake-
spearean tragedy, is among the grandest problems of historical Marxism."[115]

Kiernan himself has been eager to develop a Marxism theory of Shake-spearean tragedy. As I indicated above, in the years immediately following the Second World War, he produced a book-length manuscript on the subject (to which he has now returned). Moreover, his books *State and Society in Europe, 1550–1650* and *The Duel in European History* clearly indicate his inti-macy with the works of the great playwright, and their incorporation in his history writing. Also, his essay, "Human Relations in Shakespeare" well rep-resents what might be termed the "dialectical" character of his tragic vision of history. As much as Kiernan celebrates Shakespeare's dramatic renderings of the impermanence and demise of the feudal epoch—and the rule of aris-tocrat and monarch—he finds within the plays an appreciation of the libera-tion of human relations associated with what we might now refer to as the making of the modern world, or the transition to capitalism: "In a season of change one artist will fasten chiefly on what is bad in the situation, decline and decay, another on what is good, birth and growth. Shakespeare belongs emphatically to the second sort." [116] But this was written in the early 1960s and is likely to present Kiernan's historical vision in too "optimistic" a light. A better way of seeing it today is suggested in Margot Heinemann's "Shake-spearean Contradictions and Social Change":

> Shakespearean tragedy and tragic history implies a double view. We reduce it if we present it as wholly somber, showing history *only* as a meaningless cycle and human beings only as helpless or grotesque, doomed by fate. There is no need to replace this view by its oppo-site: that the endings (even in *Lear* or *Troilus*) must always be felt as "optimistic," or even that tragedy is not an art for socialists. In the last quarter of the twentieth century, Marxists of all people must feel acutely the contrast between what men *could* make of history and life and what they *do*. This is truly a *tragic* sense of futility and waste—and not less because so much of the suffering is avoid-able. [117]

Thus, we are returned to the issue of the *making* of history which must always be a central one for those of us who aspire to more democratic, egal-itarian, and libertarian social orders. Kiernan has long called for a "reforma-tion" of both Marxism and socialism reinvigorated by new ideas to be real-ized in the mirror of history. This again poses a question for Kiernan: In the light of the current debates about the future of Western socialism and the place of class struggle and working-class agency within it, does he align him-self with those "postmodern" socialists who contend that the working class— if it ever was so central—has been superseded by the "new social movements" of environmentalism, peace, race/ethnicity, and feminism as the primary agents of progressive social change and the making of radical democracy and/or socialism?[118]

In "Notes on the Intelligentsia" (1969) Kiernan wrote that "The barrier fortresses of class power remain, and will not fall down for any blowing of trumpets, intellectual or other. Class struggle remains as necessary as Marxism has always said." In those pages, and elsewhere since, he has insisted that "the working class remains indispensable to any thorough-going change," both for the vigor and fortitude it would instill in the socialist movement and for the sake of ensuring that its victories entailed the maximization of democracy.[119] Yet, at the same time, he has said that "There is no chosen class, any more than a chosen people," and he looks ahead with some hope to the emergence of a broad progressive alliance of workers, intellectuals, women, and young people. Moreover, he has stated that "socialism in Europe has been allowed to appear too closely linked to a single class" and, further, that Marx and Engels clearly underestimated the potential inclination towards socialism in sectors of the middle class.[120] The history of religion and art, he observes, shows how "creations of the mind" are capable of transcending their historical circumstances and—more than Marxism has allowed—the same potential exists for socialism.[121]

The formation of a socialist alliance constructed around the working class and sectors of the middle class remains, however, problematic. In one of his most pessimistic articles, "After Empire," Kiernan acknowledged: "Socialism cannot be built without the working class, which is not interested in it; it cannot be built against the middle classes, which are hostile to it." Ever ambivalent—though never indifferent—he allows that the "true nature of classes remains mysterious" and, thus, from the "autonomy which the working class has preserved, negative as it may often seem, fresh beginnings can always be looked for hopefully."[122] All of which, it seems to me, points again to the "Wordsworthian" dilemma of surmounting the divide between poet and "people." And here I am led to withdraw, or recant, my accusation of Leninism directed at Kiernan's political thought, for his sympathies and inclinations are, as I have implied throughout this essay, actually much more often Gramscian with reference to the responsibility of Left and socialist intellectuals to articulate the aspirations, ideals, and vision of socialism out of a "dialogue" with "the people."[123] Indeed, *there* is the challenge—as it has always been—for radical-democratic and socialist intellectuals. Kiernan himself proposed it thirty years ago in his review of Raymond Williams's *Culture and Society* when, for all his criticism of both Williams's book and the tradition of cultural criticism delineated in it, he asserted that "if the Tradition meant more than mere self-complacency it was because England had a record never long interrupted of popular resistance to society as it was, and of writers ready to put the feelings of the people into language."[124] We could do no better than to emulate that long and honorable tradition.

I have argued that while Hilton, Hill, Hobsbawm, Rudé, and Thompson have not been primarily strategists of socialist politics, by way of their historical practice they have been pursuing a particular political strategy. This might be comprehended as the creation of a "historical aesthetic," and their writings may be seen as contributions to the formation of a critical, democratic, and socialist historical consciousness. Though, as I have noted, Kiernan's work both intersects *and* diverges in significant ways from that of his former comrades of the Historians' Group, his wide-ranging historical efforts have consistently been bound up with this project. Here I would recall the words of the German-Jewish writer, Walter Benjamin, that "Only that historian will have the gift of fanning the spark of hope in the past who is firmly convinced that *even the dead* will not be safe from the enemy [the ruling class] if he wins. And this enemy has not ceased to be victorious." It might be said that while his fellow historians have been "fanning the spark of hope," Kiernan has been reminding us that "The enemy has not ceased to be victorious." [125]

4

E. P. THOMPSON,
THE BRITISH MARXIST HISTORICAL TRADITION
AND THE CONTEMPORARY CRISIS

In this chapter I would like to present a set of reflections on the continuing relevance of the British Marxist historical tradition in the face of the contemporary mutual crises of history and socialism, in which the great "grand-governing narratives" by which we comprehend past, present, and possible futures are being revised or rejected.[1] Thus, after reviewing the principal contributions of the British Marxist historians to history and social thought as a collective or tradition, I will consider those contributions in terms of what they offer to historical and political practice today, focusing in the latter half of the chapter on their work, especially that of E. P. Thompson, as "historical critics." I begin, however, with an autobiographical note.

When I was a child, my grandfather would come over to our house almost every weekend and on those occasions he introduced me to "the past"—or at least what I took to be the past. Most often he would read to me from a collection of Old Testament Bible stories. Other times he would tell me about coming to America as a Russian-Jewish immigrant and about growing up on the lower East Side of New York. My grandfather was a lawyer and he had a fantastic way of telling stories. Equally important, I later learned, was that he had been a young socialist before and during his years in law school. It is quite likely that his particular—perhaps "political"—renderings of the Old Testament shaped my sense of the stories. What I heard from my grandfather was a history of exploitation and oppression but, also, a history of dissent and struggle *and* exodus, redemption, liberation and revolution. I was captivated and inspired by the narrative he offered and in spite of the mediocre and unchallenging history I was taught at school, I was determined to read it at university.

Indeed, I eventually did receive a first degree in History, but I switched to the social sciences at the graduate level, assuming that I could work in what was coming to be known as historical sociology. For several reasons I was committed at the time to Latin American Studies, and specifically I wanted to write my doctoral dissertation as a historical sociology of landlord-peasant relations in Spanish America.[2] What I had found in writings on the subject was that although attention had been given to the landlords' domination of the peasantry and, increasingly, peasant resistance and rebellion, there was still little sense that the movement, the historical development, of those polities and social orders were shaped by peasant and worker struggles. The crucial conflicts were adjudged, historically, to be those between landed and mercantile elites. Of course, there were historical models available in North America for the kind of work I wanted to pursue. There was Barrington Moore, Jr.'s *Social Origins of Dictatorship and Democracy* which effectively licensed the historical-sociological enterprise for many of us; and, also, there were the studies of southern slavery by Eugene Genovese.[3] It was in Genovese's writings in particular that I found a theoretical perspective, and it was through him that I discovered the British Marxist historians, for the path from Genovese led to Maurice Dobb and the "transition question," then to Rodney Hilton and landlord-peasant conflicts, and onwards to Christopher Hill, George Rudé, Eric Hobsbawm, and E. P. Thompson. Essentially, in the British Marxist historical tradition I not only came upon a range of ideas and insights for my dissertation; I rediscovered the kind of history to which my grandfather had introduced me twenty years earlier. It recounted both the experience of exploitation and oppression *and* the episodes of dissent and struggle; it was committed and passionate; and it was connected to a larger problematic. (Little did I know that its authors were in several cases themselves raised in Old Testament traditions!)[4]

The British Marxist historical tradition is hardly singular. Consider the variety in the following. The "debate on the transition to capitalism" initiated by Maurice Dobb's *Studies in the Development of Capitalism:* originating in the deliberations of the Communist Party Historians' Group and pursued on an international scale in the pages of the American journal, *Science and Society,* the debate established the framework for most of the historians' later works.[5] "People's History": imbued in the Historians' Group by A. L. Morton's pioneering synthesis, *A People's History of England,* and the efforts of Dona Torr, exemplified by *Tom Mann and His Times,* this practice connects the senior historians with the History Workshop movement of socialist and feminist historians among the principle protagonists of which has been Raphael Samuel, a schoolboy member of the original Historians' Group.[6] "Labor History": fomented by the Society for the Study of Labour History which includes among its founders Eric Hobsbawm, John Saville, and Dorothy Thompson, this field now encompasses both the chronicles of the "Labour Movement" and the broader history of the working class.[7] "Cultural Studies": originating in the writings of Richard Hoggart, Raymond Williams, and Stuart Hall and pursued most energetically by the students and graduates

of the Birmingham Centre for Contemporary Cultural Studies, this enter-
prise was also clearly inspired by E. P. Thompson's *The Making of the English
Working Class*.[8] And yet another strand of the "tradition" (to which I shall
return), represented by the work of Victor Kiernan, Ralph Miliband, John
Saville, and Perry Anderson, and more recently Philip Corrigan and Derek
Sayer, has attended to ruling classes, power, and the state.

Nevertheless, if we treat the "core" of the tradition—which in our respective ways is what Bill Schwarz did in his article on the "Historians' Group,
1946–56"[9] and what I did in *The British Marxist Historians*—then it would
have to be said that beyond the outstanding accomplishments of the historians in their particular fields of study there have been four paramount contributions which they have made as a "collective." First has been the development of "class-struggle analysis." Derived from *The Communist Manifesto,* the
central working hypothesis of the British Marxist historians has been that
"The history of all hitherto existing society is the history of class struggle."
Thus, the medieval world was not harmoniously organized into three estates
but was an order of struggle between lords and peasants; the conflicts of the
seventeenth century were not a mere civil war but a "bourgeois revolution"
driven by struggles of the lower orders as well; the eighteenth century was
not conflict-free but shot through with antagonisms between "patricians and
plebeians" which, moreover, were expressions of "class struggle without
class"; and the Industrial Revolution entailed not only economic and social
changes but, in the course of the conflicts between "Capital and Labor," a
dramatic process of class formation determined in great part by the agency
of workers themselves. Revisions have been made to these stories but the
centrality of class struggle persists. Moreover, such struggle has not been
limited to moments of outright rebellion or revolution. The British Marxist
historians have enlarged the scope of what is to be understood as "struggle"
and, thus, in addition to rebellion and revolution we now have "resistance"
as part of our historical vocabulary.

The second contribution has been the pursuit and development of "history
from the bottom up." Perhaps the finest statement of the imperative behind
this perspective was offered by the German-Jewish critic, Walter Benjamin,
when he wrote: "Only that historian will have the gift of fanning the spark
of hope in the past who is firmly convinced that *even the dead* will not be safe
from the enemy [the ruling class] if he wins. And the enemy has not ceased
to be victorious."[10] The British Marxist historians have sought to redeem, or
reappropriate, the experience and the agency of the lower orders—peasants,
plebeians, artisans, and workers. In fact, history from the bottom up has
come to be equated with the "history of the common people" and I expect
we are all familiar with the words, quoted before in this volume, which have
become something of an "oath" for young social historians: "I am seeking to

rescue the poor stockinger, the Luddite cropper, the 'obsolete' handloom weavers, the utopian artisan and even the deluded follower of Joanna South-cott, from the enormous condescension of posterity."[11] Granted that the *Annales* historians can be seen as having initiated "history from below," they did not, however, pursue it with an interest in class struggle and popular political "agency" as have the British historians. Actually it might be said that whereas the British Marxists have been pursuing a "revolutionary" English past, the *Annalistes* seem to have been running from the demands of 1789, 1830, and 1848. Again, history from the bottom up was originally conceived to be a "perspective." As I tell my students, let's get our prepositions straight: it is not merely history *of* the bottom, but *from* the bottom *up*. Through the history of the common people we have gained much, but perhaps some revision is in order.

The third contribution of the historians has been the recovery and assemblage of a "radical-democratic tradition" in which have been asserted what might be called "counter-hegemonic" conceptions of liberty, equality, and community. In Gramscian—as opposed to Leninist—fashion, the historians have revealed not a history of political ideas originating inside the heads of intellectuals, but a history of popular ideology standing in dialogical relationship to the history of politics and ideas. Alongside the Magna Carta we are offered the English Rising of 1381; outside of Parliament in the seventeenth century we encounter Levellers, Diggers, and Ranters; in the eighteenth century we not only hear Wilkes but also the crowds of London asserting the "rights of the free-born Englishman"; and in the Age of Revolution we are reminded that within the "exceptionalism" of English political life there were Jacobins, Luddites, Captain Swing, and Chartists (the last representing the first working-class political party seeking, at the least, political democracy). At the same time, it must be noted that the British Marxists do have their "intellectuals": John Ball and his fellow priests; Milton and Winstanley; Wilkes, Paine, and Wollstonecraft; Wordsworth and Blake; and Cobbett, Owen, Jones, Marx, and Morris.

Finally, another contribution of primary importance is that by way of class-struggle analysis, history from the bottom up, and the recovery of the radical democratic tradition, the British Marxist historians have effectively helped to undermine the great "Grand Narratives" of both the Right and the Left. Their labors directly challenged the Whig version of history in which the development of English life and freedoms is comprehended as a continuous evolutionary and progressive process. And they also helped to clear away the (supposedly) Marxist presentation of history in which historical development is conceived of in unilinear, mechanical, and techno-economistic terms.[12] This may not have been their intention back in the early days of the Historians' Group, but surely their persistent stress on the *historical* in historical materialism led them to it. I hope we are all in agreement that this fourth contribution has been a liberating process though necessarily one which entails its own challenges of both a historiographical and a political nature.

It is tempting to claim that the British Marxist historical tradition has actually become an Anglo-American tradition, for the influence of the British historians on American historical writings has been remarkably extensive. Their work has shaped both American labor studies—from writings on colonial and republican artisans to those on immigrant workers and industrial proletarians—and agrarian studies—from writings on the Antebellum and Reconstruction South to those on farmers' movements in the Midwest.[13] Additionally, American historians and social scientists have taken the British Marxist tradition to such places as highland South America, Southeast Asia, Europe and even back to Britain itself. In fact, considering the aggressive and enthusiastic efforts of Robert Brenner and Immanuel Wallerstein, has not the debate on the transition to capitalism now migrated to America?[14] Moreover, British Marxism has influenced women's studies and feminist scholarship, educational, cultural, and literary studies, and the exploration of contemporary social and political questions including "critical legal studies."[15] In turn, one might register the influence of the work of American Marxist historians like Eugene Genovese and David Montgomery, on that of the British.[16]

Noteworthy in this vein is that the attacks on socialist, especially Marxist, historians initiated by Thatcher and her allies[17] have been echoed most loudly in America by Professor Gertrude Himmelfarb, a leading historian of nineteenth-century British political culture and ideas, and *the* leading voice of neo-conservative historiography in the United States. Himmelfarb's critiques of recent historiographical developments are well known. She decries the rise of the "new" social history for its neglect of politics and its rejection of a narrative style of presentation (criticisms for which I must admit to having a certain sympathy). However, as one might imagine, since the British Marxist historians' scholarly efforts are essentially "political" history framed by a specific narrative scheme, Himmelfarb's hostility to their work is of a different order. In her review article of *The British Marxist Historians* and the MARHO interviews, *Visions of History,* in the American magazine, *The New Republic,* she pursued a decidedly "Cold War" attack on their scholarship.[18] That is, she did not challenge their studies as history—at least not directly—but, rather, she conjured up a shadowy image of "Stalinism" standing behind their careers. We should not be too surprised to see that in the past few years Himmelfarb has fervently taken up Thatcher's celebration of a particular rendering of Victorian Britain, and that she is proffering it on both sides of the Atlantic.[19] Once again we are reminded that history *is* politics.

This brings us to the present juncture. After a decade of the Thatcher Government[20] with its class warfare from above against the unions, local democracy, freedom of expression, and the welfare state, and its concomitant service to Capital and centralization of state powers, it has been presumed that the Conservatives have undermined the postwar "social democratic" consensus. Excuse the sociologist in me for resorting to them, but the polls indicate that although Britons in the majority do see the country after ten years of "Thatcherism" as "richer," they also see it as "sadder"—which is not exactly the basis for a new "consensus." In fact, other surveys seem to indicate that the social-democratic consensus may not have actually collapsed for, apparently, working people still believe in the justice of a "downwards" redistribution of wealth to be carried out by the state.[21] That seems to run directly counter to the Conservatives' hegemonic ambitions. We ought not to be optimistic, however, for here's the "rub": the very same surveys indicate a widespread cynicism about the ability of the "common people" to do anything to bring about such a project. In other words, what we find is "resignation" not consensus. Of course, no historiography should subordinate itself to the politics of the moment, but surely the problem of resignation and accommodation in the face of an aggressive antidemocratic politics should make us reflect a bit, especially since the British Marxist historical tradition has been a historiography of "agency." At the same time, it must be acknowledged that the British Marxists' narrative has been essentially a long chronicle of "tragedy" or, to play with the title of a recent work by Christopher Hill, "the experience of defeat."[22] We might put a somewhat more "progressive" spin on it by recalling William Morris' words in *The Dream of John Ball:* "I pondered how men fight and lose the battle, and the thing they fought for comes about in spite of their defeat, and when it comes turns out to be not what they meant, and other men have to fight for what they meant under another name." We can probably do no better than to read the past in exactly such a manner, but at present we need to put it more starkly: "The enemy has not ceased to be victorious."

In that light I would like to offer a few thoughts on the practices fostered by the British Marxist historians considering in particular their recovery of the radical-democratic tradition and what it represents for the regeneration of a Left "public discourse" and, possibly, the making of a new grand narrative. First, regarding class-struggle analysis, it should be evident that we need to explore ever more deliberately the intimate relations between and among the experiences of class and gender and race and ethnicity. A fuller understanding and appreciation of, for example, the formation of classes and their identities—above and below—and, thus, their modes of inclusion and exclusion depends on it. Obviously, British Marxist historians have begun to take up the question of gender and class (one immediately thinks in Britain of Sheila Rowbotham, Barbara Taylor, and Catherine Hall, among others), but such work has just started, relatively speaking. As Hall states in conclusion to her contribution to *E. P. Thompson: Critical Perspectives:* "The complexities of the relation between class and culture have received much attention. It is time for gender and culture to be subjected to more critical scrutiny."[23]

Even less often explored is the articulation of class, race, ethnicity, and national identity. Very much on the political agenda and in "the news," this problematic must join the Marxist historical agenda. Perhaps on this question British historians might want to have a look at the work of American social historians of the Left, not because of the media "line" that Britain is now suffering what the States have long had, a "race problem," or because after all the benefits Americans have derived from British historians, we owe you something; but, rather, because American studies in this area indicate both the ways in which ethnicity and race presented obstacles to effective class formation *and* how such seemingly insurmountable barriers have on certain occasions been transcended.[24] I am suggesting no more than what I did for my dissertation: read the American works not for formulae but for questions and ideas. Britain has had its own *long* history of race and ethnicity intersecting with class conflicts and, most significantly, nation-state formation. In such terms consider again the notion of being "British" as opposed to Welsh, Scottish, or English (not to mention Irish). Furthermore, as Victor Kiernan recounts in "Britons Old and New," the Norman Conquest was hardly the last arrival of Europeans alone to settle on the island and greatly upset the locals.[25] Marxist historians might even wish to take the lead in deliberations on how to incorporate the historical experiences of black people into British historical education; imagine the innovations which might be effected in the tradition of the "free-born Briton" past and present in this generation and the next by way of the black and Asian presence in Britain. In this light, as a counterpart to "imperial history," Marxist historians should consider the international and multiracial "British" history proposed by Robin Blackburn's book, *The Overthrow of Colonial Slavery,* in its exploration of the connections between political and class struggles for "freedom" in Britain and the Caribbean.[26]

The second observation, or suggestion, I would make relates to history from the bottom up. Whereas some would call for a break with this approach, I would say that what is really needed is a return to a fuller idea of history from the bottom up as a "perspective," or, as Barrington Moore, Jr., put it, "a [critical] sympathy with the victims . . . and a skepticism about the claims of the victors."[27] And from that vantage point we do need to be more concerned with what Perry Anderson has called the "intricate machinery of class domination." That is, more investigation should be undertaken of: ruling-class formation, deformation, and reformation; ruling-class values, aspirations, and expectations; the state in all its complexity; modes of exploitation and appropriation; and, processes of hegemony within and without the state apparatus. We just don't know enough about these things; yet they are what makes the perspective of history from the bottom up necessary, and how are we to comprehend class *relations* without them? As F. Stirton Weaver has observed: "Class societies are not a product of nature. It takes great human effort and struggle to create and maintain a system in which some of the people do the work from which others derive the benefits"; and, as Victor Kiernan has remarked: "In general, as in Britain today, the upper classes have been in the driving seat because they are more united, more class conscious, better equipped, and politically more intelligent." [28]

Perhaps American social history and social science have something to offer here as well. I am thinking in particular of such writers as C. Wright Mills, Paul Sweezy, Paul Baran, Harry Braverman, William Appleman Williams, James Weinstein, Gabriel Kolko, William Dumhoff, and Christopher Lasch whose respective works and theoretical perspectives are quite varied, but might all be encompassed by the term "power structure studies." [29] The goal of such research and writing has been to uncover the power, wealth, and degree of cohesion of the elites, or ruling classes, and to reveal the modes of appropriation, manipulation, and political and ideological domination which they have exercised or others have exercised on their behalf. This practice is the scholarly counterpart to the radical American political tradition of decrying the concentration of wealth and power (and, thus, the emergence of an "aristocracy") as a corruption of the American democratic ideal—which, I tell my students, is derived in part from the Levellers. In one respect British socialist writers would do very well to attend to such a model, for those American scholars of the Left have not hesitated to explore twentieth-century and contemporary history—a pursuit which has been significantly absent from the British Marxist historical tradition. Otherwise, however, we should all be careful with such studies for they have characteristically denied working-class and popular agency. What is actually required is not merely power-structure studies, but class-*structuration* studies focusing on the ruling classes; and class structuration has been, as I have argued before, a central concern of the British Marxist historians.

Therefore, after considering the American studies one might return to the British tradition for, as I noted earlier, there is a strand which has concerned itself with ruling classes, power, and the state. It is best represented by the writings of Victor Kiernan, such as *The Lords of Human Kind, State and Society in Europe, 1550–1650,* and *The Duel in European History.* [30] Also, one must note the volumes on European state formation by Perry Anderson, *Passages from Antiquity to Feudalism* and *Lineages of the Absolutist State;* that on English state formation, *The Great Arch* by Philip Corrigan and Derek Sayer; and a recent work, *1848: The British State and Chartism,* by John Saville. [31] The last is an excellent study of a dramatic moment in the making of the Victorian state and ruling-class hegemony which, it should be added, makes us think again about English "exceptionalism" and reminds us that at least in the nineteenth century the propertied realized that the struggle for democracy and socialism were co-equal. Arguably, all of this has also been present, at least to some extent, at the core of the tradition; especially if one thinks about Hill's early writings on the Church, English State and Puritanism, Hilton's book, *A Medieval Society,* Thompson's *Whigs and Hunters,* and Eric Hobsbawm's magnificent trilogy on the long nineteenth century.[32]

Remember, there is always the danger that such history can have the effect of merely inspiring even greater cynicism about the worth of popular agency—unless Walter Benjamin was right when he said that working-class political struggle is "nourished more by the image of enslaved ancestors than liberated grandchildren."[33] Nevertheless, it is essential that Marxist historical study continue to work towards the recognition of the ways that the agency of the lower orders have actually *structured* power, a recognition of the fact that it has made a difference. Such agency includes revolution, rebellion, and resistance in all their variety, possibly including even accommodation, which may well signify an intense will to survive, to bear witness, and, perhaps, to fight another day. A possible starting point for what I have in mind was proposed by the English critic, Terry Eagleton, at an American conference on "The Literary Imagination and the Sense of the Past" when he said: "What is meant by reading history from the standpoint of the oppressed is not that the oppressed are the concealed, forgotten, inarticulate, abandoned 'subject' of history; it means, rather, grasping history as constructed from within the constraints that the oppressed, by their very existence impose."[34] In essence we need to reveal the faces of power and to de-reify their expressions by showing their *social* origins and indicating how they have also been determined by the dominated themselves.[35]

Lastly, then, what about the further recovery of the "radical-democratic tradition" and the possibility of a new synthesis or grand narrative of British history developed from a Marxian perspective? My call for increased study of ruling classes past and present is not at all intended to discourage the effort of mobilizing and further articulating a radical-democratic and socialist heritage. Indeed, such labors are crucial to my final suggestion, which is that at the same time that socialist historians (on both sides of the Atlantic!) continue to work within the historical discipline, they should seek the reinvigoration of the practice of historical and social *criticism.* Admittedly, this ambition arises most immediately from the growing recognition within the American Left that it has been marginalized—or, as some have argued, marginalized itself—from the realm of *public* discourse. While the Right continues to rail on (to truly myth-making proportions) about the strength and significance of the Left's presence in American academic life, Left scholars and writers are themselves ever more conscious of the fact that they have failed to adequately confront the rise of the New Right and its commanding presence in public intellectual and political debates.[36] Yet my proposal also emerges from ongoing discussions in Britain and Europe regarding the future of socialism as a movement and historical project. However skeptical I remain of the arguments of "post-Marxist" and "postmodern" socialists who believe that contemporary history has transcended "class struggles," leaving the imperative of working-class agency in its wake, they have reawakened many on the Left to the legacy of liberal and democratic thought and rhetoric and, at the same time, compelled a reconsideration of the political and moral role of intellectuals.[37] Furthermore, common to the deliberations of both the American and British Lefts, it seems, are the beginnings of a renewed appreciation of the necessity of history and the *powers of the past* in breaking the tyranny of the present. For example, John Keane has recently reiterated the importance of a "democratic remembrance of things past": "An active democratic memory recognizes that the development of fresh and stimulating perspectives on the present depends upon criticisms that break up habitual ways of thinking, in part through types of criticism which remember what is in danger of being forgotten."[38]

At the outset, the further recovery of the radical-democratic tradition is for our own edification because it will provide an essential reminder that the most effectively democratic criticism is advanced, as Michael Walzer contends in his book, *Interpretation and Social Criticism,* not by alienated or detached intellectuals equipped with new and better theories discovered on a distant mountaintop or invented in the solitude of a philosopher's study, but by "connected critics" engaged in the interpretation and original elaboration of existing or historically-recovered and grounded values and aspirations. This does not, it should be made clear, represent a commitment to the status quo. Indeed, more than others, Marxists should be sensitive to the fact that it is in the very nature of class-structured societies that there is an incoherence between ideal and reality, and that the differential experience of that reality by rulers and ruled affords an opening for political engagement: "Morality is always potentially subversive of class and power." Furthermore, as Antonio Gramsci realized, in the course of the struggle to secure its hegemony, a ruling class must necessarily take into account the interests and expectations of the ruled and, too, make sacrifices. Thus, even in a seemingly coherent social order there is a ground, a space, an opening, for criticism. As Gramsci contends in *The Prison Notebooks,* socialist critics must initiate "a process of differentiation and change in the relative weight that the elements of the old ideologies used to possess. What was previously secondary and subordinate, or even incidental, is now taken to be primary and becomes the nucleus of a new ideological and theoretical complex."[39]

On reflection, is this not what has been best in the "radical-democratic tradition" according to the British Marxist historians? As I detailed above in Chapter 1, against those who had portrayed the English Rising of 1381 as "fanatical *prophetae* mixed with disoriented and desperate masses on the very margin of society," Hilton has shown that the Rising was a uniquely class-conscious movement of peasants and artisans and, moreover, that the importance of John Ball and his fellow village clerics was that they "seem to have re-inforced the peasant demands for freedom of status and tenure by a broader articulation of contemporary feelings." Indeed, he continues: "What is remarkable is the way that their vision of a society of free and equal men and women fused with the ancient peasant demand for freedom of status and tenure, in the formulation of a programme which, though entirely incapable of realisation, given the historical forces at work in the late middle ages, did challenge root and branch the ideas of the ruling class."[40] Then there are Hill's studies of the religious and secular dimensions of the ideological origins of the English Revolution, in which he highlights the respective roles of Puritan preachers and lecturers and of "intellectuals" such as Bacon, Raleigh, and Coke in inspiring "confidence" in "the middle sort of people" by articulating and giving voice to their ideals and aspirations. And it was this "class" which made the civil war into a revolution. Similarly there are Hills's portraits of the radical religious figures, like Winstanley, whose "original" renditions of the ideas of the middle sort began to capture the imagination of the lower orders threatening a *democratic* revolution-in-the-revolution.[41]

Thompson's classic, *The Making of the English Working Class,* also reveals such a political praxis. The book magnificently illustrates how the *formation* of the working class in the Industrial Revolution entailed a broadening and deepening of the tradition of "the free-born Englishman" and, too, as Terry Eagleton denotes, the making of a *"counter-*public sphere" to that of the "bourgeois" public sphere: "In the Corresponding Societies, the radical press, Owenism, Cobbett's *Political Register* and Paine's *Rights of Man,* feminism and the dissenting churches, a whole oppositional network of journals, clubs, pamphlets, debates and institutions invades the dominant consensus, threatening to fragment it from within."[42] And even before his brilliant discussion in *The Making* of Tom Paine's role as a radical-democratic intellectual in advancing the tradition of the free-born Englishman (discussed above in Chapter 1),[43] Thompson had authored the article, "Homage to Tom Maguire," in which he appreciatively revealed a political practice that embodied in real historical terms Gramsci's "organic intellectual." Maguire, the worker, poet, and socialist organizer who was so instrumental in the establishment of the I.L.P. (Independent Labour Party) in the West Riding of Yorkshire "had been the point of junction between the theoretical understanding of the national leaders, the moral teachings of Morris and Carpenter, and the needs and aspirations of his own people."[44]

Indeed, I would propose that in their very efforts to recover the radical-democratic tradition, the British Marxist historians have themselves been working not simply as historical scholars but, at the same time, as historical critics, most especially (though not alone) Edward Thompson. Indeed,

Thompson is greatly admired for this in the United States, and in the aforementioned American discussions on the need to reinvigorate the "public
voice" of the intellectual Left his work is regularly cited as a model of historically-informed political and social criticism. For example, writing in review
of Perry Anderson's critique of Thompson's history, theory, and politics, *Arguments within English Marxism*, Marcus Rediker poses the question "How
can historians produce politically useful knowledge?" Acknowledging the
theoretical rigor of Anderson's criticisms, Rediker nevertheless endorses
Thompson's practice over that of Anderson not only because he is more sympathetic towards Thompson's view of the purpose of Marxist historical study,
but also because of the "democratic" aspirations and commitments which
characterize Thompson's thought and are expressed in his writings. In particular, Rediker recommends Thompson to us for the manner in which he seeks
to engage his audience: "Thompson writes with continual human reference,
affirming certain values over and against others, and he tries to make his
readers active valuing agents as they think about history and politics." Moreover, in contrast to Anderson, whose primary audience is "the Left, in both
its academic and institutional forms," Thompson addresses himself not
merely to the Left and to fellow historians, but as well, to a popular *and*
working-class audience.[45]

To refer once again to *The Making of the English Working Class*, it should be
recalled that it was written by a politically-engaged socialist both as a critique
of Old *and* New Left assumptions about working-class consciousness and
agency, and as a challenge to historians' and social scientists' renditions and
assessments of working-class experience and struggles in the Industrial Revolution and their contributions to the making of modern British political and
cultural life. Moreover, as an adult education tutor during the years in which
he was preparing the book, Thompson says he wrote it not for academics but
with working people and the Labour Movement in mind. In the preface to a
collection of essays by the American radical historian, Staughton Lynd,
whom he refers to as a fellow "Objector," Thompson explains that "as we
argue about the past so also are we arguing about—and seeking to clarify—
the mind of the present which is recovering that past. Nor is this an unim-
portant part of the mind of the present. For some of the largest arguments
about human rationality, destiny, and agency, must always be grounded there:
in the historical record."[46] In just this spirit, Fred Inglis, the English education critic, has described *The Making*, along with Thompson's other historical
studies, as providing the working class with "a new past to live from; it
changes the social memory so that, differently understanding how the present
came about, the agent thinks forward to a new set of possibilities."[47]

The historical imagination and intentions which have determined his study
of the past have also shaped Thompson's specifically political writings. As I
have observed before, Thompson's political interventions recall those of Tom

Paine and William Cobbett. Indeed, I recently came upon G. D. H. Cole's portrait of Cobbett from which it is worth quoting at length, for Cole's description of the Radical Cobbett might well have been provided as an introduction to Thompson.

> There are certain Englishmen who, being memorable for much besides, make me think, whenever they come into one's mind, of England. . . . Cobbett was an Englishman in this very special sense. . . . Bluff, egotistical, shrewd, capable of meanness as well as of greatness, positive in all things and desperately wrong in some—but also devastatingly right in many more—no theorist till he could see with his own eyes the human stuff of which problems are made, quick to anger and indignation but also infinitely friendly; didactical and often overbearing and yet full of sympathy; very well satisfied with himself and ever ready to hold his own experience up as an example to others; and therewith possessed of a singular power of identifying himself with the country he loved and the people for whom he fought—there you have the portrait of this tall, gawky, florid exuberant farmer who looked like a farmer. . . .
>
> Above all else, I think of Cobbett as the man who, at a wretched time in the history of the English people, put hope into their hearts, not by telling lies or painting fancy pictures, either of this world or the next, but by good solid cursing that never degenerated into a whine or a mere vapouring of despair, but bade men gird up their loins and struggle for the right. . . . He was angry, exceedingly angry; but there was always love as well as anger in his words. He loved the people on whose behalf he made crusade; and, equally with the people, he loved the land they lived in—the villages and churches, the great houses with their parks of orderly trees, the birds and beasts, the downs and valleys and rivers and streams, the crops that grew out of the earth and, last but not least, the earth itself. The smell and feel of the countryside were his tonic.
>
> For Cobbett was one of those evangelists who see the future by looking to the past. Maybe the past they think they see is not quite what really was; for they are as ready to pick out from it the things they love and value as to pick out what is bad in the present.[48]

Thompson's own anger is well known. Over the past decade it has been directed against a range of targets. In the early 1950s he spoke out against the "threat" posed by the importation of American capitalism and commercial values; then, in 1956, against the Soviet invasion of Hungary and the British Communist Party which had refused to denounce the action and, in the process, democratize itself; and, thereafter, against the politics of both the so-called "revolutionary" Left and the Labour Party leadership.[49] During the 1960s he turned to confront the new editorial leadership of the *New Left Review,* in particular Perry Anderson and Tom Nairn, who had taken over the journal from Thompson and his fellow co-founders and were proceeding to offer what they called a "global critique" of British history and society *and* the Labour Movement from the vantage point of historical and theoretical models derived from continental European Marxisms.[50] In the 1970s Thompson continued to question the "importation" of Western European Marxisms by a younger generation of theorists; most aggressively and spectacularly he challenged the ascendance of the "structuralist Marxism" developed by the French communist philosopher, Louis Althusser. But also in these years, he directed broadsides against the powers that be of the British Establishment who, in the face of a series of political and economic crises, had proceeded to trample on civil rights and liberties and threaten the social and economic gains secured in the past.[51] Finally, in the 1980s, Thompson joined in the reinvigoration of the Campaign for Nuclear Disarmament (CND) and, as a co-founder of European Nuclear Disarmament (END), energetically called for the tearing down of the Cold War blocs and opposed Thatcher's championing of Reagan's missile deployment and the military adventurism of both.[52]

It is not merely that Thompson has regularly been moved to anger and indignation, but that in venting them he has persistently sought to position himself *within* and to speak *from* English experience and traditions and, from that site, to articulate an interpretation of English history which both the Left *and* "the people" might recognize and appreciate as belonging to them and to which they have to answer. For example, in conclusion to *Out of Apathy* (1960), the collection of essays which he edited as the first "New Left Book," Thompson rejects the prevailing "extremist" visions of socialist transition, both the Fabian model of "piecemeal reform" and the Leninist model of "cataclysmic revolution," and proposes instead a "democratic strategy" of socialist "revolution" which calls for both extra-parliamentary "direct action" and, ultimately, parliamentary politics. The strategy he wishes to advance, he declares, emanates from a "democratic socialist tradition" which of all the Western nations is "strongest" in Britain. Even then he was sensitive to the likelihood of being accused of "utopianism" which was, of course, to recur in later criticisms of his political thought; yet, he expectantly counters, it is "foolish also to underestimate the long and tenacious revolutionary tradition of the British commoner."

> It is a dogged, good-humored responsible tradition: yet a revolutionary tradition all the same. From the Leveller corporals ridden down by Cromwell's men at Burford to the weavers massed behind their banners at Peterloo, the struggle for democratic and social

rights has long been intertwined. From the Chartist camp meeting to the dockers' picket line it has expressed itself most naturally in the language of moral revolt. Its weaknesses, its carelessness of theory, we know too well; its strengths, its resilience and steady humanity, we too easily forget. It is a tradition which could leaven the socialist world.[53]

In "The Peculiarities of the English" (1965), his extended reply to Anderson and Nairn, Thompson takes umbrage at their readings and assessments of English history. Their "ideal type" of revolution, drawn from (supposed) French experience, and their "critical theory," derived from continental Marxisms (which, Thompson notes, has failed to engage the English "empirical" idiom), have led them, he argues, to misconstrue the social character of the seventeenth- and eighteenth-century landed aristocracy, to "ignore the importance of the Protestant and bourgeois-democratic inheritance," and to "overlook the importance of capitalist political economy as 'authentic, articulated ideology.'"[54] His answer to their portrait of the British Labour Movement had already been offered, in great part, in *The Making of the English Working Class*. Later, in "An Open Letter to Leszek Kolakowski" (1973), Thompson refers to the literary and theoretical company he prefers to keep—in contrast to the "greats" of European philosophy.

> Take Marx and Vico and a few European novelists away, and my most intimate pantheon would be a provincial tea-party: a gathering of the English and the Anglo-Irish. Talk of free-will and determinism and I first think of Milton. Talk of man's inhumanity, I think of Swift. Talk of morality and revolution, and my mind is off with Wordsworth's Solitary. Talk of the problems of self-activity and creative labour in socialist society, and I am in an instant back with William Morris.

Further along in the "Letter" he identifies the figures of the British Marxist historical tradition as his immediate intellectual comrades—those who "sustain him"—and, once again, he defends the richness of working-class culture and values against the supposed cultural superiority of intellectuals.[55]

Then, of course, there is the famous (or infamous, depending on your view) counterattack on Althusserian structuralism, "The Poverty of Theory," in which he defends the *historical* in historical materialism against a scientifically-discovered and theoretically-elaborated version of Marxism proffered by philosophers. In the foreword to the volume in which it is published, Thompson responds to the criticism that he is merely an "English nationalist" who has failed to properly appreciate the theoretical contributions of Western European Marxists: "The 'adoption' of other traditions—that is adoption which has not been fully worked through, interrogated, and translated into the terms of our own traditions—can very often mean no more than the evacuation of the real places of conflict within our own intellectual culture, as well as the loss of real political relations with our own people."[56]

Admittedly, Thompson is capable of a certain self-indulgence and even vanity in his writing style (as I have implied by way of Cole's picture of Cobbett), but as well there is humor and a wonderfully evocative imagery to be found there, reflecting his eagerness to root himself in a specifically English historical and cultural landscape. Consider his description of himself in the "Letter to Kolakowski" as a "bustard" in comparison to the high-flying "eagles" of European philosophy; or, in the conclusion to *Whigs and Hunters,* his expression of skepticism about the orthodox Marxist assertion that "the law"—being merely a "superstructural" feature of capitalist production relations—will be dispensable in a socialism structured by "new forms of working-class power," advising us to "watch this new power for a century or two before you cut your hedges down." Or, again, in the closing lines of "The Poverty of Theory," his announcement that "My dues to '1956' have now been paid in full. I may now, with a better conscience, return to my proper work and to my own garden. I will watch how things grow."[57] (It is arguable that in his recent novel, *The Sykaos Papers,*[58] Thompson departs from this "rooting" in English experience for he resorts to the arrival on earth—to England in fact—of an "alien" in order to provide himself with a new vantage point for social criticism. However, as Walzer notes regarding the very same device having been used in the eighteenth century by another "connected critic": "If it suits their purposes, they can play at detachment, pretend to see their own society through the eyes of a stranger—like Montesquieu, the well-connected Frenchman, through the eyes of Usbek. But it is Montesquieu, the well-connected Frenchman, not Usbek, who is the social critic. Persian naivete is a mask for French sophistication." We might merely insert Thompson and Oi Pas the Oitarian for Montesquieu and Usbek the Persian.)[59]

These episodes portray Thompson as a critic of the Left, which he certainly has been, but it must be reiterated that however antagonistic his words have been, they are those of a *connected* critic arguing with his comrades on the Left from *within* their own history. Furthermore, his voice has just as angrily—and for just as long—been directed against the Right and the inner circles of the British Establishment, most expressively, perhaps, in the 1970s and 1980s on the subjects of civil liberties and nuclear disarmament. Here, too, however, Thompson has actually been concerned with articulating an interpretation of English history and the radical-democratic tradition which would serve to recall the Left and especially, in these instances, "the people" to their political and cultural "inheritance" ever aware that the Conservatives have themselves regularly sought to lay a prior claim to "the past" and, in the

process, to champion a different version of it. Speaking to a broad liberal and
Left audience in the pages of *New Society* in the midst of the political turmoil
of the early 1970s—heightened by the Miners' Strike (1972) then underway—Thompson acknowledges that "One tends to think of history as a reserve of the conservative and 'traditional.'" Nevertheless, he insists, "there is
still today an enormous reserve of radicalism stored within our culture."[60]
With this in mind he warns in 1977 that along with the increasing powers of
"The Secret State" one of the most worrying of contemporary developments
is the apparent historical amnesia of the British people. For the past twenty
years, Thompson writes, there has been "a dulling of the nerve of resistance
and outrage." He states this even more directly in his 1982 television address,
"The Heavy Dancers" (Channel 4), when, attending once again to the hidden wielders of power in the British State, he decries that "These non-elected
and self-vetted persons arrogate to themselves power which would astonish
our ancestors. . . . We've forgotten what any 'freeborn Englishman' knew
200 years ago—and what Americans still know [I hope!—H. J. K.]—that
the state exists to serve us: we don't exist by permission of the state. Why
have we forgotten? Why do we let these people get away with murder?"
Confronting this historical amnesia, Thompson reminds his fellow citizens
of both the tradition of English poets who regularly "asked where society
was going," and the "tradition of popular 'dissent' . . . the alternative nation,
with its own vibrant but unofficial culture—the true dissent of John Bunyan,
but also the political dissent of Cobbett, the Chartists, women's suffrage pio-
neers . . . [who] brought their influence to bear on the segregated world of
Britain's rulers—campaign for the vote—for the rights of press and opinion—and the rights of labour and women."[61]

Perhaps reflecting as well on his own practice, Thompson writes in "Homage to Thomas McGrath": "Yet anger demands an alternative. If the alternative be only the elegiac recollection of the past, then anger's alternative may
only be nostalgia."[62] However, even if we might argue about the priorities he
establishes it should be clear that Thompson does not seek a return to a
previous age and experience, but to inform *present* struggles and intellects
with the experiences and aspirations of the past. It may well be true, as Perry
Anderson claims, that, grounded in the "radical libertarian tradition,"
Thompson's political thought has failed to formulate a specifically *socialist*
project. Yet it must be registered that however much he seeks to articulate
the radical-democratic and socialist traditions as one, Thompson does not
equate liberal, or "bourgeois," with socialist democracy. Rather, what his historical and political writings do propose is that if socialist democracy is to be
made in Britain (or, I would add, America), it is crucial—for the sake of both
an effective democratic mobilization of popular and working-class political
participation in the present and to help secure the formation of an increasingly libertarian and democratic polity in the future—that it be developed

out of and remain connected to the radical-democratic tradition even as it seeks to broaden, deepen, and recompose it. Again, whatever their inadequacies, Thompson's writings, along with those of his fellow historians, compel the recognition that the radical-democratic *and* socialist traditions have been central to English and British political development—which is all-the-more essential today when a Conservative Government is striving once again to advance a narrative of British history in which socialism appears an "alien" thing (a process already well-effected in America).

Beyond our own political education, then, the recovery of the radical-democratic and socialist tradition, along with the history of exploitation and oppression and the conflicts to which they have given rise, is to bear witness to the creativity of popular struggles and the values and aspirations they have asserted and to secure the "dangerous memories" which might yet engage critical thought and action. Thus, it is to advance the *historical* "education of desire" and to continue the practice Victor Kiernan had in mind when he dubbed socialism "the prophetic memory."[63] At the same time, we should not fail to consider the subversions and corruptions of popular ideology and aspirations and, yes, the tragedies which have characterized past and present. To repeat my concluding argument of *The British Marxist Historians,* the objective of Marxist history must be to contribute to the formation of the kind of historical consciousness which Gramsci envisioned as the goal of a critical education "which understands movement and change, which appreciates the sum of effort and sacrifice which the present has cost the past and which the future is costing the present, and which conceives the contemporary world as a synthesis of the past, of all past generations, which projects itself into the future."[64]

As to the development of a new grand narrative to replace the old ones: well, that awaits both politics *and* the skills of historians and historical critics who can assimilate the past and imaginatively articulate the political and moral aspirations of the present.[65] Yet for those of us who are radical democrats and socialists, the real question surely is: "How *original* will that new grand narrative be?"; the answer to which, I would insist, depends in fair measure on the consequences of the historical consciousness that we help to fashion. Though we will have to find our own voices, I still maintain that we can find no better guides than E. P. Thompson and the British Marxist historians.

5

OUR ISLAND STORY RETOLD:
A. L. MORTON AND "THE PEOPLE" IN HISTORY

> To sum up, then, the study of history and the love and practice of art forced me into
> a hatred of the civilisation which, if things were to stop as they are, would turn
> history into inconsequent nonsense, and make art a collection of the curiosities of
> the past, which would have no serious relation to the life of the present.
> —William Morris, "How I Became a Socialist"[1]

The Crisis

It is now widely acknowledged that we are in the midst of a "crisis of history," both of the historical discipline and of historical consciousness. For almost a generation it has seemed as though Henry Ford's dictum that "History is bunk!" has prevailed. Historical education has been in decline, increasingly displaced by social sciences in schools curricula; historians perceive their activities and efforts to be peripheral to public culture and discourse; and political culture has reflected what American sociologist, Russell Jacoby, has termed "social amnesia: memory driven out of mind by the social and economic dynamic of society."[2]

Of course, crises are characterized by paradoxes and that of history is no exception. Ironically, in the very same years that historical study and thought have been recognized as in decline and crisis, there has emerged a tremendous, seemingly insatiable, demand for "the past" which has given rise to a thriving commerce in popular history, museums and historical recreations, and, also, a wide assortment of nostalgia enterprises—all of which have come to be referred to as the "Heritage Industry."[3] Moreover, making the crisis all-the-more galling to historians is the paradoxical fact that concurrent with the marginalization of historical education in schooling, historical scholarship itself, by almost all accounts, has been expanding and flourishing. Clearly, this has been due to the phenomenal growth and development of *social* history, which has entailed the incorporation of ideas and methods drawn from the social sciences, and the "democratization" of the past by way of history *from the bottom up,* which has emphasized the experience and actions of the "common people."

Indeed, it has been argued that the crisis of history is due especially to the latter development, that is, historical study and thought have "become" pe-

116

ripheral to education and public culture because they have largely ceased to serve the purpose of contributing to elite ideology and the persistence of the status quo. In any case, in Britain it obviously has been the New Right and Mrs. Thatcher's Conservatives who have been most energetic in placing the crisis of historical education on the political agenda, both through their "Victorian values" rendition of the British past and their initiatives to reform and nationalize the historical curriculum.[4]

This crisis, and the public attention which it has generated, have instigated numerous assessments and suggestions as to how historians ought to respond in order to prevent the discipline from joining the classicists in the dustbin of academic history and to reconnect historians with public debate. Usually these proposals are fairly pragmatic and limited to merely academic initiatives, but the more imaginative entail extra-curricular projects. Perhaps the most intriguing among them is the call for the elaboration of new syntheses, or "grand narratives," out of the innumerable, varied and seemingly unconnected histories recovered in the course of the social and cultural explorations of the past carried out during the last quarter-century. Crucial here is that the new narratives are to be cultivated and propagated not only in textbook and classroom settings but, at the same time (assuming it can be accomplished), via the major media in order to reach as wide an audience as possible.

In Britain such a proposal has been presented in a most aggressive fashion in the scholarly pages of both the *Times Literary Supplement* and the journal, *Past & Present, and* on BBC Television (on at least one occasion), by the Cambridge don, David Cannadine.[5] Recognizing that neither the classic Whig version of the British past, nor that of the welfare-state Whiggism of the postwar period, are any longer capable of accommodating late twentieth-century experience; sensitive to the apparent decline of both domestic and overseas interest in British history; and well aware that the countless socio-historical monographic studies now available had yet to be brought together in a meaningful manner, Cannadine has called for the making of a new grand narrative adequate to the times and powerful enough to reinvigorate British historical thought. In his words: "We must fashion a new version of the national past which can regain its place in our general culture and become once again an object of international interest."

A People's History of England

The question which arises in these terms is: Where do we commence the development of a new grand narrative entailing the synthesis of the best of the past generation's "new history"? However we answer this, in preparation we might well start where we ask our students and lay readers to begin—in the past. It is in this light that I recommend the reconsideration of A. L. Morton's book, *A People's History of England,* for it was both a pioneering work and something of a model for the scholarship of many of the most important figures in the development of British (and international) social history and the perspective known as history from below or the bottom up.

First published in 1938 by Victor Gollancz as a Left Book Club selection,[6] *A People's History* was reissued in 1945 by Lawrence & Wishart and has remained in print and available on bookstore shelves at an exceptionally popular price ever since. Though no accurate figures are available, the publishers estimate that well over one hundred thousand copies have been sold in the U.K. alone; and it is worth noting that in addition to thirteen translations, the book remains in print in the United States.

This lengthy (approximately 550 pages) but paperback-sized volume surveys British history from the times of Iberian and Celtic tribes to the end of the First World War. Written in extremely clear and crisp English, *A People's History* focuses on political and economic history but also attends throughout to military affairs and the history of ideas/ideology as they shaped national political development. Also significant is that Morton regularly situates English history in the European and international contexts in which its leaders and their followers played such central roles in the making of the modern world.

The shape of the book's seventeen chapters is given by the author's apparent view that the three major phases of pre-twentieth-century Anglo-British development were medieval feudalism, the English Revolution of the seventeenth century, and the triumph of industrial capitalism; the last encompassing the Industrial Revolution, the emergence of the working class, and the formation of the British Empire. This seems reasonable, but in several ways the book is strikingly different than most historical studies of then and now. For a start, *A People's History* is almost completely free of footnotes (the few there are can actually be found at the foot of the page, as was the custom!). This break with scholarly convention was possible because Morton was himself not an academic don, but a former schoolteacher and journalist intent on writing a popular text on English history from a Marxist perspective.

As a Marxist study, *A People's History* set out to enlarge the scope of historical understanding. Feudalism, for example, was presented not only as a contract between lord and vassal, but as a social structure and historical mode of production characterized by particular relations of exploitation in both town and country. Moreover, feudalism was not conceived as a harmonious order of three estates (i.e., those who pray, those who fight, and those who labor: priests, lords, and peasants), but as a conflict-ridden society in which the struggles between classes—including the everyday resistance and rebellions of the peasants against those who ruled them—were central to the movement and development of medieval English history. Not only the Magna Carta, but the Peasants' Rising of 1381 also had an important place in Morton's narrative. Indeed, Morton reminds us that the 1381 Rising was ignited by the imposition of a poll tax perceived "as an oppressive class measure."

In a similar fashion the English Civil War was portrayed as having been "a class struggle . . . revolutionary and . . . progressive." However subject to revision this appears today, it must be recognized that such a proposition opened up a rich vein of exploration and analysis of the struggles of the seventeenth century which had for so long been called the Puritan Revolution. Moreover, it should be remembered that Morton did not construe the world-historic consequences of the revolution merely as the development of capitalism and later Industrial Revolution. As he wrote: "We do not need to idealize the bourgeoisie of the 17th century, who had most of the faults common to their class in all ages, but it is possible to say that just because they were the historically progressive class of their time, they could not fight for their own rights and liberties without also fighting for the rights and liberties of all Englishmen and of humanity as a whole."

Leslie Morton

Born in July, 1903, to a Suffolk farming family, Leslie Morton went up to Cambridge in 1921 where he read history and English and became a socialist. (Morton's father was himself a Tory, but all accounts indicate he was not inflexible and, in fact, Leslie dedicated *A People's History* to him.) Maurice Cornforth, his longtime comrade and companion in the Communist Party, describes the political situation of the day:

> At that time, the immediate post-war years of the early twenties, intellectuals who felt concern about society and politics had to stand up and be counted as to whether they were for or against the Russian Revolution, for or against the [1926 British General] strike demands, particularly of railwaymen and miners, and for or against taking industries into national ownership and starting up measures to relieve poverty and unemployment, and for a more equal distribution of wealth. Leslie found himself in the Labour Club among those who were "for"—a very small minority in the University.[7]

Following university, Morton taught at a grammar school in Sussex. However, as a consequence of his public support for the strikers in 1926, the school governors saw fit to relieve him of his post. After a period of unemployment he applied for a teaching position at A. S. Neill's experimental school, Summerhill, where he taught for a year.

Having entered the Communist Party in 1928, Morton joined the staff of the *Daily Worker* in 1934, where one of his first assignments as a reporter was to cover the 1934 Hunger March from East Anglia. (Cornforth notes that it was this experience covering the march that introduced Morton to the East Anglian folk songs with which he was afterwards "often to entertain" his friends and acquaintances.) He stayed with the newspaper for three years, performing a variety of jobs, but left it and London in 1937 to move back to the family farm in Suffolk so that he could concentrate on writing *A People's History*. Again, Cornforth relates: "Before beginning to write, Leslie went on a solitary walking tour for several weeks, along the ancient Icknield Way, in winter, to gather local colour and think things out. Then he quickly wrote the opening chapters—whereupon he found himself "stuck" and unable to write anymore. The trouble, he decided, was living in London. The city no longer suited him, and there were too many distractions—particularly, demands of local party work."[8] Thus, back in the country, he was able to complete the book in a year's time.

Following the war, during which he served in the Royal Artillery, Morton returned for a few years to teach at Summerhill. In 1950, he and his wife, Vivien, moved to the village of Clare in the Stour Valley, where they had purchased a small, converted twelfth-century chapel. There they lived together for the next thirty-seven years (until his death in October, 1987). *A People's History* was merely his first historical study. Amongst his many later works written at the Old Chapel are: *The English Utopia* (1952); *The British Labour Movement, 1770–1920* (1956) with George Tate; *The Matter of Britain* (1966); *The World of the Ranters* (1970); and editions of *The Life and Ideas of Robert Owen* (1962); *Three Works of William Morris* (1968); *Political Writings of William Morris* (1973); and *Freedom in Arms: A Selection of Leveller Writings* (1975). Also, a collection of his own poems which he had written between the wars was published in 1977.[9]

In spite of Morton's many writings and the success of *A People's History*, his scholarly reputation has been limited, no doubt due to the fact that he was not a university-based historian and because so much of his work seemed bound up with his political commitments and activities with the British Communist Party (of which he remained a member until his death—unlike so many of his historian comrades who left the Party in 1956–57). However, his contributions to British historiography should not be underestimated. Though a "popular" text, *A People's History* influenced the thinking of that most remarkable generation, or cohort, of British labour and social historians involved in the Communist Party Historians' Group in the years 1946–56, including Rodney Hilton, Christopher Hill, Eric Hobsbawm, George Rudé, John Saville, Victor Kiernan, and Dorothy and E. P. Thompson. For example, Dorothy Thompson, the leading historian of Chartism, remembers "cutting her historical teeth" on Morton's book in the late thirties and early forties. Also, Eric Hobsbawm recalls that along with Maurice Dobb's *Studies in the Development of Capitalism* (1946), *A People's History* was central to the discussion and debates of the Historians' Group. And Christopher Hill terms

Morton a pioneer in the study of the politics of the radical religious groups of the seventeenth century, which is evidenced in particular by his book, *The World of the Ranters*. (This work was followed up by Christopher Hill in 1972 in his book, *The World Turned Upside Down*.) It might be said that the original narrative which the members of the Historians' Group struggled with was provided by Morton's history of England.[10]

Beyond A People's History?

In recommending *A People's History* as a starting point for a new grand narrative of British history, I am not suggesting that it merely be revised and updated. That would be an unrealistic and foolish notion, for the book has obviously been "dated" by fifty years of historical scholarship and experience. Moreover, the panorama of history which it offers—that is, the "rise of the bourgeoisie" followed thereafter by the "forward march of the working class" to challenge and (eventually) overthrow the rule of the former—is far from acceptable in the form in which it is presented. It remains to the credit of *A People's History*, however, that so much of the historical study which has superseded it was originally informed and inspired by the book itself.

Nevertheless, Morton's volume affords a model for the "literary" reconstruction of British historical narrative. First, it represents an example of a committed work whose priorities are clear; that is, rather than offering a history consisting of "one damned thing after another" or a "total history" which fails to make choices and agglomerates all manner of experience as if the past were a jumble/rummage sale, *A People's History* advanced a political and economic history which did seek to integrate other dimensions of social change and continuity—even if in comparison with historical studies today it may seem narrowly drawn. (In this vein, it should be noted that Morton occasionally intervenes in his narrative to make a historical comparison between past and present. For example, writing in the ever-darkening skies of 1937, he reflected on the outbreak of the late-medieval Hundred Years' War that "It was a situation characteristic of an age on the edge of a great social transformation and can be paralleled by the equally blind and suicidal impulse driving the bourgeoisie today towards war and Fascism.")

Second, it offers a judicious mix of narrative and analysis and generalization and detail. Indeed, Morton even allowed appropriate space for individuals—and their intrigues!—in the long course of events (thus, Elizabeth I and her domestic and foreign rivals find a special place in the narrative). Too often the "new history" with its social scientific orientation has entailed a disavowal of biography; we need to develop ways of treating not only the typical but, also, the outstanding personages in social history. (I am not, however, in favor of psychohistory.)

Third, even as the book was laying some of the groundwork for the writing of history from the bottom up by insisting on a central place for the experience and struggles of peasants, the common people, and the working class, it continued to attend to the actions and efforts of the elites and dominant classes who have lost hold of the reins of power only on rare occasions. Any reinvigoration of the British historical narrative must respond to the findings of the many studies of the "lower orders" and the relations of gender and the family, and also find a means of handling both the histories of the Celtic regions and the varied experiences of "black Britons" and ethnic minorities. Yet, it is also essential that social historians integrate these in such a way that the rulers of the land and people are kept fully in sight.

Finally, and most crucially, perhaps, *A People's History* is imbued with the understanding that *history is a process of struggle,* a view of the past and the making of the present to which even Mrs. Thatcher and her Tory colleagues have apparently subscribed—though, it need hardly be added, in a form and with a content quite different from the one advanced by Leslie Morton. I would stress this aspect of Morton's presentation of Anglo-British history and recount an experience I had while on sabbatical in Britain earlier this year (1987). It so happened that I was called in for some "historical advice" by a British television company involved in a joint Canadian-American-British production of a ten-part series on "The Struggle for Democracy." In the course of conversations on their treatment of the "historical background, origins and development," it became apparent that they were going to represent the historic struggles for freedom and equality by focusing on the signing of the Magna Carta. This "episode" appeared to have been all but wrapped up and it seems quite likely that there will be little reference to the Rising of 1381, the English Revolution, or the Chartists. However much the media may wish to reject the Left's version of the past, such a rendition of history will not do.[11]

I would like to conclude this essay with an immediate suggestion for my British colleagues, directed, perhaps especially, at those involved in the History Workshop movement. 1988 is the fiftieth anniversary of the original publication of *A People's History of England.* It would seem an appropriate time to honor the work by convening a conference at which we might consider, discuss, and debate "what is to be done" towards refashioning and reinvigorating British historical narrative. In the meantime, we might all re-read Morton's book.[12]

Postscript: A Challenge to Socialists to Remake Britain's Grand Narrative

In the midst of the current debate about the future course of the Left instigated by Thatcher's third election victory (1987), we must not lose sight of the past. Historians on the Left will be familiar with the fact that two crises have been developing concurrently: the crisis of historical study and thought, *and* the crisis of socialism. Yet there has been little recognition of the relationship between them.

History is in crisis both as an academic discipline and as a form of consciousness. . . .

The crisis of socialism is even better known. The Soviet Union ceased to inspire long ago;[13] the Third-World struggles which captured hearts and minds in the 1960s may still attract sympathy but offer little for Western socialists; and the socialist and Eurocommunist parties of the West seem incapable of offering an alternative vision beyond that already provided and effectively besieged by conservatives and neo-conservatives. Here in Britain—though not here alone—Thatcher and the New Right Conservatives have waged, for more than a dozen years now, unceasing political and ideological campaigns against the postwar social-democratic consensus and, also, the grand historical narrative which was engendered by it. This history was articulated most succinctly by the late sociologist, T. H. Marshall, in *Citizenship and Social Class*. The British state was portrayed there as the product of three stages in the expansion of rights: first, following the seventeenth century, civil and legal rights; next, in the course of the nineteenth and early twentieth centuries, political rights (universal adult suffrage); and, finally, in the twentieth century, social rights (education, health, housing, etc.). Marshall's narrative implied that the establishment of these rights was an evolutionary process in which the freedoms and equality of citizenship triumph over the inequality and restrictions of class and, moreover, that the development of social rights was not yet complete.[14] This view of modern British history, a grand example of welfare-state Whiggism, is no longer adequate or accurate (as David Cannadine has argued).

The crisis of British historical narrative represents, then, a problem—*and* a challenge—not only for professional historians, but also for the Left and the Labour Party. Of course, Labour's leadership must give first priority to a reappraisal of its platform if it is to effectively confront the political, economic, and cultural realities of Britain's changing social and class structures. Yet, however much it may feel the need for a break with the past, it must at the same time attend all-the-more to history, not simply in the immediate sense of trying to comprehend the historical sociology of current change (and what it portends for future election campaigns), but, just as strenuously, to the longer view of past and present—to begin to fashion a new historical narrative which can speak to contemporary experience and contribute to the making of an alternative vision of the future.

The foundations for such a narrative already exist in the work of a generation of senior historians, a generation of British Marxist historians which includes Rodney Hilton, Christopher Hill, George Rudé, Eric Hobsbawm, Victor Kiernan, John Saville, and Edward and Dorothy Thompson. In their writings we encounter the Peasant Rising of 1381; Puritanism, Levellers, and the radical religious sects who made a civil war into the English Revolution; popular support for "Wilkes and Liberty"; the assertions by radical artisans and agricultural workers of their rights as free-born Englishmen against political oppression and exploitation; and Chartist demands for the extension of democracy to the working class.

To read the studies of these historians is to participate in the recovery of those popular and class struggles for liberty and equality without which the securing of civil, political, and social rights would never have come about. Obviously, this history must be revised in the light of current work on questions of gender and race/ethnicity; nevertheless, it provides a critical basis for the remaking of British historical narrative.

It is essential that the Left not pursue this project in the exploitative and abusive fashion of Thatcher and the Conservatives. Rather, we must engage the past respectfully and in such a way as to reinvigorate our own historical imaginations. For example, as I have argued in my book, *The British Marxist Historians,* socialists have for too long suffered from the simplistic model of collectivism *vs.* individualism, yet the experiences rescued—in E. P. Thompson's memorable words, "from the enormous condescension of posterity"— by the Marxist historians reveal a continuity of struggles by peasants, artisans, and workers for liberty, equality, *and* democratic community which attest to an alternative conception and vision of "individualism" to that being purveyed by Thatcher and the Tory Right.[15]

In its own way this may appear to be another Whig reading of the past, but it is a Whig history from the bottom up, which accords an active role to the "lower orders" or common people. And, in contrast to the classic Whig view, it might well be seen to be an accounting of historical tragedy; one which might resonate well with the experience of Thatcherism. It is even arguable that the Tories themselves have provided the grounds for the redemption of a supposedly outmoded historical narrative. Cuts and the inadequate provisioning of social services; episodes in the miners' strike (1984–85) and the removal of teachers' negotiating rights; recent efforts to limit the freedom of the press—not to mention the enclosure and sale of common/public properties to private hands: by reversing the forward march of citizenship against the domain of class, Thatcherism has raised up the image of "lost rights" which inspired popular movements from the fourteenth to the nineteenth century (a story told so beautifully in Christopher Hill's "Norman Yoke Theory" and the central chapters of Dona Torr's *Tom Mann and His Times*).[16] Finally, in the effort to revitalize British historical narrative we should remind ourselves, first, that it was the attempted imposition of a poll tax which ignited the Peasant Rising of 1381 and, second, that however immediate a catalyst this was, it did not prevent the development and expression of a grander vision of a Britain without overlords.[17]

6

CAPITALISM AND DEMOCRACY IN AMERICA: LEO HUBERMAN'S WE, THE PEOPLE

These are the times that try men's souls. The summer soldier and the sunshine
patriot will, in this crisis, shrink from the service of their country; but he that stands
it *now*, deserves the love and thanks of man and woman. Tyranny, like hell, is not
easily conquered; yet we have this consolation with us, that the harder the conflict,
the more glorious the triumph.
—Thomas Paine, *The American Crisis* (1776)

The issue which I was addressing in Chapter 5, Our Island Story Retold,
especially in the retrospective on A. L. Morton's *A People's History of England,*
might be restated in this way: After a generation of producing critical histories by recovering the experience and agency of the exploited and oppressed,
can we hope to articulate—in the face of the crisis of historical study and
thought and the aggressive use and abuse of the past by the New Right—an
alternative or oppositional narrative to that of capitalism which not only
seeks to portray the making of past and present but, also, contributes to the
making of a *new* history increasingly libertarian, egalitarian, and democratic?
And, if we can, how are we to proceed in molding the syntheses out of the
innumerable and varied studies pursued, as we say in America, "from the
bottom up"? My calling attention to *A People's History of England* was not to
propose simply that we attempt to revive *the* narrative which Morton had
provided in the book, but that in our deliberations we consider his work as
a model possessing qualities not to be lost in the process.

Upon the original publication of that essay, a number of British colleagues
asked if I was familiar with what struck them as the American counterpart to
A People's History, referring me to Leo Huberman's *We, the People* (1932)
which, like Morton's book, was first published in its British edition by Victor
Gollancz and the Left Book Club (1940). Apparently, for many of them,
Huberman's book, either in its original or a later edition, had been their
introduction to American history. I had to admit (with some embarrassment)
that although I had read Huberman's classic of economic history, *Man's
Worldly Goods* (1936), I was actually unaware of *We, the People;* however, I
was intrigued and, before departing England, I found a secondhand copy of
the Left Book Club Edition intending to take it up as I had Morton's book.
Ensuing political events compelled me to do so.

Revival Show for the American Left?

The 1988 U.S. presidential campaign and Republican victory were a very sobering experience and I found myself over and over again looking back on the previous twenty years of American political life. I was hardly alone in looking back. George Scialabba in the *Village Voice Literary Supplement* opened his essay, "A Thousand Points of Blight: What Ronald Reagan Left Behind," with these words:

> When Martin Luther King was killed 20 years ago, Kenneth Clark remarked bitterly: "You have to weep for this country." Yet in retrospect, 1968 seems like the middle of a long golden age. American prosperity had just rounded its phenomenal peak and the bill for the Vietnam war had not come in. Blacks and college students had mobilized *en masse* and had not yet succumbed to media hype, Leninist dogmatism, or government infiltration. An unpopular president had been, in effect, deposed. Victories had been won; more would soon follow, as the women's movement, environmental movement, the welfare-rights movement, the consumer movement were born and flourished.[1]

And yet, as Scialabba sadly observes: "By now most of those hundred flowers have withered. The American economy and polity are turning into a vast wasteland."

The hopes and tragedies of the sixties have made for exciting and extremely popular history and sociology courses in American colleges and universities; however, the "lessons" of that decade, especially for those of us on the Left, are not to be found within those years alone but just as much in the 1970s with the formation and rise of the New Right coalition of corporate free marketeers, cold warriors, traditional and neo-conservatives, and Moral Majoritarians. The 1960s had been years of Democratic Administrations still operating within the "liberal consensus" that had been forged by the Roosevelt Democrats in the New Deal of the 1930s and the defeat of Fascism in the Second World War, and then tempered in the course of the Cold War and McCarthyism. Allen Hunter describes this American counterpart to the "social democratic" consensus of postwar Western Europe thus:

> From the end of World War II until the early 1970s world capitalism experienced the longest period of sustained economic growth in its history. In the United States a new "social structure of accumulation"—"the specific institutional environment within which the capitalist accumulation process is organized"—was articulated around several prominent features: the broadly shared goal of sus-

tained economic growth, Keynesianism, elite pluralist democracy, an imperial America prosecuting a cold war, anticommunism at home and abroad, stability or incremental change in race relations and a stable home life in a buoyant, commodity-driven consumer culture.[2]

The liberal consensus was to be severely strained by the struggles and social movements of the sixties, but not until the bills were delivered for the expansion of the Welfare/Warfare State in the face of the economic crises of the 1970s—along with the Oil Crisis of 1973–74 and the combined political effects of the withdrawal from Vietnam and the Watergate scandal—were its limits reached. And it was at that moment, in the midst of the crisis of the liberal consensus, that the movements which came to make up the New Right coalition began to mobilize ever more successfully. Crudely put, the failure of the Left was its inability to formulate an alternative progressive vision—alternative, that is, to the liberal consensus—which might have brought together the "new" social movements for racial and gender equality with the social-democratic aspirations of labor and the white working class. To imagine having effected such a coalition is, perhaps, to engage in utopian thinking and to forget the divisions wrought by the battles of the 1960s; but it is exactly that vision of the respective struggles of blacks and other minorities, women, and the working class (along with Left intellectuals) coalescing in a radical-democratic movement which threatened corporate and conservative interests and against which the forces of the New Right were to mobilize so effectively. Indeed, despite their hostile views of each other, both corporate conservatives and (supposed) liberals appear to have shared the view that *the* problem of the American polity in the wake of the turmoil of the 1960s was that there was "an excess of democracy." The rest is history.[3]

It is true that after the Trilateral-Commission supported the Carter Administration and, far more significantly, eight years of the Reagan Administration, the Right has yet to secure its political and intellectual victories and predominance in a new postliberal consensus, a new hegemonic framework. That is, the primary efforts and values of the New Deal and the Great Society do appear to persist. Nevertheless, in one important respect the Right has succeeded: political expectations and aspirations are apparently lowered and *capitalist* democracy is secured. Moreover, in spite of the "thousand points of blight," the Left has still not developed a vision and strategy to counter the New Right and, following an uninspired election campaign, Americans have seemed most eager simply to return to the problems of everyday life—that is, to a politics of resignation and privatism—and away from the "making of history."[4]

Arguably, there are signs of life, perhaps even reasons to be hopeful. Politically, not only do liberal ideals survive in the American experience and imagination (at least according to opinion polls and surveys) but the Jackson campaign of 1988, with all its problematic baggage, has shown that a populist-progressive initiative can capture broad sympathy and support. Thus, although I am extremely doubtful that Jackson himself can make it happen—or even should be the one to do so—a broad progressive coalition remains possible.[5] Developments emanating from the academic arena are also presenting possibilities for renewal on the Left.

Though not at all to the extent that their paranoid and McCarthyite antagonists assert, it is true that a generation of New Left scholars has "secured" itself with tenure and professorships in college and university humanities and social science programs. Moreover, having done so according to the traditional rules of the academy—with, perhaps by necessity, a bit more verve and imagination than is usual—they have achieved positions of some import in their departments and professional associations. In accomplishing this, however, the sixties' generation has most often directed its intellectual efforts and agency to merely scholarly fora and academic politics (personifying, unfortunately, Foucault's "specific intellectual" as opposed to Gramsci's "organic intellectual"). Russell Jacoby has stated the problem most acutely and self-consciously in his recent book, *The Last Intellectuals: American Culture in the Age of Academe.*

> The final report on universities and the New Left is not yet in. The complexity and size of higher education forbid confident conclusions. The general tendencies, however, are clear. The academic enterprise simultaneously expands and contracts; it steadily intrudes upon the larger culture, setting up private clubs for accredited members. That it is difficult for an educated adult American to name a single political scientist or sociologist or philosopher is not wholly his or her fault; the professionals have abandoned the public arena. The influx of left scholars has not changed the picture; reluctantly or enthusiastically they gain respectability at the cost of identity. The slogan that was borrowed from the German left to justify a professional career—"the long march through the institutions"— has had an unexpected outcome: at least so far, the institutions are winning.[6]

This pattern, however, may well be subject to change. Not only are Left intellectuals aware of the anemia of American political democracy and sensitive about their own isolation and marginalization from extra-academic public debates, but increasingly they are acknowledging that their marginality is in part a product of their own actions and, furthermore, that the reinvigoration of the American polity depends to some degree upon their capacity to reform their own practices and reassert a Left voice and presence in American

public life. For too long, we now realize, we have been alienated and discon-
nected from public debates and the movements and struggles to which we
originally contributed so much. This awareness may be due to the fact that
conservative and neo-conservative academics, with New Right and corporate
backing, have begun organizing against the Left once again,[7] or because,
now, as working and family people we are all the more involved with, and
concerned about, the institutional and political settings we were previously
critical of from a distance, such as schools, churches, and public and private
firms and agencies. Whatever the catalyst, the generation of Left intellectuals
of which I am a part has in recent years begun to seek out a new critical voice
and more effective ways of connecting with and shaping public life.[8]

It is not that American Left intellectuals are *en masse* rejecting the Marxist
and neo-Marxian ideas which they originally redeemed from Stalinist orthodoxy in order to critique the political economy and culture of late twentieth-
century America (though, admittedly, many have), but that they have become ever more conscious of the limits of "critique" alone and, thus, they
have begun to explore the traditions of liberal and radical-democratic
thought and struggle which have been so central to American political development. Indeed, the imperative of addressing liberal and radical-
democratic traditions has arisen not only in reaction to the New Right's efforts to monopolize the American past (and future), and in recognition of
the fact that if the Left is to break out of its academic corner it will have to
articulate both a critique *and* a vision of America in terms which engage
working people's experiences, values and aspirations, but also in response to
the historical scholarship pursued during the past twenty years by scholars
informed by Marxian theory.[9] Their histories of class, race, ethnic, and wom-
en's struggles have challenged the simpler grand narratives of Right and Left
and compelled more critical attention to, and appreciation of, the actual making of the modern world—in particular liberal and democratic freedoms and
practices and, too, past and present resistance and hostility to them.

Thus, we find such writers as Samuel Bowles and Herbert Gintis in *Democracy and Capitalism,* and Frances Fox Piven and Richard Cloward in *The
New Class War* eschewing their previous functionalist analyses and pursuing
a reconsideration of American history in which the making of democracy is
comprehended as a struggle within and against capitalist political economy;
and, in a related work, *Making History,* Richard Flacks explores the political
and cultural role and contributions of the American Left tradition within
their revised historical narrative, and reflects on the prospects and possibilities of renewing both the Left tradition and the making of *democratic* history
in contemporary America.[10] Also, there are studies such as Michael Walzer's
Interpretation and Social Criticism and *The Company of Critics,* Jim Merod's
The Political Responsibility of the Critic, Henry Giroux's *Schooling and the
Struggle for Public Life,* and Walter Adamson's *Marx and the Disillusionment of*

Marxism[11] addressing the theory and practice of social, political, and cultural criticism and the question of how Left intellectuals ought to situate themselves in relation to "power" and "the people" for the sake of democratic struggle. A primary characteristic of these writings is their disavowal of an "elitist" (Leninist) conception of the political role of the critic and intellectual in favor of a Gramscian-inspired model which entails interpretation, connection, dialogue, and articulation.[12] In this vein should also be noted Norman Birnbaum's recent book, *Radical Renewal,* in which he surveys and critically assesses the scholarly and intellectual efforts of the academic New Left during the past twenty years to discover what might be garnered for the purpose of informing a revival of the American radical-democratic political tradition. Along with his salvage job—in the course of which he finds reason for hope and even optimism—Birnbaum stresses the necessity of linking up Left scholarly labors and intellectual initiatives with the classical American vision, or ideal, of the democratic *citizen.* In conclusion, he states:

> We do know that American social science has, in large measure abandoned its earlier search for the conditions of citizenship. The idea of progress in knowledge was its bastard substitute for belief in human progress, a substitution all the more fatuous for its origins in a mistaken conception of science. If we are to reenact, in contemporary terms, the early American belief in a republic of virtue, we shall have to find a new philosophical basis for both social inquiry and politics. That is a matter for further reflection.[13]

Of course, it remains to be seen whether or not these concerns and aspirations can be translated into an actual Left presence in public debate. And, ultimately, even more important is the question of whether or not this "New" Left can formulate a vision and strategy capable of inspiring the coalition of American working people (black, white, Hispanic . . .) and new social movements, the possibility of which so worried corporate and conservative elites in the 1970s.

"We, the People"

In view of the resources available to the political Right, Old and New, the relative absence of Left voices from America's prevailing public culture cannot be attributed simply to the Left's own doing. Nevertheless, there is much truth to Russell Jacoby's argument in *The Last Intellectuals* that the now-maturing sixties generation of intellectuals—of whom so much of a "public" nature might have been expected—has expended most of its energy and activism, thus far, on securing tenure, promotion, and status in the academy. At the same time, now that the predicament is recognized, a "radical renewal" might yet be in the making. Of course, if it is to happen, it will require, first, the articulation of an engaging vision, or narrative, of America's past, present, and possible futures capable of challenging those engendered and promoted by corporate capitalism and, second, their being communicated to extra-academic audiences and, as C. Wright Mills said it, "publics."[14]

After a generation and more of pursuing in Robin Hood–like fashion the recovery of historical experience from the "powers that be" past and present, radical-democratic and socialist American historians should have a great deal to contribute to such a project. Indeed, so successful have been these reappropriations that a foremost question increasingly seems to be that of how to actually integrate the "pluralistic" historical studies of class, race, ethnicity, and gender into a new synthesis or narrative that might inform a truly *democratic*-socialist politics. The answers we provide to this question will have to be our own, derived from our own experience and addressing the world as it is today. Nevertheless, as historians and historical thinkers we might do well to follow our own advice to others: reflect on the experience of our predecessors for the sake both of perspective, to better perceive continuities and changes, and of imagination, to better inform our own efforts with their critical aspirations, visions, and practices.

In this spirit I would recall a classic text of American radical historiography, *We, the People,* by Leo Huberman. First appearing in 1932 in the depths of the Depression and on the eve of the New Deal Administration of Franklin Roosevelt, the book sold extremely well in its first American edition and, again, in a revised edition of 1947; and, even now, it remains a popular paperback title for Monthly Review Press, which picked up the rights to the work from its original U.S. publisher, Harper. In fact, *We, the People* would eventually be published abroad not only by the Left Book Club in Britain, but also in translation in a number of foreign languages (Italian, Portuguese, Spanish, Greek, Danish, German, Swedish, Finnish, and Marathi).[15]

His first book, Huberman wrote *We, the People* to provide a narrative of American development from a Marxian perspective. Moreover, it was to be a "people's history" in two ways. First, it was to be a history for a popular audience, not a textbook for academics and/or their students alone. And, in this respect, its sales reveal that it was not unsuccessful. Second, it was a people's history in that it was a history told *not* through the lives and actions of leading figures or presidential administrations one after another but, rather, through the agency and experience, economic and social, of the generations of American working people and their rulers. Not at all a simple chronology, the chapters of the book are thematically organized offering an "interpretative" history of the United States from the bottom up. There was, as we might expect, very little "radical" historiography upon which Huberman could draw for his Marxian synthesis and, thus, he states in his preface and clearly acknowledges in his notes that he was necessarily "guided"

through the events and processes of American history by a selection of leading authorities. Most notably, he appears to have been influenced by Frederick Jackson Turner and *the* Progressive historian, Charles Beard, both of
whom, in their respective ways, as David Noble has observed, saw the antagonism and conflict between "capitalism" and "democracy" as central to the
story of the nation's development. In this respect it is arguable that Huberman was picking up from where they left off.

Writing late in the nineteenth century (and into the early years of the twentieth), Turner advanced his now-classic thesis that the original and unique
formation of American democratic political life had been engendered in the
"frontier experience" and freehold property pattern which grew out of it. Yet
he wrote not for the purpose of celebrating the country's past, but to warn
that this exceptional history was coming to an end with the closing of the
frontier. The world-historical process of industrial capitalism and its accompanying property structures and mode of civilization would, ultimately, over-
whelm American experience.[16]

Beard did not accept Turner's prophecy. Although, as Noble explains, there
are dramatic differences between his early and later writings, Beard's work
represents a persistent attempt to "revitalize the American jeremiad as the
narrative structure of historical writing." It might be said that he sought to
re-open the closing frontier. In his early studies Beard did so by reconceiving
the historical implications and possibilities of industrial development; that is,
he contended that industrialism was not inevitably linked to capitalism and
that actually industrialization was creating the new material foundations necessary for the fulfillment of American political democracy. The new Progressive political order Beard envisioned was to be "classless" and "regulated by
social and economic planning"—an "industrial democracy" of equal and par-
ticipatory citizens no longer subject to a capitalist aristocracy. This was a
model not unrelated to those proposed by varieties of socialists (I often think
of the Progressives and Fabians as cousins, but being Americans the former
appear to have been more "democratic" in spirit!). Nevertheless, the Progressives were *not* socialists; their project portrayed "enlightened citizens"—
aided, in Beard's view, by "public-spirited" social scientists—battling in the
public arena against monopoly interests, not working-class struggles against
Capital and the State. Beard himself had a particular interest in worker education and improvement (he was a founding figure of Ruskin Hall, Oxford),
and he was most definitely influenced by an economistic reading of Marx; yet
these interests did not engender a Marxian conception of class conflict on
Beard's part. In this very respect it must be noted further that following
World War I, although Beard persisted in believing that the American
"people" would assure the triumph of American democratic life, his "progressive" conception of the process of industrialism and its special promise
for the United States was to give way to an increasingly nationalistic and

isolationist worldview ever more hostile to "universalist and internationalist philosophies," and the pursuit of a specifically *American* cultural tradition upon which democratic development might be cultivated further. Moreover, in *The Rise of American Civilization* (1927) which he co-authored with his wife, Mary Beard, the American people are portrayed essentially as the American "middle classes," less so the working classes, white and black proletarians.[17]

Huberman solidly incorporated Turner's thesis about the frontier experience into the narrative of *We, the People* and it is accorded character-forming influence: "The pioneer . . . was a new person. Many of those qualities we think are typical of Americans in general were the result of the frontier life. What were the things this battle with the wilderness taught the pioneer? It taught him to be independent. . . . It gave him a feeling of self-confidence. . . . He believed that one man was good as another." There was to be no question about it; the frontier was *determining* of the "character" of American development, but not only in the geographic and environmental sense in which these shaped the emerging patterns of social and economic life. Writing as a Marxist and "pioneer" of history from below, Huberman was not about to marginalize class struggle and the agency of *working* people. Thus, in Chapter 3, "Are All Men Equal?" having described the early American class structure (the ruling and upper class of royal officials, rich merchants, rich plantation owners, holders of large estates; the yeoman farmers; the free laborers, skilled and unskilled; the indentured white laborers and servants; and Negro slaves) he asks: "Did no one challenge the right of the rich to manage things?" And, though acknowledging the role of both the small farmers and urban artisans and workers—and, too, the fear that their mobilizations struck in the hearts and minds of the wealthy and powerful, especially in the Revolutionary war years—he nominates the frontiersmen as having been the progenitors of the American democratic ideal: "[They] demanded a say in running things. They demanded the right to help make the laws for themselves. The American idea of all men being equal first came from the frontier. This idea had been talked of in Europe before, but it was first put into practice in America. It was a very, very important notion which later affected the whole world" (p. 41).

The history of the United States has been very much a *geographical* history, a history of *spatial* expansion marked by regional variation. *We, the People* captures well both the dynamic of territorial expansion and the features of American regionalism, presented in chapters such as "The Manufacturing North," "The Agricultural South," "A Rifle, An Axe [the near frontier]," and "A Strange, Colorful Frontier—the Last [the West]." In these terms the narrative presents the experience of the men and, though admittedly to a *much* lesser extent, the women who *made* these regions, their economies and their richness; and, again, the experience is consistently portrayed in "materialist" terms, both that of "man's" engagement with the environment and the relations and confrontations of working people with those who would be their masters.

From Turner he got the frontier thesis, but without closure; from Beard—though very much a feature of classical Marxism, as we know—he took a new frontier, the dynamic and promise of economic transformation. Following his chapter on the U.S. Civil War, "Land Lords Fight Money Lords" (in which he declares: "in this second American Revolution Negro slavery was overthrown, and with it the rule of the slaveowners"), Huberman presents two chapters on the agricultural and industrial revolutions in the United States in the latter half of the nineteenth and first part of the twentieth century. Like Marx, he commences with a certain admiration for the capitalists, but he does not leave it at simple celebration.

> Materials, men, machinery and money—all together they made the United States the richest country of the world. The capitalists who came into power with the Civil War were the driving force. They combined the natural resources, the labor and the capital and made modern America. They developed the country—sometimes by foul means. They became rich. They became powerful. More and more wealth of the country became concentrated in the hands of the few. Their power grew with their riches. They became the real rulers of America.

Indeed, like Marx, he makes it very clear from whence the capitalists' riches were and *are* derived.

> This was the army of labor, the men, women and children who did the actual work of digging, building, making. These were the people who chopped away at chunks of coal deep down in the bowels of the earth; these were the people who by steady toil from dawn to dusk carefully nursed their crops through blizzard, heat, drought, and flood; these were the people who drove red-hot rivets into steel girders, while dangerously perched hundreds of feet in the air on the framework of some skyscraper; these were the people who tended the speeding machines in factories. Many of them were newly arrived immigrants from faraway countries. (pp. 188–189)

Beyond Turner and Beard, Huberman not only foregrounded the material and social experience of rural and urban American working people, the American farmers and working classes, he placed their struggles against capitalist oppression and exploitation at the center of his narrative, and articulated those struggles as the dynamic of democratic development and the promise for economic and political freedom. The industrial-capitalist incorporation of agriculture compelled American farmers to fight: "He [the farmer] had a grievance against the grain elevator men. . . . against the money-lenders, the banks, the moneyed-class in general. . . . The farmer was bitter against the capitalists. . . . From the 1870s through to 1896 the farmers translated their grievances into action. They followed the advice of one of their leaders who said, 'what you farmers need to do is to raise less corn and more hell' " (p. 202). The greatest political expression of these grievances was the People's Party, the Populists of the 1890s; but as Huberman bluntly states: "the capitalists were too strong for them." There were attempts to link the movements of agrarians and workers—the Populists themselves sought such a combination. However, the respective classes were themselves internally divided so it is not surprising that the cross-class alliance was never accomplished.

Huberman critically, but appreciatively, recounts the formation of the American labor movement and the development of trade unionism noting— as we now well know from the writings on American artisans inspired by E. P. Thompson's *The Making of the English Working Class* (1963)—that "The earliest American unions were not those of oppressed factory workers: They were unions of highly skilled craftsmen who were forced to combine in self-defense." Then, reproducing the rather economistic history proposed in *The Communist Manifesto* that "working-class organization grew with capitalist development," he observes that the middle decades of the nineteenth century were "a story of ups and downs" until, that is, the growth period after the Civil War. These later decades of the century were a period of fierce class war: "facing the working class in its struggle for unionization was a capitalist class which increased its ruthlessness as it increased its wealth" (pp. 225–26). Here Huberman introduces us to the Knights of Labor (1869–1880s), the American Federation of Labor (founded 1886), and the Industrial Workers of the World (founded 1905), each of which advanced a particular "way of fighting capital." The Knights stressed the "dignity of labor" and declared the "idealistic aim of elevating the whole laboring class through organization, education and cooperation." In spite of their failings, Huberman asserts, they contributed much to the experience and reformation of the American working class. In particular, they *educated* workers: "largely through their agitation for political reforms such as the income tax, the abolition of child labor, workmen's compensation . . . [etc.]" (pp. 225–28).

The American Federation of Labor (AFL), Huberman explains, was "totally unlike" the Knights. In contrast to the Knights' idealism and commitment to the interest of all the working class, the AFL represented "business unionism"—that is, "practical-thinking of better conditions now"—and concerned itself "only with the skilled workers who were in the organization." The "uplift" sought by the AFL was to come with "higher wages, shorter hours, and better conditions." The AFL, led by Samuel Gompers, was, Huberman grants, "aware of the realities of the capitalist system" and, too, they were conscious of the conflicts between workers and their bosses, but "they kept their eyes on immediate goals." The AFL's contribution was to survive, thereby providing a solid, disciplined labor organization, but its mode of survival cost the labor movement dearly, all but leaving the unskilled workers out in the cold.

Yet not completely so, for there appeared early in this century the Industrial Workers of the World (IWW), who called for "revolutionary unionism" in "one big union." Though their numbers never exceeded seventy-five thousand, writes Huberman, they were not without significant influence, reaching hundreds of thousands with their message. Most successful in attracting members from among the unorganized, the unskilled, and migratory workers, the militancy of the IWW and its "fearless and magnetic leaders" like "Big Bill" Haywood injected fear into the American ruling class, and during and after the First World War employers and the state pursued the suppression of the "wobblies." And thus, Huberman regretfully notes, "By 1924 they were practically out of existence" (pp. 233–34).

Capitalist hegemony was established through coercion and economic and political power and influence, and *all* union organizing struggles were hard and difficult because, as Huberman states in words which remain meaningful today: "The employing class saw in labor unions a challenge to its power." Not only was force wielded—Huberman sadly quotes capitalist Jay Gould's boast that "I can hire one-half of the working class to kill the other half"—but ideology too: "the employers have had control of the opinion-making forces—the press, the schools, the church, etc. The newspapers have printed, the teachers have taught, and the clergymen have preached, in the main, the capitalist side of the struggle" (p. 235).

Also, in contrast to Turner's and Beard's versions of the "promise" of America, Huberman placed the immigrant experience at the very front of *We, the People.* Chapter 1, "Here They Come!" commences with: "From its very beginnings America has been a magnet to the peoples of the earth. . . . White people, black people, yellow people, brown people. . . ." Indeed, immigration, the coming to America, is offered as a continuous *and* shared experience of the American people; yet he does not fail to acknowledge its variations and its contradictions and to stress that the diversity was not only ethnic and religious but, crucially, class in character in terms both of property possessed and of one's own status *as* "property"—free, indentured, or slave: "And so they came, both the willing and the unwilling." Sensitive to the tragedy of the slave trade and the South's "peculiar institution," Huberman also relates the horror and tragedy of the relations between Euro-Americans and native American Indians; and, though he does so in language we would necessarily eschew today, Huberman's sympathy and respect for the "victims" are evident.

Leo Huberman

Huberman was born to a Jewish American family in Newark, New Jersey, on October 17, 1903. As he wrote in a two-page autobiographical note found in his files after his death (in November 1968): "I was . . . the last but one of eleven children, of whom six had died before my birth. My parents were worker intellectuals who became middle-class." He was obviously a hard working young man, spending his summer vacations in paid employment: "At the age of eleven, I worked in a celluloid factory, nights from 6 P.M. to 6 A.M. I was a 'runner' for a Wall Street brokerage house, a salesman at Nedick's, a laborer in a glass factory, an electrician's helper, a clerk in a post office, and a night 'checker' in a telegraph company." These "industrial" experiences were all acquired before his graduation from high school at sixteen. Following high school, Huberman spent two years at the teacher's college in Newark and on receipt of his diploma began work as an elementary schoolteacher in the same city. He married a high school classmate, Gertrude Heller, who had also become a schoolteacher, and their honeymoon involved hitch-hiking from New Jersey across the country to California and back again (an excellent preparation for writing *We, the People!*). Huberman remained a hard worker—again, in his own words: "My schedule in those early teaching years was rather full. I would teach in Newark till 3:15 P.M., take a bus and a train to New York for afternoon classes at New York University, then train and bus back to Newark, where I taught English to foreigners." Completing his degree in 1926 he took a position teaching at a private experimental school in New York.[18]

Writing *We, the People* in his spare time, its success on publication in 1932 significantly altered Huberman's life. His publishers commissioned him to write a history of the world next. In order to do so he gave up his teaching post and went to study at the London School of Economics *and,* as he adds, the British Museum (perhaps to commune with Marx's ghost). The product of this sojourn (1933–34) was his phenomenally successful book, *Man's Worldly Goods: The Story of the Wealth of Nations* (1936), which has sold internationally over one million copies. Returning to the United States, he held a variety of employments in publishing, education, and journalism from the mid-1930s to the late 1940s, including work as associate editor of *Scholastic Magazine,* chairman of the Department of Social Science, New College, Columbia University (1938–39), and director of the Department of Public Relations and Education for the National Maritime Union, CIO (Congress of Industrial Organizations). Additionally, in these years, he spent his evenings writing books and pamphlets. Notable among these is *The Labor Spy Racket* (1937, reprinted 1971). One of the first paperbacks in modern American trade publishing this work sold fifty thousand copies in the first fortnight!

Altogether, Huberman would write or co-author eleven books and co-edit six more. The co-produced volumes were done in partnership with his long-time friend and comrade, the Marxist economist, Paul Sweezy, with whom, in 1949, he founded the independent socialist magazine *Monthly Review* (*MR*) and, in 1952, established Monthly Review Press (the first title of which was I. F. Stone's *The Hidden History of the Korean War*). Huberman and Sweezy co-edited *MR* until the former's death in 1968 (at which time Sweezy was joined as co-editor by Harry Magdoff with whom he continues to super-vise the magazine).[19]

There is not room to take up the story of *Monthly Review,* the international friendships and contacts which Huberman and Sweezy established (and the recognition received), or the challenges and tensions of the 1950s and 1960s, but we must note two things more of a biographical nature. First, Huberman was an active labor educator before and after the founding of *MR*. In the previously-noted autobiographical statement (apparently written in the early 1950s) he proudly gives over a whole paragraph to his work with the National Maritime Union:

> Evenings and vacations were spent in teaching, in schools for work-ers. Our Leadership Training Program at the National Maritime Union became justly famous. *Time* magazine, reporting on our union bookstore (the first in the United States), and our union pamphlets said: "NMU's apparatus includes some of the slickest trade union literature in the world, most of it the work of Leo Huberman. Members are laboriously trained [at the union school] in procedures. Skippers have learned to respect and fear the ship-board committees who handle seamen's beefs."

And the second biographical point is that Huberman's politics and commit-ments to the labor and socialist movements resulted in his being called to testify before Joseph McCarthy's Senate subcommittee in 1953. This was his response (worth quoting at length):

> I am a Marxist and a socialist. I believe in working together with others, including Communists, to the extent that their aims and methods are consistent with mine.
> I have never sought to conceal what I think or where I stand. I am anxious that my ideas and beliefs should be known to as many people as possible; anyone interested in them can readily satisfy his

curiosity by reading my books and *Monthly Review.* I have nothing to hide—quite the contrary.

So much have I stated under oath, not because I concede the right of this Committee to ask for such information, but because I want to make it crystal clear that Communism is not an issue in this and to focus attention on what *is* the issue—my right as an author and editor to pursue my occupation without interference from Congress or any of its committees. To assert this right, I have refused to answer any further questions put to me by the McCarthy Committee concerning what I think, or what I believe, or with whom I associate. That, in accordance with good old American tradition, is my own business—to be discussed only with whom I choose. I do not choose to discuss it with the McCarthy Committee.[20]

Referring back to the relative absence of Left intellectual voices in American public culture, it is significant that in *The Last Intellectuals* Russell Jacoby refers admiringly to both the American radical-history tradition—"seeking to rediscover the untold history of a nation or labor or women or minorities . . . they have wished not simply to reclaim the past but to reclaim it for the participants—for a public"—*and* the *Monthly Review* school of political economy and social science—noting in particular Paul Sweezy, Paul Baran, Harry Braverman, and Harry Magdoff—for their having "formed a school that in coherence, originality, [clarity], and boldness no other American Marxism has come close to matching."[21] Yet, surprisingly, Jacoby fails to register the figure of Leo Huberman, which is rather unfortunate since Huberman's intellectual and political career links together in a pioneering way these two experiences and, moreover, his scholarly and political labors represent an especially critical model of intellectual practice. That is, it might be said that Huberman embodied Gramsci's conception of an organic intellectual: an intellectual emerging from the working class whose energies and initiatives as a socialist remain linked in a pedagogical and dialectical fashion with the labor movement. In this vein, Huberman's writings can be seen as having emanated from his pedagogical concerns and activities. In fact, there are those who have written off his work as *mere* "popularization." But, as Paul Sweezy insists, we are seriously mistaken if we undervalue the task of the "popularizer."

Leo was much more than a popularizer, but before I come to that I want to express our emphatic dissent from the attitude, fashionable in some quarters, which looks down on the work of popularization as being somehow beneath the dignity of a real intellectual. What

foolishness! The talent and understanding required of a good popularizer . . . is far above what is required of the run-of-the-mill spe-
cialist. And the work of bringing knowledge to masses of people is
surely more important than that of adding a little to some special-
ized branch of knowledge. In a world of rapidly increasing special-
ization in which most brainworkers are obliged to learn more and
more about less and less, there is a crying need for more and better
popularizers, men and women who can understand what goes in
the various special fields, relate them to each other and to the physical and social world as a whole, and express their findings and ideas
in language intelligible to a literate public—a public which includes, or should include, the vast majority of the specialists themselves.[22]

Sweezy appreciatively adds that the principle which shaped Huberman's
work and which he brought to *Monthly Review* was "We must be clear."

We, the People is not only *clearly* written. It was accurately described in *The
New York Times* as "unique and stimulating . . . stirring and thrilling." Indeed,
the book's subtitle, *The Drama of America,* aptly conveys the manner in which
Huberman presents the narrative of the country. Consider that after six decades the book remains a pleasure to read even though we are often told that
social and economic history cannot compete with the traditional narrative
style of political history and the stories of individual actors (by which is
meant usually elite figures). It is not only that Huberman never loses touch
with the human element and the aforementioned dynamics of material
struggle, environmental and political, but that he weaves into his narrative
well-chosen anecdotes which seem to capture the spirit of the people in their
respective times. There are some splendid ones. Unfortunately, space does
not permit the repeating of the best, but we might note a short and pointed
one illustrating what he believed to be the popular democratic sensibility of
Westerners: "In a crowded meeting in the West certain officials were trying
to force their way through to the platform. 'Make way there,' they cried. 'We
are the representatives of the people.' . . . 'Make way yourselves,' came the
quick retort. '*We are* the people'" (p. 106). Also, Huberman does not hesitate
to make the light of the past shine on the conditions of the present and vice
versa. For example, when he states (remember it is 1932): "*Except in the poll
tax states of the South today,* you have the right to vote if you are a citizen with
the proper age qualification. In colonial America . . ." (p. 37, my italics).

At the same time we should not fail to acknowledge here the contributions
to the text provided by the artist Thomas Hart Benton (1889–1975). Originally from Missouri, Benton spent the 1920s and early 1930s in New York
City. Strongly influenced by Marxism during these years in the East, Benton

himself was eager to connect his understanding of Marxist thought with American history. Especially, he pursued the development of a pictorial form and content which would express the experience of working people in a democratic and popular fashion. This took the shape of a series of murals which he titled the *American Historical Epic*. Indeed, through this project Benton essentially pioneered the muralist movement in the United States which was to emerge as one of the major art forms of the New Deal years (though, curiously, Benton himself never produced any work for the Roosevelt Administration).

In the course of the 1930s, Benton rejected Marxism, and though he remained a "populist," he moved to the Right politically, becoming increasingly anti-internationalist and "nativist" in his views—leading him to break with his friends on the Left and to depart New York City in the middle of the decade. In 1931, however, Benton was still in the city and his project to render American social history in visual terms intersected with the historical-literary project of his friend, Leo Huberman. Thus, together they would relate the making of the country through the experience and agency of working people. So close were Huberman's and Benton's aspirations that Henry Adams is able to write in his recent book, *Thomas Hart Benton: An American Original*, that "*We, the People*, in fact, serves well as a guidebook to the social message of Benton's paintings of this period."[23] Along with original pieces, plus a series of maps emphasizing the economic and geographical growth of the United States (but, also, attending to America's regionalism), Benton clearly drew upon his previous work for the *American Historical Epic*. In particular his illustrations communicate the frontier experience and movement westward (Benton too had written of the influence of Frederick Jackson Turner on his own work), the violent and sad encounter of Europeans and Indians, the look and labors of town and country, and the energy—human and mechanical—of industrial activity. Most of the pictures are of working people engaged in their livelihoods and everyday activities, though there are a variety of illustrations recalling the experiences of social confrontation, political and industrial. Notably, there are no depictions of specific political events or personalities.

The American intellectual historian, Richard Pells, writes that in the later 1930s under the influence of the Popular Front period, the "aesthetic of social protest was to be supplanted by a literature of 'democratic affirmation' which would allow the 'progressive' artist to express his 'sense of solidarity' with the American citizenry. . . . One of the most important results of this romance between the intellectuals and the 'people' was a growing fascination on both sides with the American past."[24] Huberman's and Benton's respective and joint projects were pioneering—or, if I may be so bold, in the "vanguard"—of those interests, commitments, and endeavours.

"We, the People" Today

We, the People was written six decades ago. Even allowing for the 1947 revised edition, too much has transpired for us to treat it as an adequate introduction to American History. It is not only that there have been such great changes and developments these past sixty years, but that the historical questions themselves have been revised and the scholarship resulting has dramatically refashioned our knowledge and portrait of the past. Any attempt today to create a work such as *We, the People* will not only have to take into account the developments of the intervening years, it will have to address the complex experiences of class *and* race, ethnicity and gender which we now know so much more about after a generation of critical and pluralistic politico-economic, social, and cultural historical study.[25]

Nevertheless, I would argue that Huberman's work remains of value to us and not merely in *historical* terms, that is, as a document revealing and expressing a particular moment in the history of the American Left and an especially original and imaginative rendition of its sense of past and present at that time. First, *We, the People* offers a valuable reminder to us of the possibility of actually providing a lively and dynamic reading of United States history. In fact, Huberman's work should challenge us to seek to create new popular syntheses of our national experience.[26] But there is more to it. Not only should we draw inspiration and ideas from Huberman's spirited and creative writing (a point to which I will return); we should consider once again the "materialisms" to be found there. To repeat: I am not urging the simple appropriation of his arguments. However, I would say, in the light of the phenomenal growth of the field of "cultural studies" and its near-equation with Left scholarship, that we must take all-the-more seriously Huberman's attentions to the "confrontations" between humanity and the natural environment and, too, those between *classes* in all their complexity. Regarding the latter, political economy and class-structured experience and relations have been submerged in too much of recent Left scholarship in favor of postmodernist perspectives which lack the *political* edge and promise of even the mass culture and society (that is, elites and masses) approach. Changes and discontinuities do indeed mark our lives and contemporary experience, but we should not be blind to the dramatic *continuities*. As Leo Ribuffo soberly reflected in "The Burdens of Contemporary History":

> Despite notable shifts in belief and behavior, our society has many affinities with, not only the 1920s and 1930s, but with the order created at the turn of the century. By 1900 large corporations dominated the economy and, now operating internationally, they continue to do so. . . . Most Americans underestimate this historical continuity partly because pundits, concentrating on styles instead

of power relations, warn them of change so rapid that it portends "future shock." . . . Equally important, a nostalgia industry channels vivid personal memories into stylized patterns and makes even recent events seem like they happened long ago. . . .

Old problems reoccur, not because "those who forget the past are condemned to repeat it," but because sturdy power structures and tenacious world views link past and present.[27]

To return to Huberman's project of articulating a synthesis of American history from a Marxian perspective for a popular readership: *We, the People* should also serve to remind us that we have, as Russell Jacoby and others have argued, too often limited ourselves (at least in the U.S.A.) to academic endeavors. I am referring to both our research and pedagogical pursuits. It is not merely that radical historical scholarship in its very success and excitement has usually taken the form of monographs and journal articles, and that we will thus have to reconsider our literary styles if we are to address and engage non-academic working people, but also that we educate and train our students in a fashion which teaches them to write and express themselves *as* and *to* academics. The overwhelming majority are *not* future academics and scholars, but they could be public intellectuals. In other words, we need to consider and elaborate means by which our students and we ourselves develop the skills and knowledge of historical study *and,* at the same time, the language and modes of communication to enable us to engage "the people" and begin, or continue, the refashioning of our public discourse in an ever more democratic direction.[28]

As we know, historians "naturally" tend to resist or oppose the practice of "generalization" in favor of "specification," but—while holding on dearly to the value of the ideal and pursuit of historical objectivity and accuracy (though not neutrality)—I would argue that synthesis, the making of "grand narratives," remains a possible and necessary aspiration, though one to be approached most critically. That is, if it is not to be imposed on the past and/ or the present—as the New Right has been attempting to do for almost a generation now—then we must *connect,* and connect *with,* the diverse experience of working people yesterday *and* today. More precisely, we must recognize that although we might pursue syntheses which contribute to radical-democratic development, new grand narratives will emerge not purely from the pens of critical historians but from the dialectic of the making of history. Remembering that should help to energize our efforts, but also to maintain our modesty. To imagine otherwise could too easily allow a return to elitism.

It is arguable that I am no longer speaking of the discipline of history but of another practice which might better be called "historical criticism." However, the fundamental imperatives of historical study—perspective, critique, consciousness, remembrance, and imagination—and the researches they inform are the foundations upon which any good *historical* criticism must be practiced. In other words, critical history and historical criticism may not be exactly co-equal, but they are tightly bound together and should be recognized as mutually dependent on each other. And, in any case, in the context of the social orders in which we live, and will continue to live for some time, the best critical history will necessarily be perceived as historical criticism (and should be!).

Finally, then, we might well draw something else from *We, the People*, though, as I have explained, it was not original to Huberman's work. That is, even though it will need to be rewritten in the light of history and historiography, the conception of American history as a conflict over, if not between, capitalism and democracy continues to present itself. And, indeed, there are historians and historical social scientists who continue to assert it as *the* central dynamic and narrative.[29] But the loudest voices in American public debate today continue to emanate from the Right, and they are speaking of the "end of history" and the mutuality of capitalism and democracy. The thing to realize, however, is that they are anxious voices, for however compatible capitalism and democracy may seem to appear, at the heart of the former is a dynamic of conflict out of which anticapitalist and democratic working-class struggles have emerged projecting a yet more developed form of democratic life.

This was a point to which Leo Huberman returned in his 1947 revised edition of *We, the People*. Allowing himself to reflect on the significance of the New Deal years—"a revolution in ideas, not in economics"—he wrote in words so very relevant today:

> The common man must not forget the New Deal. It was a valuable experience. It gave the workers and farmers a sense of their own power. They learned that in order to be able to get any of the things they wanted they had to organize both politically and economically. And today, when the New Deal is rapidly becoming a memory, they must remember that lesson. They must redouble their economic and political activities. They want jobs and peace. They must take the initiative in getting them. And they will learn through their struggles that jobs and peace are attainable only under a system of production for use, not for profit. (p. 351)

JOHN BERGER AND THE
QUESTION OF HISTORY

John Berger has been a presence on the cultural Left for almost forty years. In the course of these four decades he has worked as an artist, art critic and historian; novelist, screenwriter and filmmaker; essayist, social critic and sociologist; and since the middle of the 1970s—to use the ascription to which he would respond most favorably—a storyteller. During the 1980s his work became the subject of critical assessment and appreciation in a variety of disciplines. Indeed, at the same time that our political cultures of the transatlantic English-speaking world have been dominated by the figures of Margaret Thatcher and Ronald Reagan, John Berger it would seem has become that to which he would respond most unfavorably, a celebrity. Not only have numerous articles appeared in academic journals which survey and critique his fictions and aesthetic and social commentaries and visions; he has also been celebrated in the pages of selected glossy periodicals, including the *New York Times Sunday Magazine*.[1] Berger's writings have also provided the basis for a book-length exposition and discussion of his career in which the author describes him as "one of our greatest writers" and Berger is seen as developing his own critical theory of art and society, dubbed "spiritual materialism."[2] Perhaps most curious, however, is that because Berger has been living in a peasant village in southeastern France since the mid-1970s and has not made himself too accessible otherwise, those writers who have sought an interview or conversation with him have had to journey—one is tempted to say "make a pilgrimage"—to his home in the Savoy.

Lest my tone be misinterpreted, I too am an admirer of Berger's work and have sought to contribute to his recognition, his "celebrity" status, by way of appreciative scholarly essays. For those of us who have grown increasingly intolerant of academic boundaries, Berger's writings have represented models in the evasion—better, confusion—of disciplinary categorization, not only because they have extended across a range of subjects and modes of communication, but also because there has been no divorcing his aesthetic, sociological, and fictional efforts from each other. He has not been frivolous in his interests. There are continuities in his work and certain concerns are persistently re-emerging: the active experience of looking, seeing, and telling; the individual and collective sense of time and space; and the role of the artist and intellectual in states and social orders of exploitation, alienation, and oppression. It has been my contention, moreover, that bound up with these has been an even more pervasive concern. Throughout his writings one encounters the problematic of historical thinking and consciousness. I return again to Berger's work not merely to update my earlier assessments, but also to indicate that whereas I once felt strongly that Berger's initiatives had major contributions to make to the discourse about the "crisis of history" *and* to the project of reinvigorating historical thought and consciousness, in the light of his more recent writings I have become somewhat ambivalent about what he has presently to offer. I still find him a most engaging and committed writer, and I continue to be drawn to his superbly evocative storytelling; however, I find myself impatient with his criticism and his "vision."

Historical Perspective

Although Berger's own historical perspective has changed in the course of forty years, reflecting his shifting sense of the possibilities of transforming the corporate and state-dominated regimes of the late twentieth century, he has remained committed to the necessity of critical historical thought and consciousness. Expressed in his art and social criticism and in his fictions from the 1950s through the 1970s is the imperative to oppose the cultural alienation and mystification characteristic of class-structured societies. In *A Painter of Our Time* and *Permanent Red,* his first novel and first collection of art criticism, respectively, Berger argued that capitalism was in its dying stages and, thus, we were witnessing the "cultural disintegration of the West," more specifically, "the ideological disintegration of the bourgeoisie." In the arts, anxiety about the meaning of contemporary developments was reflected, according to Berger, in the rejection or disavowal of historical thinking in favor of a view which ahistoricized or "universalized" aesthetic production and experience.

In *Permanent Red,* he wrote that "All appreciation of the art of the past is one-sided and to some extent distorted. Above all the art of the past gives a sense of false security. It offers too easy a confirmation of the continuity of human culture." And in *A Painter of Our Time,* on seeing art in historically-specific terms, Berger writes—via the diary of the central character, Janos, an exiled Hungarian artist:

> Those who think that art is transportable, timeless, universal, understand it least of all. They put a Hindu sculpture next to a

Michelangelo and marvel at the fact that in both cases the woman has two breasts! But it is the differences which are essential to our sense of fraternity. Each of us works for different ends, under different pressures, a few of them personal, most of them social and historical.

The task of the "revolutionary" artist and intellectual, therefore, was to insist on the historicity of art both to de-reify aesthetic experience and to recover its history.

Contrary to the presumed radical project of "breaking" with the past—an enterprise that Berger showed to be actually central to the cultural disintegration of capitalism, and which was, tragically, mirrored in state socialism—truly progressive artists and intellectuals had the responsibility of asserting the "continuity" of art and through their works assuring the continuity of hopes into the future. He wrote of the Dutch artist, Frisco Ten Holt, that "artists like Ten Holt . . . will be seen to have been heroes. Not because they were politically conscious heralds of that new society—that is another way of living; but because they obstinately believed in the *continuity of art* at a time when most, doubting the continuity of their own way of life, wanted to destroy all continuity. And to believe in continuity is to be modern, is to be—for us who can respect nothing else—revolutionary." The twentieth century in Berger's view is preeminently the epoch of people "claiming the right of equality." Thus, the question he poses as a critic is "Does this work [of art] help or encourage men to know and claim their rights?" which does not require that the artist work for a particular cause but that the work "increase our awareness of our potentiality."[3]

Berger's perspective on contemporary development in the late 1950s was that it was a period of transformation which, however uneven, complex, and contradictory it might seem, was that of the transition from capitalism to socialism: "We live in a period of transition to Socialism, transition to Communism." But the transition was not mechanical, nor the outcome determined. Such change necessarily involves consciousness—*historical* consciousness: "Historical necessity does not of itself make heroes, but the realization of historical necessity can make heroes . . . organization and discipline are necessary, as well as an understanding of history. . . . Our historical understanding is enabling us to change the world."[4]

Berger's optimism was strengthened in the course of the sixties. It was not that history had somehow sped up, but that a fundamental truth had now been realized: "The world is a single unit and it has become intolerable." The recognition of this truth, he observed, was "an historical achievement" which had been struggled for: "It was born of the determination of the exploited to fight—not even, to begin with, for economic justice, but for their identity." Vietnam, the Prague Spring, May '68 in Paris, and growing student movements in Western Europe and North America: "In 1968, hopes nurtured more or less underground for years were born in several places and given their names." *And yet,* in the very same year "these hopes were categorically defeated."[5]

In the shadows of the defeats of 1968 Berger's historical perspective was dramatically shaken; however, his commitment to historical thought and consciousness, though seemingly characterized by moments of doubt, persisted with a renewed appreciation of the powers of both coercion and ideological domination available to the late twentieth-century state. In *Ways of Seeing* (1972), his extremely influential book on art history and visual experience intended as a critical response to Kenneth Clark's television series and book, *Civilisation,* Berger returned to the exploration of the process of cultural alienation and mystification in advanced industrial capitalism.

> The past is never there waiting to be discovered, to be recognized for exactly what it is. History always constitutes the relation between a present and its past. Consequently, fear of the present leads to a mystification of the past. The past is not for living in; it is a well of conclusions from which we draw in order to act. Cultural mystification of the past entails a double loss. Works of art are made unnecessarily remote and the past offers us fewer conclusions to complete in action.

He explained that if we were able to *see* the art of the past we would be able to situate ourselves in history, but "When we are prevented from seeing it, we are deprived of the history which belongs to us." The consequences of cultural amnesia are historically consequential because "A people or class which is cut off from its own past is far less free to choose and to act as a people or class than one that has been able to situate itself in history." The political question raised is "Who benefits from this deprivation?"; to which Berger's response was that "the art of the past is being mystified because a privileged minority is striving to invent a history which can retrospectively justify the role of the ruling classes."[6]

Memory and Storytelling

The period before 1968 was for Berger (and many others) a "time of expectant hopes" and "revolutionary expectations." The period immediately thereafter was to be a time of crisis and reevaluation. His novel *G.*—for which he was awarded the prestigious Booker Prize—was written over the years 1965–71 and reflects much of the period for Berger. It is the story of a "Don Juan," the out-of-wedlock son of a married Italian merchant and an American woman, who is raised by relatives in England but moves across Europe to Trieste, around the turn of the century. It is equally the story(ies) of the women he comes to know.

The narrative in *G.*, one is tempted to say, is very much like life itself—forever shifting. It is constructed of the author's narration; the spoken, thought and felt words of the characters; the author's explanation of the "history" within which the experiences are transpiring—a history which moves parallel, into and out of the characters' lives; and the author's (Berger's) own meditations on sex and history.[7]

In *G.*, Berger quotes Collingwood on historical consciousness: "All history is contemporary history: not in the ordinary sense of the word . . . but in the strict sense: the consciousness of one's own activity as one actually performs it. History is thus the self-knowledge of the living mind" (*The Idea of History*). There is, however, another way that this concern is expressed, reflecting his expectation of change (transition). That is, Berger presents us with moments of a character's experience which are "historically" charged but which cannot *yet* be understood or articulated. For example, Beatrice, G's older cousin and guardian with whom he first has sex, and who, according to one very reasonable interpretation, represents the English gentry, experiences the following:

> She could not explain her feelings to herself. There is an historical equivalent to the psychological process of repression into the unconscious. Certain experiences cannot be formulated because they have occurred too soon. This happens when an inherited world-view is unable to contain or resolve certain emotions or intuitions which have been provoked by a new situation or an extremity of experience unforeseen by that world-view. . . .
>
> A moment's introspection shows that a large part of our own experience cannot be adequately formulated: it awaits further understanding of the total human situation. In some respects we are likely to be better understood by those who follow us than by ourselves. Nevertheless, their understanding will be expressed in terms which would be alien to us. They will change our unformulated experience beyond our recognition. As we have changed Beatrice's.
>
> She is aware that there is another way of seeing her and all that surrounds her, which can only be defined as the way she can never see. She is being seen in that way now. Her mouth goes dry. Her corsets constrain her more tightly. Everything tilts. She sees everything clearly and normally. She can discern no tilt. But she is convinced, she is utterly certain that everything has been tilted.[8]

The sense of change—of becoming—not yet understood, reflects Berger's own experience at the time of writing.

At the same time, this was a period not only of expectation but also of rebellion, rebellion *defeated*, which challenged not only Berger's historical perspective, but seems also to have challenged—though it did not in the end undermine—his concern for historical consciousness. This is evidenced in part by his interest in experience outside of "normal time," or, more accurately, experiences of timelessness, which in *G.* is sex.

Berger's interest in experiences outside of normal time was not original to *G.* or to that period of his work. For example, in *A Painter of Our Time,* the specific *act* of artistic creation is referred to in terms of timelessness. Other examples exist. Also, other interpretations of the role of sex in *G.* are possible. However, the persistent reference to sex as timeless when contrasted to normal time and history seems to indicate a search for an alternative—to the intolerability of the world? and the tragedy which is contemporary history?: "(Passion must hurl itself against time. Lovers fuck time together so that it opens, advances, withdraws upon itself and bends backwards. Time which their hearts pump. Time whose vagina is moist with timelessness. Time which spends itself when it ejaculates generations.) We have no time, Nusa, he said" and "In an indeterminate world in flux sexual desire is reinforced by a longing for precision and certainty: beside her my life is arranged. In a static hierarchic world sexual desire is reinforced by a longing for an alternative certainty: with her I am free."[9]

This was clearly a difficult time for Berger (and not for him alone). In an essay on the Grunewald Altarpiece he explained how, between 1963 and 1973, his way of seeing had changed, which altered the way in which he viewed the work and the world around him: "In a period of revolutionary expectation, I saw a work of art which had survived as evidence of the past's despair; in a period which has to be endured, I see the same work miraculously offering a narrow pass across despair."[10]

His despair was also expressed through his other fictions of this period. These took the form of films—*The Salamander* (1971), *The Middle of the World* (1974), and *Jonah, Who Will Be 25 in the Year 2000* (1976)—pursued in collaboration with Alain Tanner. In *The Middle of the World,* the affair between the Italian migrant worker waitress and the Swiss engineer, which ends in their separation, is discussed in terms of *normalization,* which means that a relationship between two parties (people or countries) is established but nothing changes. And in the third fiction-in-film with Tanner, *Jonah,* the defeats (and despair) of '68 are illustrated through a group of young people and their attempts to find alternatives to politics. (At the same time, we should note that this last film does conclude in a common recognition of the need for fellowship and community.)[11]

Although it is true that his historical perspective no longer comprehended the world in terms of imminent change, Berger's despair did not lead him to a rejection of history and historical consciousness. To some extent his changed perspective could be described by way of the quote from Antonio Gramsci's *Prison Notebooks:* "The crisis consists precisely in the fact that the old is dying and the new cannot be born; in the interregnum a great variety of morbid symptoms appear." But this is stated too negatively, for, as Berger himself has said, "One of the great illusions of the left is to believe that everything can always be resolved, that one doesn't actually have to *live* perhaps a whole lifetime with contradictions."[12] He still saw contemporary history in terms of a transition, but he now saw the process of change in terms of a *longue duree*.[13] In other words, Berger's historical perspective had changed, but his concern for historical consciousness had intensified. In fact, what had always been a concern became a problem to which he committed himself.

In the early 1970s, Berger and Jean Mohr, his photographer-colleague on a previous book, *A Fortunate Man* (1969), produced their study of migrant workers in Europe titled *A Seventh Man* (1975).[14] Berger has said that in carrying out the project he came to realize that he did not know enough about the origins of the migrants, most of whom had come from the countryside. Thus, in 1974 he moved to a peasant village in southeastern France. (He had already "exiled" himself from London to Geneva in the 1960s; he was now "emigrating" from urban to rural Europe.) Although Berger has remained active in art criticism, visual studies, and essay writing as evidenced by his books, *About Looking, Another Way of Telling, The Sense of Sight* (the British title is *The White Bird*), and *And our faces, my heart, brief as photos,*[15] his major work has been in fiction, that is, the novels, *Pig Earth* and *Once in Europa*, the first two volumes of a trilogy entitled *Into Their Labours*.[16] The move to the countryside has not only entailed changes in Berger's subject matter—now peasants as opposed to "urbanites"—it has also determined changes in the form of his writing, alterations in his historical perspective, and a further evolution in his perception of the problem of historical thought and consciousness. Indeed, it is the "crisis of history"—which has been so much a part of contemporary public discourse—that provides the framework for the first book, *Pig Earth*.

Both volumes of *Into Their Labours* are different in form from Berger's earlier novels. As opposed to a single story, both works are actually collections of stories and poems. As well, *Pig Earth* includes two essays. The first considers the practice of peasant storytelling and the second, which is presented in the form of a "Historical Afterword," discusses the peasants as a "class of survivors" who are now, however, disappearing from the European countryside, and what this means in historical terms. That the two books took the form they did was not something Berger had expected, nor was he originally prepared for it. He has said that he discovered that if his writing was "to hold and embrace their [peasant] experience" he would have to "relearn," or learn anew, how to write. Apparently much to his surprise and pleasure he found that the peasants he lived amongst were to be his "teachers," educating him to a new way of telling. In public conversation with

Berger, the sociologist Teodor Shanin reflected that "I think you relearned not only writing, you also relearned how to live."[17]

Berger's primary understanding of peasant experience is that they are a class of survivors.

> Peasant life is a life committed completely to survival. Perhaps this is the only characteristic fully shared by peasants everywhere. Their implements, their crops, their earth, their masters may be different, but whether they labour within a capitalist society, a feudal one, or others which cannot be so easily defined, whether they grow rice in Java, wheat in Scandinavia, or maize in South America, whatever the differences of climate, religion or social history, the peasantry everywhere can be defined as a class of survivors.[18]

Survival, however, must not be construed as passive, for it is not; it is active, it is a struggle. As Berger had earlier written in *Art and Revolution,* we have to rethink the concept of "courage" such that it comprehends "the obstinacy of victims who resist their victimization: it becomes their ability to endure until they can put an end to their suffering." In this way we are forced to acknowledge "the courage of a people or class, not as represented by their professional armies, but made manifest in the actions of the entire population, men and women, young and old." And such courage is "not proved by their risking their entire existence: on the contrary, it is proved by their endurance and their determination to survive."[19]

Yet Berger also had to acknowledge that the class of survivors is vanishing: "For the first time ever it is possible that the class of survivors may not survive. Within a century there may be no more peasants. In Western Europe, if the plans work out as the economic planners have foreseen, there will be no more peasants within twenty-five years." As Teodor Shanin said to Berger, "You may be the last witness, poet, painter of a world which is dying."[20]

Berger insists that he does not seek by his writing to save peasants from extinction: "In a just world such a class would no longer exist." Neither does he wish to romanticize peasant life; in fact, he writes of contemporary peasant experience in part to bear witness against the mystification of peasant life characteristic of our commodity culture. However, because of its persistence and survival over thousands of years, he does claim for peasant experience a special historical validity which should not be dismissed. That is, there are aspects of peasant culture from which we might learn, among the first of which, Berger says, is the peasant "suspicion of progress," *the* common principle and aspiration of both capitalism and socialism. For when we acknowledge the way the peasantry is disappearing—it is being eliminated—and consider what is replacing it, we see that this suspicion has not been "altogether misplaced or groundless." Similarly, he contends, we need to reconsider the meaning of "peasant conservatism" which, in contrast to the conservatism of landlords and petty-bourgeoisies, seeks neither privilege nor power over other classes: "Peasant conservatism scarcely defends any privilege . . . it is a conservatism not of power but of meaning. It represents a depository (a granary) of meaning preserved from lives and generations threatened by continual and inexorable change."[21]

A depository of meaning: here we encounter the most important feature of the peasant culture of survival from which we might learn, for it directs our attention to historical consciousness. Berger does not propose that peasant experience offers the "correct" historical consciousness but that in their struggles for survival peasants have developed cultural practices by which they could maintain their links with the past (and the future), specifically, storytelling and memory: "Memory implies a certain act of redemption. What is remembered has been saved from nothingness. What is forgotten has been abandoned . . . with the loss of memory the continuities of meaning and judgement are also lost to us."[22] It is important to note, memory does not refer merely to that which is remembered from the past of one's own life. As Berger writes: "Experience is indivisible and continuous; at least within a single lifetime and perhaps over many lifetimes. I never have the impression that my experience is entirely my own, and it often seems to me that it preceded me."

The stories in *Pig Earth* bear witness to the disappearance—elimination— of the peasantry (in Europe, at least). The people in the stories are old, for the young have migrated. Yet the old continue to work and remember. For example, Marcel, a sixty-three-year-old man, explains his planting of new apple trees—even though his sons have left to work in the city: "Working is a way of preserving the knowledge my sons are losing. I dig the holes, wait for a tender moon and plant out these saplings to give an example to my sons if they are interested, and, if not, to my father and his father that the knowledge they handed down has not yet been abandoned. Without that knowledge I am nothing." And there is Catherine, a peasant woman of seventy-four years, being helped by her brother and a neighbor in locating and repairing a pipe which brings water to her house from a nearby spring, who says to them regarding its location: "It's buried one metre deep. . . . I can hear Mathieu telling me that. One metre deep. . . . Fifty years is a long time, but I remember him saying it was one metre deep." Elsewhere, Berger recounts how he was impressed by a peasant's memory of events which preceded his *lived* past but had remained very much a part of his *living* past: "Once I was walking in the mountains with a friend of seventy. As we walked along the foot of a high cliff, he told me how a young girl had fallen to her death there, whilst haymaking on the *alpage* above. Was that before the war? I asked. In 1833, he said."[23]

Evidently, Berger's concern for storytelling and remembrance has been de-

rived from his living amongst what may possibly be the last generation of
French peasants, but it also expressed a continuing intimacy with the ideas
of the German-Jewish writer, Walter Benjamin (1892–1940). The first part
of Berger's television production and later book, *Ways of Seeing,* was greatly
influenced by Benjamin's essay, "The Work of Art in the Age of Mechanical
Reproduction"; and Berger's understanding of what it means to work as a
storyteller surely owes much to Benjamin's essay, "The Storyteller: Reflections on the Work of Nikolai Leskov." From Benjamin—and increasingly
from the researches of historians and social scientists in peasant studies working "from the bottom up"—we get a clearer sense of the practical and political importance of the storyteller within the peasant community. As Benjamin
wrote: "Memory is the epic faculty *par excellence.* . . . Memory creates the
chain of tradition which passes a happening on from generation to generation." The storyteller is the "people's remembrancer" (as the Welsh historian,
Gwyn Williams, has said), entertaining and/or providing "counsel," but, also,
as the living village archive the storyteller practices a mode of resistance
against the *longue duree* of exploitation and oppression which others have
exercised over peasants. Through the storyteller, memory, as history, waits to
be acted upon.[24]

In his essay, Benjamin spoke of the epochal changes underway which were
devaluing experience in favor of "information," and of how the practice of
storytelling, which had already declined in relation to the rise of the novel,
was becoming all-the-more rare in the context of "the dissemination of information." Fifty years later, Berger offers a similar assessment of contemporary
developments, but from the vantage point of the countryside he makes even
more explicit an argument evident in Benjamin's essay. That is, the decline of
storytelling and the remembrance of experience are due to the continued
development of the forces of the industrial market economy and the steady
elimination of the peasantry: "there is the historic role of capitalism, a role
unforeseen by Adam Smith or Marx . . . to destroy history, to sever every
link with the past and to orientate all effort and imagination to that which is
about to occur. . . . Henry Ford's remark that 'History is bunk' has generally
been underestimated; he knew exactly what he was saying. Destroying the
peasantries of the world could be a final act of historical elimination."[25]

In our so-called "post-1968 era" when, first, cross-class alliances and, now,
the "new social movements" are presumed to have replaced "class politics,"
and intellectuals and European socialists speak of "postmodern" culture and
politics in yet another effort to "break" with the past, Berger's own strategy
has been to move *towards* the past in order to confront industrial-capitalist
development at its least conspicuous, but perhaps most dramatic, point of
expansion in time and space. In a sense it seems that Berger has recognized a
point made by Barrington Moore, Jr., that

The chief social basis of radicalism has been the peasants and the smaller artisans in the towns. From these facts one may conclude that the wellsprings of human freedom lie not only where Marx saw them, in the aspirations of classes about to take power, but perhaps even more in the dying wail of a class over whom the wave of progress is about to roll. Industrialism, as it continues to spread, may in some distant future still these voices forever and make revolutionary radicalism as anachronistic as cuneiform writing.[26]

Obviously, Berger is under no illusions that the peasantry of Western Europe any longer represents a radical force as they did in 1381 or the Revolution of 1789. It is their cultural modes of resistance, storytelling, and remembrance, which he seeks to redeem or rescue so that they might be turned against the "social amnesia" of industrial capitalism and state socialism.

This project was also central to his continuing work with Jean Mohr to develop an alternative photographic practice—alternative, that is, to the public uses of photography currently pursued by science, administration, publicity, and entertainment—the task of which is "to incorporate photography into social and political memory, instead of using it as a substitute which encourages the atrophy of any such memory."[27] Again, for Berger, this entails confronting the elimination of alternative "histories" by the forces of progress, for the logic of progress has entailed the expulsion, or suppression, of any sense of experience, of time *or* timelessness, other than its own. That is, Berger says, "history and time" have been "conflated . . . become indivisible, so that we can no longer read our experience of either of them separately."[28] I was reminded of this by James O'Connor's recent observation that "Today, the concept of history has itself become suspect. We tend to experience time as 'enlarged simultaneity' rather than as a link with the past and future. In the crisis, it seems that 'there is only one time—the present.'"[29] This sense of one-dimensionality in time had previously been opposable, Berger states, by the rare moments of revolutionary action but also, and ever more often, by both the "faculty of memory" and the "living of certain moments which defy the passing of time . . . because, within their experience, there is an imperviousness to time." But, he declares, these too are subject to subversion and incorporation. He avers, however, that people are not merely the "passive objects of history"; there has been resistance, "popular ingenuity," and he finds within the private use of photography one of those modes of resistance.

In this case such ingenuity uses whatever little there is at hand to preserve experience, to re-create an area of "timelessness," to insist upon the permanent. And so, hundreds of millions of photographs, fragile images, often carried next to the heart or placed by the side

of the bed, are used to refer to that which historical time has no
right to destroy.[30]

Inspired by the promise which is revealed in the private use of photography, Berger and Mohr propose a photographic practice of storytelling by way
of photo-montage, in which the visual narratives offered are to be "presented
as images belonging to a *living* memory." The sentiments expressed and
theory developed are inviting, but how does it translate into practice? They
themselves provide an experimental effort, a sequence of photographs titled
"If each time . . . ," intended to be a narrative of an (imaginary) old peasant
woman remembering experiences of her life. The photographs employed are
actually drawn from a variety locales and "experiences," which is strange for
it challenges the very notion of a *"living* memory"—that is, whose memory?
that of the imaginary old peasant woman? Berger's and Mohr's? the reader,
who is presumably living in an urban center in the industrial west?[31]

Berger himself, prior to *Another Way of Telling,* had proposed the aspiration
for the alternative public use of photography when he wrote that "Narrated
time becomes historic time when it is assumed by *social* memory and *social*
action."[32] The narrative which Berger and Mohr offer is intriguing, but it is
not clear how it represents a meaningful alternative practice that would contribute to more than private and personal readings. This, however, does not
efface the theory, the intentions, or the possibility of developing such a practice. Indeed, I would direct attention to a work published about the same
time as *Another Way of Telling,* which I believe well exemplifies the alternative
practice Berger envisions, that is, Susan Meiselas's *Nicaragua, June 1978–July
1979.*[33] Her personal epigraph introduces the practice and the aspiration to
be found in the narrative:

> NICARAGUA.
> A year of news, as if nothing had happened before, as if the roots
> were not there, and the victory not earned. This book was made so
> that we remember.

As a storyteller, Berger came to see himself even more clearly as an "artic-
ulator of experience" whose duty is "to describe the world we live in as not
being inevitable. Life with its enormous and crushing necessities often does
not allow for something that is happening to be other than what it is. Literature always allows for that."[34]

History Without Politics?

In the work which followed *Pig Earth* and *Another Way of Telling,* Berger's
writings continued to attend to modes of resistance to the "crushing neces-

sities," but the modes were ever more private and personal in character to the extent that "accommodation," though still not surrender, might be a more appropriate term than resistance. Whereas in the first volume of *Into Their Labours* the primary theme was storytelling and remembrance resisting the histories of domination, in *Once in Europa* and the related book, *And our faces . . .* , the central theme is love and the search for a "home" in a world capitalist economy which enforces alienation, separation, and homelessness.

Berger's essays from the 1970s collected in *The Sense of Sight/The White Bird* attest that love and separation and time and timelessness have long been among his concerns. As stated above, my own interpretation was that such interests, especially Berger's fascination with the idea of the experience of timelessness (e.g., in the novel *G.*) reflected moments of doubt and disillusion about historical thinking in the aftermath of the late sixties. I may or may not have been correct as to what it indicated in his thought during the 1970s, but it now appears that Berger has found in the "universals" of love and the search for a home a transcendent yet historically-significant hope, possibly even a promise or vision. His most direct statement of this is to be found in *And our faces . . .* when he offers the experience of the migrant worker as the paradigmatic example—in the extreme—of the displacement, homelessness, and alienation of our time. "What can grow on this site of loss?" From within modern experience, he replies, two new expectations have emerged. The first, "passionate romantic love," though historically-constructed, seems to escape history; and yet its very "primacy" imbues it with a special meaning in the face of contemporary alienation and the absence of a home, "a centre." The second expectation is built on the recognition that there is, indeed, no return to the village—nor for humanity a return to the village as "the centre of the world." Thus, Berger declares: "The one hope of recreating a centre now is to make it the entire earth. Only world-wide solidarity can transcend modern homelessness." The leading prophet of this *historical* vision he reminds us was Marx. But is such a vision historically possible? In spite of all that has transpired, Berger confesses, he can still "imagine it."[35]

Although history is present in each story in *Once in Europa*—indeed, the work affirms Fred Inglis's remark that Berger is forever trying "to write each personal history as if it were the history of the world"[36]—the stories do not express the historical vision of transcending the present, but rather the search for a home and the "hope of completion" within romantic love. In Berger's own words this second volume of *Into Their Labours* is a "collection of love stories set against the disappearance or 'modernization' of village life." An appreciative critic, Bruce Robbins, writes: "The five stories . . . are about the basic hinges of love and death. And on all the hinges peasant life swings shut." The first story, "The Accordion Player," is about solitude and loneliness. Felix, a middle-aged peasant bachelor whose mother had died more than ten years earlier, lives alone: "Today he was alone, alone to decide the risks, to cut the hay, to ted it, to turn it, to transport it, to unload it, to pack it, to level it, to quench his thirst, to prepare his own supper. With the new machines he did not have to work harder than in the first half of his life; the difference now was that he was alone." He continues to work and to play at other people's weddings but remains alone (an old friend had said to his mother: "It's not like our time. . . . Nobody wants to marry a peasant today.") In "Boris is Buying Horses" a peasant ends up committing suicide, having been used by a woman from the city who (with her husband) inherits his property and turns his farmhouse into a souvenir shop; and in "The Time of the Cosmonauts" a young peasant woman leaves the mountains and the old peasant cowherd with whom she has been intimate to marry a migrant Italian woodcutter whose dream, which is fulfilled in the story, has been to own a grocer's shop. Then, in the title story, "Once in Europe," a peasant girl has a love affair with an immigrant worker employed in the factory which surrounds the farm of her father (who resists all offers to be bought out). But the man is killed in an accident in the works, leaving the young woman alone with their child. Later she marries a shopkeeper who, too, had been a worker in the factory, but had lost his legs in an earlier accident in the plant. Here again the peasant becomes a towndweller. And in "Play Me Something," a peasant visiting Venice becomes involved with a woman worker of the city— an "erotic and political encounter," as Robbins puts it, in which the peasant's "philosophy of cyclical stasis" comes face to face with the worker's "philosophy of progress." He departs on the bus with his compatriots but it is quite possible he will return to the city permanently, seduced.[37]

The stories are beautifully told, and even though the resistance of remembrance and storytelling has apparently succumbed to the logic of progress, the peasants in Berger's stories are still respected as agents of their own lives. Within and against the "crushing necessities" they remain *willful:* "His achievement wasn't only his herd of thirty cows. It was also his will. Every day now, old and alone, he found no answer to the question. Why go on? Nobody ever replied for him. Every day of the summer he found the answer himself."[38]

Indeed, against his own intentions, Berger's stories bear witness to the disappearance of the peasants not merely as victims but, accommodating themselves to history, as *"willing* the changes" themselves.[39] That is, in the face of their elimination as a class they persist in making choices: whom to love, where to live, and when to die. Such decisions are indeed present in his stories and Berger will no doubt be pleased to have them revealed, for, as he noted above, he is intent upon drawing out the "resistance" to contemporary history even in the most seemingly universal and extra-historical experiences. Thus, in *And our faces . . . ,* he proposes that "The sexual thrust to reproduce and fill the future is a thrust against the current of time which is flowing

ceaselessly towards the past. The genetic information which assures reproduction works against dissipation. The sexual animal—like a grain of corn—
is a conduit of the past into our future."[40] This is the "spiritual materialism"
of which Geoff Dyer has spoken.

Sharing the chronicle of historical tragedy in this century has been state
socialism. Set within the shadows of its darkest moments and locales is the
play, *A Question of Geography*, which Berger co-authored with Nella Bielski, a
Soviet emigre writer.[41] It treats the lives of a group of former political prisoners who, having been released from labor camps—it is 1952, the year
before Stalin's death—are still required to live in Siberia in the immediate
darkness of the horrors of the Gulag and with the ever-present threat of
rearrest. The question which Berger and Bielski pose through the experiences
of the characters is "How can people, deprived of everything which we
understand by security continue to survive, and not only survive, but make
meaning of their lives?" The making of choices, however immediate as opposed to the traditionally heroic; the intimacy of friendship and love; the will
to bear witness: these oppose the logic of the Gulag, these reject that which
the "Zeks" (the political prisoners) were to have become. The will to bear
witness entails holding onto the tenuous past and future in the experience of
the present; but the sense of space—"a question of geography"—is definitive
of the present from the scale of a continent to that of the body. Consider the
exchange between Ernst, one of the Zeks, who as a doctor is allowed out of
the camp during the day and spends a few hours of "domestic" intimacy with
Dacha at her apartment, and Dacha's son, Sacha, who has come from Len-
ingrad to visit his mother whom he has not seen for fifteen years. The boy
has become involved with a man, a former sea captain, who plans a "heroic"
escape by sea across the Bering Straits to America.

> Ernst: The grains on which we live are invisible. You come here.
>   I'm not sure what a boy of your age thinks. . . . Probably
>   you find us colourless, a peculiar mix of passivity and ner-
>   vousness.
> Sacha: That's not true!
> Ernst: I'm sure you believe that somehow we can choose. Choose
>   like Ignatiev to put out to sea and cross the Bering Straits!
>   You are wrong. Ignatiev has been arrested. Here there are
>   no choices—choices as you imagine them.
> Sacha: None of you can choose?
> Ernst: Everything outside prevents it. The choices we make are
>   inside.[42]

Earlier, at the outset of the 1980s, I contested both those who saw Berger
still believing in the possibility of imminent radical change and those who

had begun to conclude that Berger had nothing to offer to contemporary political action.[43] It was my view that the former had failed to recognize the changes which had occurred in Berger's historical perspective. Despairing of urban-industrial life and impatient with democratic politics, Berger's intellectual struggle against cultural mystification, alienation, and amnesia had led him to the margins, or wake, of industrial-capitalist development, where he had discovered the peasants' culture of survival. Having himself acknowledged that the struggle against contemporary historical development would necessarily be a long one, he found in the culture of survival a historical perspective which "may well be better adapted to this long and harsh (struggle) than the continually reformed, disappointed, impatient progressive hope of an ultimate victory."[44] And, against those who saw Berger as ceasing to offer any direction, I argued that they had failed to recognize that he was working to redeem the practices of storytelling and remembrance— "another way of telling"—that they might be renewed to *rub history against the grain*.

Geoff Dyer has claimed that Berger is one of our greatest writers because his work affords us "a glimpse of ourselves, what we might become"; and in a sympathetic fashion, though less assured than Dyer of Berger's achievement, Bruce Robbins has written that although Berger does not actually provide us with a vision of the "global feeling" or experience, which Berger says he "can still imagine," nevertheless, he makes us "desire" it.[45] As I indicated at the outset, in the light of Berger's most recent writings I am somewhat less confident about his contribution. I continue to admire his storytelling, and his commitment to bearing witness deserves our utmost respect and reflection. In its best moments his writing is capable of making us desire the "worldwide solidarity" which, it should be recalled, Berger asserts is the only real alternative to the alienation and homelessness of the contemporary order. However, in conjuring up this desire in the way he does, it appears that Berger's perspective is trapped in the extremes of apocalypse and utopia. Perhaps this is the product of his bleak view of urban-industrial life and democratic politics,[46] and of his bearing witness to the elimination of the class of survivors from the European landscape—a process, it must be *remembered*, which, however tragic, is neither the Holocaust nor the Gulag. (I should make clear that I do not believe that Berger himself has ever forgotten this.)

The argument presented in a recent article by Berger should help illustrate the basis for my ambivalence. In the essay, Berger proclaims that the central political question of modern history has ceased to be that of "Who governs?" and has become that of "How to survive?" He acknowledges that the question of survival may seem "minimalist" but he insists that in fact it is "total."[47] And therein lies the problem. The circumstances in which we live in the industrial-capitalist and *democratic* West are not those of the Gulag (again, Berger knows that); the tyrannies we face are not those enforcing modes of accommodation alone. Admittedly, the question of survival must be at the forefront of our thinking, the horror and threat of nuclear war demand it. But that very prospect makes the question of survival inadequate and the question of *who* governs all-the-more crucial, for should the day of nuclear destruction come, there will be *no* choice, *no* accommodation, *no* hope. Moreover, the danger exists that the proposition of the question of survival in terms of a "maximalist" vision of fear/hope will merely contribute further to the political resignation currently characteristic of capitalist democracies.[48]

Nevertheless, I am not prepared to divorce myself from his project, for whatever my concerns about the implications of his current historical and political perspective, he continues to assert the necessity of historical thought and consciousness—"a sense of history has become a condition of our survival"—against those voices, right and left, which would so eagerly break with the past. Indeed, in spite of his too ready displacement of the question, "Who governs?" with that of "How to survive?" I most definitely do subscribe to his closing remarks of the same article:

> The most urgent task today for those intellectuals who might once have been traditional intellectuals is to invoke the historical experience of the ruled, to underwrite their self-respect, and to proffer—not to display—intellectual confidence.

I would merely add—and, I assume, Berger would agree—that this is not only to support the struggle for survival but at the very same time the struggle over *who governs*.[49]

8

PAST AND PRESENT:
NOTES ON HISTORY AND POLITICS

The Death of the Past?

It is more than twenty years since the original publication of J. H. Plumb's
The Death of the Past (1969).[1] Still in print and widely read by students and
others, we might well ask in what ways its arguments remain relevant. In the
book, whose chapters originated as lectures, Plumb sought to comprehend
what he perceived to be the ongoing collapse of our *grand governing narratives* (a term he did not himself use)—defined by the late Terrence Des Pres
as the "presiding fictions that allow us to behold ourselves and make sense of
the historical world"[2]—and, thence, to draw out its implications for the
scholarly and intellectual practices of historians. It was Plumb's contention
that across all areas of our experience "the hold of the past is weakening." He
made very clear that he understood "the past" and "history" to be two very
different things. Whereas the former is "ideology," formulated to "control
individuals, motivate societies, or inspire classes," history is a critical intellectual activity pursuing "what happened, purely in its own terms and not in
the service of religion or national destiny, or morality, or the sanctity of institutions."[3]

Plumb referred to the place of the past in the lives of all social strata but,
in particular, he treated the continual relationship between the past and the
powerful. This was characteristic not only of ancient and medieval orders.
With a view toward the modern world he wrote that "every literate society
which has so far existed has needed to use the past for the same fundamental
purpose. The past has always been the handmaid of authority."[4]

Nevertheless, Plumb insisted, today "the past is dying," citing as evidence
the spreading debility of the governing narratives of religion, both Christian
and Marxist, and those of nation-states, such as the English-Liberal Whig
interpretation of history, the French Revolutionary and Napoleonic traditions, and, increasingly, the American sense of exceptionalism with its visions

of equal opportunity and Manifest Destiny. He explained the enfeeblement of the past as being due to modernization, especially the revolutions in science, technology, and geography. These, he said, had the effect of revising the West's conception of both its own past and that of humanity: "The past acquired multiplicity, both in time and place."[5] The dramatic and traumatic events and experiences of the present century have merely amplified this.

Also crucial to undermining "the past," he claimed, and very much bound up with the Western-initiated revolutions of modernity, has been the development and pursuit of *history*, "the attempt to see things as they were, irrespective of what conflicts this might create with what the wise ones of one's own society might make of the past." History, in other words, is subversive, or, as Plumb himself appreciatively put it, "destructive," noting the irony that "History, which is so deeply concerned with the past, has, in a sense helped to destroy it as a social force, as a synthesizing and comprehensive statement of human destiny."[6] But it was not to be left at that, for the demise of the past liberates historians to play a more constructive role.

Clearly revealing his optimism, Plumb openly proclaimed his belief in *progress*: "It is to me the one truth of history that the condition of mankind has improved, materially alas more than morally, but nevertheless both have improved." Having contributed to the undoing of "the past," *here,* according to Plumb, lies the new task for historians: "Man's success has derived from his application of reason . . . and it is the duty of the historian to teach this, to proclaim it, to demonstrate it in order to give humanity some confidence in a task that will still be cruel and long." He then proceeded to argue that although history can no longer fortify the pasts of the powers-that-be, it "can still teach wisdom, and it can teach it in a far deeper sense than was possible when wisdom had to be taught through the example of heroes." In this way Plumb looked forward to the possibility that while "the past has only served the few; perhaps history may serve the multitude."[7]

Two decades later we can see that Plumb was too optimistic. First, he had, arguably, too much faith in his colleagues, for historiographical studies have revealed not only that the work of honest scholars has frequently reflected or been made to reflect the needs of the governing classes (out of whose ranks historians often emerged) but, also, that historians themselves have all-too-frequently been eagerly recruited to their projects—in the blunt words of Hugh Trevor-Roper, "Historians in general are great toadies of power." Second, Plumb failed to see the way in which a "scientific" and "progressive" view of society and history might itself entail a "past," a governing narrative which would function as an ideology bolstering the authority and status of the "new class" of technocrats and managers and their corporate and bureaucratic masters. Third, Plumb seemed not to recognize, as David Lowenthal and others have reminded us, that the past is all around us: "the past is not dead, as J. H. Plumb would have it, it is not even sleeping. A mass of memories and records, of relics and replicas, of monuments and memorabilia, lives at the core of our being."[8] (As if we needed to be reminded in this age of heritage and nostalgia!) And, to return to the political vein, neither did Plumb realize that the contemporary exhaustion of the grand governing narratives heralded not the termination of the past but a condition more akin to what he had himself referred to in speaking of earlier political and social crises, that is, "warring pasts"—conflicts in which historians would seem to have a crucial part to play!

Indeed, recent years have provided powerful reminders that even if our grand narratives have become problematic, the past is far from moribund and the relations between the past and power, and history and politics, remain intimate. Surely, the most dramatic reminder of the use and abuse of the past was to be that of the Soviet Union where, as part of *glasnost* and *perestroika*, Gorbachev called upon scholars to "fill in the blank pages" of the country's history, realizing that the success of the reforms being initiated required a critical confrontation with the legacy of Stalin and his successors—a past which was continuing to shape (and, no doubt, will continue to haunt) the present and future. As we would expect, after decades of suppressing the truth or making it adhere to Marxist-Leninist orthodoxy, the process of "retrospective openness and restructuring" was to be painful and threatening— equally so to Soviet historians themselves, most of whom had for many years followed the dictates of the state, but who, after some initial hesitation, seemed to enthusiastically take up the challenge. At the same time, we should expect to see a new wave of creations of "the past" as the governors of the several republics emerging from the Soviet Union, or Empire, seek to assert or reassert their national identities and destinies.[9] Closely related to events in the Soviet Union, of course, have been those taking place in Eastern—or, as it has been urged in various quarters—*Central* Europe. There the past and history also have been pivotal. For example, in Poland and the now-independent Baltic Republics much seemed to hang on the period and experience of the Hitler-Stalin Pact; and in Hungary the 1956 "Revolution" was central to the call by the oppositional Committee for Historical Justice for "objective, multifaceted historical reconstruction" of the country's development since 1945.[10]

Of course, it might well be protested that Plumb's thesis about the death of the past was advanced as a description of the liberal-democratic West *not* the now-collapsed Soviet bloc (and, even less so, China, where the suppression of the 1989 student movement for democracy has been accompanied by an Orwellian suppression of history). Yet struggles over the past have also been center-stage in the West. In the course of the 1980s, the West German Christian Democratic government of Chancellor Helmut Kohl—which was later to be the prime political beneficiary of the bringing down of the Berlin Wall and the rush to German reunification—was extremely eager to develop a more conservative and "patriotic" national identity among the country's citizens and it showed itself to be quite willing to recruit the past to its purposes, even finding support for its efforts among various neo-conservative historians whose writings attempted to "normalize" the German past by relativizing or, in certain cases, rationalizing and, thereby, "justifying" Hitler's war and the Holocaust.[11] Similarly, in Japan a new nationalism has been pursued by the long-ruling conservative Liberal Democratic Party, entailing certain revisions of Japanese history, including the omission from school texts of the atrocities committed by the Japanese military during the Second World War.[12]

Then, too, there have been the Thatcher and Reagan (now Major and Bush) regimes, in which they and their New Right supporters have mobilized and sought to impose particular renditions of our respective national histories as part of still larger projects to further undo the increasingly problematic postwar social democratic and liberal consensuses, reverse the social changes wrought in the 1960s, *and* fashion a new, conservative, capitalist hegemony. Here we should also note the occasion of the Bicentennial of the French Revolution, for the public discourse of the Western political elites, assisted by the corporate media and "fashionable" historians, communicated not so much a celebration as a funeral. Indeed, it was to be the burial not only of the French but of all social revolutions; not so much in the interest of history as to broadcast the supposed "end of history." As Daniel Singer observed of the rhetoric forthcoming: "The age of revolution is over. There was history, but it has no future. The reign of capital is eternal."[13]

In the light of both the aforementioned criticisms and the events and developments transpiring since its publication one might well wonder what is left of any substance in *The Death of the Past*. Plumb's view of historical "improvement" or "progress," and his proposal that in the wake of the demise of the past the historian's task becomes that of testifying to it, must surely be treated warily (if not, as the conservative British historian, Geoffrey Elton, originally demanded, rejected).

I am not, however, prepared to discard Plumb's book, for even if it is not the model he had optimistically intended us to follow, *The Death of the Past* does afford us a persistently relevant vision of historical practice. Having focused attention at the outset on the continuous efforts by the powers-that-be to fashion and secure renditions of the past which legitimate and enhance their rule, *and* stressing the inherent antagonism between critical history and those "pasts," Plumb—although, arguably, exaggerating the commitment of historians past (and present) to pursue it—forwards to us a conception of historical practice in which the primary challenge for historians is that of confronting and contesting the myths of the rulers (and, too, those of the ruled!), a conception of history very much in the democratic spirit of "serving the multitude."

Yet, I would amend Plumb's argument. In view of developments in historiography these last two decades, especially the pursuit of history "from the bottom up," I would contend that the project of *critical* historians—to invoke the powers of the *historical* past—is both destructive *and* constructive.

The End of History?

The publication and promotion of an article entitled "The End of History?" in the summer of 1989 in the neo-conservative journal, *The National Interest,* sparked a storm of controversy, prompting numerous scholarly commentaries here and abroad, and filling pages of weekly newsmagazines and daily newspapers.[14] But scholars, at least, too often missed the real significance of the ruckus. At issue, ultimately, is not just the particular thesis of the article, but also the state and practice of academic scholarship in disciplines like history, *and* the role of scholars in the creation of public discourse and political thought.

Clearly inspired by the remarkable events in the Soviet bloc stemming from *glasnost* and *perestroika,* the article in *The National Interest* was written by Francis Fukuyama, (then) deputy director of the State Department's policy planning staff and a former Rand Corporation analyst.[15] Mr. Fukuyama argued that what we are seeing is not simply the "end of ideology" or a "convergence between capitalism and socialism," but the "unabashed victory of economic and political liberalism."

The point for scholars is that the political origins and overtones of his argument also figure in a dilemma that historians and historical social scientists have been confronting in their work. For some time, historians have been debating what to do about the so-called "crisis of history," that is, the paradox that in an era in which popular demand for historical "roots" has risen and in which, by most accounts, historical scholarship has been flourishing, there has also been an apparent devaluation and decline in its study at all levels of education. Perceiving their growing marginality, historians have not failed to propose strategies to return history to the center of educational and public life. Unfortunately, however, they have focused only on the problem of the social and professional "status" of their discipline, ignoring the fact that the "crisis" has a *political* component. What we must do is to forge a grander and more critical conception of the role which history might play in schooling and public culture.[16]

Both the Fukuyama article and the crisis of history originated in the same political project, an attack by neo-conservatives on what had been, since the Second World War, a liberal consensus in scholarship and public life. For Francis Fukuyama, the "end of history" means the end of historical development—the lasting triumph of Western capitalist democracy. Self-consciously invoking the theories of German philosopher Georg Friedrich Hegel, Fukuyama states, "What we may be witnessing is not just the end of the Cold War but . . . the end point of mankind's ideological evolution and the universalization of Western liberal democracy as the final form of human government."[17] In short, this article represents the latest attempt by the neo-conservative and intellectual Right to create a new, postliberal consensus. Emerging in the course of the dramatic political and economic events of the 1970s—defeat in Vietnam, the oil and energy crisis, Watergate and the end of the long postwar economic boom (variously referred to as the "crisis of legitimacy," "twilight of authority," and "crisis of democracy")—and inspired by the fear that the new social movements and labor in unison with Left intellectuals might form a broad Left coalition, a New Right coalition of old and new conservatives effectively mobilized the frustrations and anxieties of the time.

Having captured the Republican Party and the Presidency in the 1970s, along with a host of other elective offices, the New Right ever since has been trying to translate its political successes into a new national consensus. This effort—what Marxists call "the struggle for hegemony"—has necessarily entailed fashioning a new grand governing narrative. We have seen this effort aggressively pursued for a decade now. Remember that a prime ideological practice of the Reagan Administration, initiated by the President himself, was the incessant use and abuse of "the past" to legitimate its domestic and foreign-policy initiatives. For example, recall not only Reagan's construction of a supposedly "lost" America which prevailed some time before "the sixties" and/or the New Deal of the 1930s (depending upon his audience) but, also, his continual reference to the Nicaraguan Contras as "freedom fighters" in the tradition of the "Founding Fathers" of the United States, and his even cruder statements regarding his visit to the Bitburg cemetery in 1985, comparing Nazi SS officers with the victims of the concentration camps.

On campus, neo-conservatives have sought to revise and reorient the teaching of history and the cultural past by using the "crisis of history," with the concomitant decline in student interest and enrollments, to serve their cause. Essentially directed against the work of social historians (who have been, broadly speaking, on the Left), the neo-conservative attack asserted that the way history was taught in the 1960s and 1970s had produced a decline in Americans' knowledge of their own history and the Western tradition, undermining our common culture and "shared values" and threatening our national welfare and security. The curricula that they have advanced to deal with the crisis propose an acritical and almost one-dimensional narrative in which the United States is seen as direct heir to the "Western Heritage" and its final fruition. Perhaps even more significant, the curricula they offer ignore the underside of American and world history and their historic traditions of dissent and struggle from below. There is, indeed, a crisis of historical understanding, but it is not necessarily the one enunciated by the New Right.

The end-of-history thesis emanates from this New Right and neo-conservative attempt to fashion a new political consensus and governing narrative, and now after ten years of rule by the Right, one specifically intended to sanctify the present order of things. The goal is to portray it as the culmination of history, the best of all possible worlds, beyond which the choice is either more of the same or economic and political retrogression.

In such terms, the crisis of history is not simply about the status of the discipline, but, even more importantly, the very purpose and promise of historical study and thought. For, beyond the historical discipline, what is ultimately at stake in our response to the crisis is the vision of the past, present, and possible future which will prevail in our public culture and discourse. The questions we should be asking ourselves are: Is the study of the past and its relations with the present to be pursued for the sake of creating a consensus in favor of the world as it is? Or, is it to be pursued so as to enhance critical reflection on the past and the present in order to better inform our own deliberations and agency with the experiences, struggles, and aspirations of previous generations as we seek to make new history?

Against historians as consensus-builders I would advance a vision of historians as social critics, invoking the *powers of the past*—perspective, critique, consciousness, remembrance, and imagination—to comprehend and consider the present in order to contribute to the charting of new directions in the future. It is not a matter of restoring the old liberal consensus about the triumph of the Welfare State nor the historiography which accompanied it. The conflicts of class, race, and gender we have been witnessing in American society for over a generation now, as well as the pluralistic historical studies accomplished, should warn us against a simple synthesis.

The answers we bring to the crisis should also condition how we respond to the controversy surrounding Francis Fukuyama's article. What should be the response of historians, especially those of us who, unlike Fukuyama, do not believe that the contemporary social and political order, even in its most advanced and humane liberal-democratic form, represents the end or culmination of history? Some writers would argue that critical historians should take the lead in developing a new historical synthesis, a new governing narrative, to be conveyed to students and the general public. I am not so sure that will work. As neo-conservatives themselves may be learning, such an initiative depends on the existence of a consensus or movement toward it—something that appears to be missing thus far, and fortunately so, for given the politics of the day, it would likely be supportive of the powers that be. At the same time, I am *not* arguing, as do some postmodern philosophers, that we have transcended the age of grand narratives or stories. But they simply cannot be spun out by historians.

Thus, it appears all-the-more necessary to recall the conception of historical practice that originally attracted so many of us to the discipline in the

1960s and early 1970s, a vision of critical scholarly and pedagogical activities linked to the experiences and struggles of working people and the oppressed. In part this means continuing the labors we have been pursuing—revealing the structures and relations of exploitation and oppression past and present, *and* recovering "from the bottom up" the lives and voices of those who have suffered and resisted them. But this alone is not adequate, and here we should recognize what the neo-conservative and intellectual Right has already proposed: history and politics are intimate. It is not enough, therefore, to merely recover these histories. They must be *communicated* and in that fashion *connected* to the experiences and aspirations of people today. In this way, I would argue, we might contribute to the development of a new "politics" out of which there might be engendered a new, more original narrative envisioning not the end of history but the extension and continuing development of the ideals and relations of liberty, equality, and democratic community.

The Death of Marxism?

What an exciting and worrisome time to be alive. As Charles Dickens observed of an earlier age: "It was the best of times, it was the worst of times, it was the age of wisdom, it was the age of foolishness. . . ." And how especially enthralling for Marxist historians—that is, for those of us whose comprehension of the making of socialism is that it entails the extension and refinement of the classical ideals of the Age of Revolution: liberty, equality, and democratic community.

The collapse of communism, of the Soviet bloc or empire, and the related termination of the Cold War dramatically revise the contemporary world and our sense of possibility *and* anxiety about the future. These developments will, and should, have a significant impact on the writing of history. Of course, this will be so far more in certain fields—such as "Soviet," Russian, Ukrainian . . . and East European Studies, and American foreign and military affairs—than in others.

The real question presented here, however, is the supposed "death of Marxism." We must begin by restating what has been apparent in intellectual and academic arenas for some time (in spite of the best efforts by neo-conservative and New Right figures to portray it otherwise): there has been no single Marxism, no *one* Marxist theory and thought. Aside from the absurd and comical carryings on of the so-called Marxist splinter groups and currents, there has emerged, especially since the 1960s, a diverse and in many ways rich variety of "marxisms" shaped, respectively, by the intellectual disciplines in which they have emerged, the theoretical ideas upon which they have drawn, and the problems they have sought to engage and address. Just consider the differences determined by the academic division of labor: political economy, sociology, anthropology, literary and cultural studies, philosophy, *and,* as E. P. Thompson proclaimed, "the queen of the Humanities," history (though my more radical-democratic Americanism prefers a less monarchical imagery).

Marxism as dogma, doctrine, orthodoxy, or set of transhistorical laws deserved to be buried long ago, and the East European revolutions of 1989 along with the dissolution of the Soviet Union in late 1991 have, in this respect, merely piled more rubble on its grave. Unfortunately, as a consequence of the propaganda campaigns long waged by Cold War politicians and ideologues equating *all* Marxist thought and study with the ideology— and I use this term in its harshest sense—of Marxism-Leninism-Stalinism and the horrors and brutalities it was intended to rationalize, it is quite likely that the various traditions (not all of which, admittedly, are to be celebrated) of Marxian enquiry and scholarship will find themselves further alienated from public culture and discourse and holding out in the academic and university centers where they have been developing for a generation and more. *Or might it be otherwise?*

Though not at all sufficient as it is, Marxian thought continues to offer the most critical questions or hypotheses with which to engage past and present. In particular, what better place is there to start one's exploration and study of history—whatever time or place—than with a social order's relations of exploitation and oppression and how they shape and determine human experience and agency and, indeed, how these are expressed in manifold forms of "class" and other modes of struggle? Actually, it is rather remarkable, after what we have seen both in the United States and in Britain for almost a generation now, that such an approach to history has not come to be the dominant popular discourse. I refer here to what has clearly been, as shown by all the standard indices, a decade and more of "the rich getting richer, the poor getting poorer." Moreover, this has not been a process transpiring merely at the margins, that is, an experience lived by the poor and homeless at one end of the hierarchy and by those who pursue the lifestyle of the rich and famous at the other—leading American observers and critics to speak of a "decade of greed" and, their British counterparts, of a return to "Two Nations." It was a central feature of the radical "politics of inequality," the political economies of class, pursued by the Reagan Administration and the Thatcher Government. In fact, what we have seen—in decided contrast to the liberal and social-democratic settlements and consensuses of the postwar period (1945–70s)—has been a "class war from above" entailing the defeat of the American and British labour movements and the fragmentation of the "new social movements" (feminism, anti-imperialism, environmentalism, consumerism) which arose in the course of the long decade of the sixties. We too often assume that class conflict is something which erupts into more organized and vehement forms *from below,* but we should realize from our historical study that "class politics" in its most identifiable modes usually commences *from above* in such phenomena as "revolts of the nobility." The work which many of us have accomplished on the 1970s reveals just such a moment.[18]

In this vein, the continuing worth of a Marxist perspective on past and present, especially, what I have elsewhere termed, *class-struggle analysis,* applies no less to the past forty-five years of East European and Soviet life. The structures and practices of exploitation and oppression which characterized those states warrant serious study and, indeed, the risings and upheavals which brought an end to Communist dictatorship and rule should be especially intriguing and challenging to Marxian historians and historical-social scientists. The actions and struggles of workers and intellectuals in Poland (Solidarity was one of the clearest cases of radical working-class struggle of the latter half of the twentieth century!) and throughout the "region" are just the sort of movements we have been *expecting,* however *surprising* to us they were.[19]

I could proceed to cite chapter and verse directly from Marx and Engels, attesting to their prescience. *The Communist Manifesto* is not only of *historic* interest but remains particularly apposite as a starting point for an *historical* appreciation of the development of capitalism as a revolutionary mode of production. The development of the world economy since the fifteenth century, now increasingly characterized by global corporations whose operations, priorities, and identities apparently transcend the "particular" interests of the nation-states out of which they grew, is captured especially well in its pages. Never have I felt that prescience is a characteristic to be admired in a historian whatever the theoretical persuasion, but it does imply that the questions and insights which Marx and Engels proffered remain most worthy of serious consideration as we try to make sense of the making of the modern world.

A Marxian approach to past and present is all-the-more imperative in the face of the initiatives on the part of the political and economic elites—in the ancient and grand tradition of ruling classes—to present the contemporary world as the *culmination* of history. In this respect, the more than decade-long use *and* abuse of the past by Reagan, Thatcher and associates; their campaigns to redirect American and British historical curricula *to the Right* under the guise of the (indeed necessary!) reinvigoration of historical education; and the recent emergence of the "end-of-history" thesis are all of a piece. Arising from the same aspiration, that of creating conservative consensuses, they are intended as contributions to the fabrication of governing narratives which legitimate the status quo and the rule of corporate capital, and, at their most hopeful, see the present *as* future.

Practiced critically, Marxian historical study and thought has invoked and wielded the *powers of the past*—perspective, critique, consciousness, remembrance, and imagination—against the freezing or closure of history by the powers that be. By *perspective* I mean the understanding that the way things are is not the way they have always been nor the way they will, or must, be in the future. *Critique* is more specific, entailing a deliberate notion of "breaking the tyranny of the present" by revealing its *social* as opposed to supposedly extra-human origins. *Consciousness* refers to an appreciation of the making of history, an awareness, as Antonio Gramsci put it, of "the sum of effort and sacrifice which the present has cost the past and which the future is costing the present." *Remembrance* acknowledges, as John Berger reflected, that while "the past is not for living in, it is a well of conclusions from which we draw in order to act." And *imagination* insists that we comprehend the structure, movement, and possibilities in the contemporary order of things and consider how we might act to prevent the barbaric and develop the humanistic.

Here, I necessarily have in mind and point again to the work of that generation of British Marxists which includes Rodney Hilton, Eric Hobsbawm, George Rudé, Christopher and Bridget Hill, Edward and Dorothy Thompson, John Saville, and Victor Kiernan. Writing "from the bottom up" these historians revealed the historicity of modern Britain and the industrial-capitalist world and both the experience and agency of the common people in its making and the values and visions which motivated them, and that might yet be relevant as we deliberate and act upon history. There are those who would deny the value and strength of the historiography developed by the British Marxist historians and now being carried forward on both sides of the Atlantic by younger generations. We hear such declamations not only from those of the Right, who persist in their McCarthyite rhetoric but, also, from those who, claiming to speak from the Left, contend that we live in a *post*modern age in which there is no continuity between past and present and no reason to hope that the future might yet be different, and thus in effect, also serve the powers-that-be by offering a mirror image of the end-of-history thesis. Of course, changes in Marxist historical study and thought are in order, urgently so. As Christopher Hill once wrote: "History has to be rewritten in every generation, because although the past does not change the present does; each generation asks new questions of the past, and finds new areas of sympathy as it re-lives different aspects of its predecessors." Or, once again, as George Rudé persistently has reminded us, in the very words of Marx and Engels: "All history must be studied afresh."

And yet, the project remains that of pursuing the historical education of desire.

NOTES

Introduction

1. On these developments in Britain, see Andrew Gamble, *The Free Economy and the Strong State* (London, 1988). For those in the U.S.A., see Sydney Blumenthal, *The Rise of the Counter-Establishment* (New York, 1986); Sydney Blumenthal and Thomas Byrne Edsall, eds., *The Reagan Legacy* (New York, 1988); and Philip Mattera, *Prosperity Lost* (New York, 1990). Also, for a comparative study, see Joel Krieger, *Reagan, Thatcher and the Politics of Decline* (New York, 1986).

2. See, for example, Ralf Dahrendorf, *Reflections on the Revolution in Europe* (New York, 1990), and Paul Starr, "Liberalism After Socialism," *The American Prospect* 7 (Fall 1991), pp. 70–80. But, also, for a welcome and highly "public" reassertion of the democratic ideals and imperatives of socialism, see Paul Berman, "Still Sailing the Lemonade Sea," *New York Times Magazine*, 27 October 1991, pp. 32–34, 78–79.

3. See Krieger, *Reagan, Thatcher and the Politics of Decline*, p. 23; Edward Greenberg, *Capitalism and the American Political Ideal* (New York, 1985); and Alan Wolfe, *The Limits of Legitimacy* (New York, 1977).

4. For a somewhat similar assessment of American political culture, see Jeffrey C. Goldfarb, *The Cynical Society* (Chicago, 1991).

5. For such an argument regarding "schooling," see Harvey J. Kaye, "Should the Fact That We Live in A Democracy Make A Difference in What Our Schools Are Like?" in Joe Kincheloe, ed., *Thirteen Questions: New Perspectives on American Education* (New York, 1992).

6. Fred Halliday, "The Ends of Cold War," *New Left Review* 180 (March–April 1990), p. 23.

7. See E. P. Thompson, *William Morris: Romantic to Revolutionary* (New York, 1976; originally published in 1955), esp. pp. 717–30. And on the necessity, or purpose and promise, of critical historical study and thought, see Harvey J.

Kaye, *The Powers of the Past: Reflections on the Crisis and the Promise of History* (London, 1991).

8. Harvey J. Kaye, *The British Marxist Historians: An Introductory Analysis* (Oxford, 1984).

9. H. J. Kaye, ed., *The Face of the Crowd: Selected Essays of George Rudé* (London, 1988); *History, Classes and Nation-States: Selected Writings of V. G. Kiernan* (Oxford, 1988); and *Poets, Politics and the People: Selected Writings of V. G. Kiernan* (London, 1989). Two additional volumes of Kiernan's essays are projected; the first will be a collection of his writings on imperialism, and the second will be those on intellectuals.

10. Michael Walzer, *Interpretation and Social Criticism* (Cambridge, Mass., 1987), and *The Company of Critics* (New York, 1988).

Chapter One

This chapter is a revised version of an article which originally appeared in *Italian Quarterly* 97–98 (Summer–Fall 1984).

1. E. H. Carr, *What is History?* (New York, 1961), p. 142.

2. See Harvey J. Kaye, *The British Marxist Historians: An Introductory Analysis* (Oxford, 1984).

3. See, for examples, Eric Hobsbawm, *The Forward March of Labour Halted?* (London, 1981); and E. P. Thompson, *Writing by Candlelight* (London, 1980), *Exterminism and Cold War* (London, 1982), and *The Heavy Dancers* (London, 1985).

4. Karl Marx, *The Poverty of Philosophy* (New York, 1963), p. 174.

5. These points are made throughout Marx and Engels, *The Manifesto of the Communist Party;* see K. Marx, *The Revolutions of 1848,* ed. David Fernbach (New York, 1974), pp. 65, 79, 80. Also, see the discussion in Ralph Miliband, *Marxism and Politics* (Oxford, 1977), pp. 17–41, 117–21.

6. In the days during which I was revising and preparing this chapter there was an unsuccessful coup in the Soviet Union against the presidency of Mikhail Gorbachev. Although defeated, the coup instigated the dissolution of the U.S.S.R. and the Soviet state in favor of "independent republics" from the Baltic to Central Asia.

7. For a basic survey of Marxist ideas about this question, see John Molyneux, *Marxism and the Party* (London, 1978).

8. The essential study of Marx is David McLellan, *Karl Marx: His Life and Thought* (London, 1973).

9. For one of the British Marxist historians on Lenin, see Christopher Hill, *Lenin and the Russian Revolution* (Harmondsworth, 1971). But note, this book was originally written in 1947.

10. V. I. Lenin, *What Is To Be Done?* (Moscow, 1947), pp. 31–32.

11. Georg Lukács, *History and Class Consciousness* (London, 1971; originally published in 1922).

12. Herbert Marcuse, *One Dimensional Man* (London, 1964), and Louis Althusser, "Ideology and Ideological State Apparatuses," in *Lenin and Philosophy* (London, 1971). Also see on this problem Martin Jay, *Marxism and Totality* (Berkeley, 1984).

13. See Rosa Luxemburg, *The Russian Revolution and Leninism or Marxism?*, ed. Bertram Wolfe (Ann Arbor, 1971).

14. Eric Hobsbawm, "The Great Gramsci," *New York Review of Books,* 4 April 1974, p. 39.

15. See Harvey J. Kaye, "Antonio Gramsci: An Annotated Bibliography of Studies in English," *Politics and Society* 10 (1981), pp. 335–53, and Geoff Eley, "Reading Gramsci in English: Observations on the Reception of Antonio Gramsci in the English-speaking World 1957–82," *European History Quarterly* 14 (1984), pp. 441–78. On Gramsci's life and political work, see John M. Cammett, *Antonio Gramsci and the Origins of Italian Communism* (Stanford, 1967); G. Fiori, *Antonio Gramsci, Life of a Revolutionary* (London, 1970); and Dante Germino, *Antonio Gramsci* (Baton Rouge, 1990).

16. There are now several excellent discussions of Gramsci's thought: Walter L. Adamson, *Hegemony and Revolution: Antonio Gramsci's Political and Cultural Theory* (Berkeley, 1980); Joseph V. Femia, *Gramsci's Political Thought* (Oxford, 1981); Leonard Salamini, *The Sociology of Political Praxis* (London, 1981); and Carl Boggs, *The Two Revolutions: Gramsci and the Dilemmas of Western Marxism* (Boston, 1984).

17. See Gramsci's essay, "The Revolution Against Capital," in P. Cavalcanti and P. Piccone, eds., *History, Philosophy and Culture in the Young Gramsci* (St. Louis, 1975). For examples of Gramsci's writings, see *Selections from the Prison Notebooks,* ed. Q. Hoare and G. Smith (London, 1971); *Selections from Political Writings (1910–20)* (New York, 1977); *Selections from Political Writings (1921–26)* (New York, 1978); and *Selections from Cultural Writings* (Cambridge, Mass., 1985).

18. Quoted in Femia, *Gramsci's Political Thought,* p. 42 from Gramsci's *Prison Notebooks.*

19. On the concept of "ideology," see Terry Eagleton, *Ideology* (London, 1991). Though I do not agree fully with their arguments, see the survey offered by N. Abercrombie, S. Hill, and B. Turner, *The Dominant Ideology Thesis* (London, 1980).

20. Eugene Genovese, "A Reply to Criticism," *Radical History Review* 3 (Winter 1977), p. 98. In this context it must be noted that one of the finest historical analyses of a hegemonic process is, arguably, Genovese's *Roll, Jordan, Roll: The World The Slaves Made* (New York, 1974).

21. Femia, *Gramsci's Political Thought,* p. 43.

22. Gramsci, *Prison Notebooks,* p. 326.

23. Ibid., pp. 327, 333.

24. Ibid., pp. 330–31.

25. See Jerome Karabel, "Revolutionary Contradictions: Antonio Gramsci and the Problem of Intellectuals," *Politics and Society* 6 (1976), pp. 123–72.

26. Gramsci, *Prison Notebooks*, pp. 355, 353.

27. Ibid., pp. 324, 411, 465, 436–37, 449, 369. Also, see Esteve Morera, *Gramsci's Historicism* (London, 1990).

28. See Gramsci's *Letters from Prison*, translated, edited and introduced by Lynne Lawner (New York, 1973), pp. 79–82. Also, see J. A. Davis, ed., *Gramsci and Italy's Passive Revolution* (London, 1979).

29. Gramsci, *Prison Notebooks*, pp. 344–45. A native of Turin, Piero Sraffa, the Cambridge economist, arranged an account to allow Gramsci to purchase books for himself while in prison. Also, he tried without success to secure a new trial for his dear friend.

30. Gramsci, *Letters from Prison*, p. 273.

31. Gramsci, *Prison Notebooks*, pp. 52–55, 96, 13.

32. One must note: in Britain, the works of Perry Anderson, "The Antinomies of Antonio Gramsci," *New Left Review* 100 (1976), pp. 5–78; Gwyn Williams, "Gramsci's Concept of 'egemonia,'" *Journal of the History of Ideas* 21 (December 1960), pp. 586–99, and *Proletarian Order: Antonio Gramsci and the Origins of Italian Communism* (London, 1975); in the United States, John Cammet, *Antonio Gramsci and the Origins of Italian Communism* (Stanford, 1967); and Eugene Genovese, "On Antonio Gramsci," in his *In Red and Black* (New York, 1971), pp. 391–422; and in Australia, Alistair Davidson, *Antonio Gramsci: Towards an Intellectual Biography* (London, 1977).

33. Carr, *What is History?*, p. 168.

34. See Troian Stoianovich, *French Historical Method: The Annales Paradigm* (Ithaca, 1976), and Peter Burke, *The French Historical Revolution: The Annales School, 1929–89* (Stanford, 1990).

35. Maurice Dobb, *Studies in the Development of Capitalism* (New York, 1946, rev. ed. 1963); Rodney Hilton, ed., *The Transition from Feudalism to Capitalism* (London, 1976); Immanuel Wallerstein, *The Modern World System*, vol. 1 (New York, 1974); Perry Anderson, *Lineages of the Absolutist State* (London, 1974); and T. H. Aston and C. H. E. Philpin, eds., *The Brenner Debate* (Cambridge, 1985).

36. See Kaye, *The British Marxist Historians*, esp. pp. 221–41.

37. Eric Hobsbawm, "Tthe Historians' Group of the Communist Party," in *Rebels and Their Causes*, ed. M. Cornforth (London, 1978), pp. 21–48.3

38. For writings on the historians by writers whose positions have been quite different than my own, see the two volumes produced by the Centre for Contemporary Cultural Studies: John Clarke, Chas Critcher, and Richard Johnson, eds., *Working Class Culture* (London, 1979), and R. Johnson, et al., eds., *Making Histories* (London, 1982).

39. Christopher Hill, "Antonio Gramsci," *The New Reasoner* 1 (Spring 1958), pp. 107–8. The essay was actually a review of *The Modern Prince and Other Writings* (London, 1957), a collection of Gramsci's writings edited by Louis Marks, one of Hill's former students.

40. Victor Kiernan, "Gramsci and Marxism," in H. J. Kaye, ed., *History, Classes and Nation-States* (Oxford, 1988), pp. 66–101; "Gramsci and Other Continents," *New Edinburgh Review* (1974), pt. 3, pp. 19–24; and "The Socialism of Antonio Gramsci," in K. Coates, ed., *Essays in Socialist Humanism* (Nottingham, 1972), pp. 63–89. I discuss Kiernan's work (and his considerations of Gramsci) in Chapter 3 of the present work.

41. Hobsbawm, "The Great Gramsci," and "Gramsci and Political Theory," *Marxism Today* 21 (July 1977), pp. 205–13. Hobsbawm's interview with Giorgio Napolitano of the Italian Communist Party, *The Italian Road to Socialism* (London, 1977), should also be noted in this context.

42. Eric Hobsbawm, *Primitive Rebels* (Manchester, 1971; originally published in 1959). See "Interview with Eric Hobsbawm," pp. 112–13, 115–16.

43. Eric Hobsbawm, *The Age of Capital, 1848–1875* (London, 1977), p. 15. For Hobsbawm's discussion of "hegemony" in this period see especially pp. 291–92. At the same time, it must be added that Joseph Femia criticizes Hobsbawm's application of "hegemony," because, he argues, Hobsbawm too readily equates it with "ideological predominance" and thus seems not to properly appreciate the complex and contradictory character of the process (Femia, *Gramsci's Political Thought*, pp. 23, 257 fn. 1).

44. "Interview with Eric Hobsbawm," *Radical History Review* 19 (Winter 1978–79), p. 123.

45. Anderson's instigating piece is "Origins of the Present Crisis," *New Left Review* 23, (Jan.–Feb. 1964), reprinted in P. Anderson and R. Blackburn, eds., *Towards Socialism* (London, 1965), pp. 11–52. Thompson's reply is "The Peculiarities of the English," originally in *The Socialist Register 1965*, reprinted in *The Poverty of Theory* (London, 1978, 4th impression), pp. 245–302. Anderson's response to Thompson's essay is "The Myths of Edward Thompson, or Socialism and Pseudo-National Culture," in A. Cockburn and R. Blackburn, eds., *Student Power* (Harmondsworth, 1969), pp. 214–84; also see Anderson's book, *Arguments Within English Marxism* (London, 1980). Nairn's essays are all in *New Left Review*: "The British Political Elite," vol. 23 (1964), pp. 19–25; "The English Working Class," vol. 24 (1964), pp. 23–57; "The Anatomy of the Labour Party," vols. 27 and 28 (1964), pp. 38–65 and 33–62. On the Thompson-Anderson exchange, see Keith Nield, "A Symptomatic Dispute? Notes on the Relation between Marxian Theory and Historical Practice in Britain," *Social Research* 47 (Autumn 1980), pp. 479–506.

46. Anderson, "Origins of the Present Crisis," p. 29.

47. See, for examples, Thompson's "The Moral Economy of the English Crowd in the Eighteenth Century," *Past & Present* 50 (February 1971), pp. 71–136; "Patrician Society, Plebeian Culture," *Journal of Social History,* 7 (Summer 1974), pp. 382–405; *Whigs and Hunters* (originally published in 1975; reprinted with

new postscript, Harmondsworth, 1977); and "Eighteenth Century English Society: Class Struggle Without Class?" *Social History,* 3 (May 1978), pp. 133–65. Thompson's long-awaited book on the eighteenth century, *Customs in Common,* will apparently be published in 1992.

48. Thompson's eighteenth-century studies are discussed at length in Kaye, *The British Marxist Historians,* pp. 193–203. Also, for a splendid example of the application of Gramsci's concept of hegemony to eighteenth-century England, see the essay by Thompson's colleague, Douglas Hay, "Property, Authority and the Criminal Law," in D. Hay, et al., eds., *Albion's Fatal Tree: Crime and Society in Eighteenth-century England* (New York, 1975), pp. 17–64.

49. E. P. Thompson, *The Making of the English Working Class,* (originally published in 1963; rev. ed. Harmondsworth, 1968).

50. Marc Bloch, *Feudal Society* (originally published in 1940; Chicago, 1961); M. M. Postan, *The Medieval Economy and Society* (Harmondsworth, 1975); and George Duby, *The Early Growth of the European Economy* (London, 1974).

51. John Merrington, "Town and Country in the Transition to Capitalism," in R. Hilton, ed., *The Transition from Feudalism to Capitalism,* p. 179.

52. Rodney Hilton, *Bond Men Made Free: Medieval Peasant Movements and the English Rising of 1381* (London, 1973).

53. Ibid., pp. 130–34, 220.

54. Ibid., p. 221.

55. Rodney Hilton, "Wat Tyler, John Ball, and the English Rising," *New Society,* 30 April 1981, p. 173.

56. Rodney Hilton, "The English Rising of 1381," *Marxism Today* (June 1981), p. 19.

57. Hilton, *Bond Men Made Free,* p. 235.

58. N. Cohn, *The Pursuit of the Millenium* (New York, 1961, rev. ed.), p. 217.

59. Hilton, "Wat Tyler, John Ball, and the English Rising," p. 173, and "The English Rising of 1381," p. 19.

60. Christopher Hill, *The World Turned Upside Down* (originally published in 1972; rev. ed. Harmondsworth, 1975), p. 15.

61. On the economy and social structure of the seventeenth century see Hill's *Reformation to Industrial Revolution: A Social and Economic History of Britain, 1530–1780* (Harmondsworth, 1969), pp, 44–60.

62. Gramsci, *Prison Notebooks,* p. 334.

63. Christopher Hill, *Society and Puritanism in Pre-Revolutionary England* (London, 1964), pp. 32–33.

64. Ibid., p. 38.

65. See Hill's "Puritans and 'the Dark Corners of the Land,'" in Hill, *Change and Continuity in Seventeenth-Century England* (Cambridge, Mass., 1975), pp. 3–47.

66. Hill, *Society and Puritanism,* p. 46.

67. Christopher Hill, *Intellectual Origins of the English Revolution* (Oxford, 1965), pp. 9, 87, 289.

68. See, on the last point, Hill's book, *Some Intellectual Consequences of the English Revolution* (Madison, Wis., 1980).

69. Hill, *The World Turned Upside Down*, p. 343. Also relevant on this are his writings, "The Norman Yoke," in *Puritanism and Revolution* (London, 1958), and *Antichrist in Seventeenth-Century England* (originally published in 1971; new ed. London, 1990).

70. Christopher Hill, "Why Bother about the Muggletonians?" in *The World of the Muggletonians* (London, 1983). Also, see his *The Experience of Defeat* (London, 1984), and *A Turbulent, Seditious and Factious People: John Bunyan and His Church* (Oxford, 1988)—in the U.S.A. it is titled *A Tinker and A Poor Man: John Bunyan and His Church* (New York, 1988).

71. Also, on Thompson, see Chapter 4 of the present work.

72. On Chartism, see Dorothy Thompson's book, *The Chartists* (New York, 1984).

73. Thompson, *The Making of the English Working Class*, p. 12.

74. Ibid., pp. 11–12.

75. Ibid., p. 9. Also, see Thompson's "Commitment in Politics," *Universities and Left Review* 6 (Spring 1959), pp. 50–55.

76. Ibid., p. 86.

77. Ibid., pp. 84–110.

78. Ibid., esp. pp. 780–820 on "The Radical Culture."

79. It is not my intention to derogate trade unionism, but only to insist that working people have not only been capable of establishing trade unions but also of fashioning a vision of an alternative social order and a means of achieving it.

80. George Rudé, *Ideology and Popular Protest* (New York, 1980).

81. On Rudé's book and American labor studies, see Jim Green, "Culture, Politics, and the Workers' Response to Industrialization in the U.S.," *Radical America* 16 (January/April 1982), pp. 101–28.

82. E. H. Carr, *The New Society* (London, 1951), p. 18.

83. Kaye, *The British Marxist Historians*, esp. pp. 241–49.

84. Paolo Spriano, *Antonio Gramsci and the Party: The Prison Years* (London, 1979).

Chapter Two

This chapter originally appeared as my introduction to *The Face of the Crowd: Studies in Revolution, Ideology and Popular Protest—Selected Essays of George Rudé* (London: Harvester-Wheatsheaf of Simon & Schuster International; and Atlantic Highlands, N.J.: Humanities Press, 1988).

1. Paul Preston, "A Review of *Criminal and Victim*," *British Books News*, February 1986.

2. George Rudé, *The Crowd in the French Revolution* (Oxford, 1959; rev. ed. London, 1983); *Wilkes and Liberty* (Oxford, 1962; rev. ed. London, 1983); *The Crowd in History, 1730–1848* (New York, 1964; rev. ed. London, 1981); and *Paris and London in the Eighteenth Century* (London, 1970; U.S. ed., 1971).

3. George Rudé, *Revolutionary Europe, 1783–1815* (London, 1964; reprinted ed., 1967), and *Europe in the Eighteenth Century: Aristocracy and the Bourgeois Challenge* (London, 1972; paperback ed., 1974).

4. E. J. Hobsbawm and George Rudé, *Captain Swing* (London, 1969; rev. ed., 1973); and G. Rudé, *Protest and Punishment* (Oxford, 1978), and *Criminal and Victim* (Oxford, 1985).

5. On "history from below" or "the bottom up," see Harvey J. Kaye, *The British Marxist Historians: An Introductory Analysis* (Oxford, 1984), especially pp. 222–32. I prefer the term "history from the bottom up"; George Rudé prefers "from below." In this instance, I defer to him and will most often use "history from below."

6. For a complete bibliography of Rudé's books and articles, see Frederick Krantz, ed., *History from Below: Studies in Popular Protest and Popular Ideology in Honour of George Rudé* (Montreal, 1985), pp. 35–40.

7. I must acknowledge the introductory articles to Rudé's *Festschrift, History from Below* (referred to in note 6), in particular Frederick Krantz, "*'Sans érudition, pas d'histoire'*: The Work of George Rudé," and Hugh Stretton "George Rudé." Together, those two essays provide the most comprehensive survey of Rudé's writings, life, and thought, and I have referred to them at a variety of points in the writing of my own essay.

8. G. Rudé, *Robespierre* (London, 1975). Fred Krantz provides a full and appreciative discussion of this book in his essay, referred to in note 7.

9. The family name was actually Rude, without the accent, but George changed it while at school in England. This biographical sketch is drawn from conversations with George in 1986–87 in Green Bay (Wisconsin), Rye (Sussex), and Montreal (Canada); but also draws heavily on the essay by Hugh Stretton referred to in note 7.

10. See V. G. Kiernan, "Herbert Norman's Cambridge," in *E. H. Norman: His Life and Scholarship,* ed. R. Bowen (Toronto, 1984), pp. 25–45; reprinted in H. J. Kaye, ed., *Poets, Politics and the People: Writings of V. G. Kiernan,* vol. 2 (London, 1989).

11. For Rudé's comments on his fellow British Marxist historians, see "Marxism and History," in H. J. Kaye, ed., *The Face of the Crowd: Selected Essays of George Rudé* (London, 1988), pp. 43–55.

12. See, for example, Rudé, "Feudalism and the French Revolution," in ibid., pp. 124–34.

13. E. J. Hobsbawm, "The Historians' Group of the Communist Party," in *Rebels and Their Causes,* ed. M. Cornforth (London, 1978), p. 37.

14. See Rudé's recollections in "The Changing Face of the Crowd" (1970) in *The Face of the Crowd,* pp. 56–71.

15. For Rudé on Lefebvre's work, see his essay, "Georges Lefebvre as Historian of Popular Protest in the French Revolution" (1960) in ibid., pp. 107–14, and Rudé's introduction to Lefebvre's classic work, *The Great Fear of 1789* (Paris, 1932; English trans. London, 1973). Also, see Lefebvre's *The Coming of the French Revolution* (Princeton, 1947) with a preface by R. R. Palmer.

16. See Albert Soboul, *The Parisian Sans-Culottes and the French Revolution* (Paris, 1958; English trans. Oxford, 1964) and also his book, *The French Revolution, 1787–1799* (Paris, 1962; English trans. London, 1974).

17. See Richard Cobb, *The People's Armies* (1961; English trans. New Haven, 1987), and *Paris and Its Provinces* (Oxford, 1975). Cobb has been an extremely prolific scholar and writer; for a bibliography of his work, see the *Festschrift* in his honor, G. Lewis and C. Lucas, eds., *Beyond the Terror* (Cambridge, 1983).

18. For example, see Rudé's introduction to *Paris and London in the Eighteenth Century,* p. 12.

19. G. Rudé, "The Gordon Riots: A Study of the Rioters and their Victims," is reprinted in ibid., pp. 268–92.

20. See Stretton, "George Rudé," pp. 45–46. Also, on the crisis of 1956 and the reactions of the British Marxist historians, see Kaye, *The British Marxist Historians,* pp. 17–18.

21. G. Rudé, *Ideology and Popular Protest* (London, 1980).

22. G. Rudé, *The French Revolution* (London, 1988).

23. G. Rudé, *Europe in the Eighteenth Century,* p. 94.

24. G. Rudé, *The Crowd in the French Revolution,* p. 2, and *The Crowd in History,* p. 8.

25. G. Rudé, *The Crowd in the French Revolution,* p. 3, and *The Crowd in History,* p. 7.

26. G. Rudé, *The Crowd in the French Revolution,* p. 5 (my italics).

27. G. Rudé, *Paris and London,* p. 280, and *Wilkes and Liberty,* p. 15.

28. G. Rudé, *Paris and London,* p. 10.

29. G. Rudé, *The Crowd in History,* pp. 10–11.

30. Ibid., pp. 11–12. Rudé always gave primary importance to the archives, discussing them at the outset of his text, rather than in a footnote or appendix.

31. Barrington Moore, Jr., *Social Origins of Dictatorship and Democracy* (Boston, 1966), pp. 521–23.

32. G. Rudé, "The Changing Face of the Crowd," in Kaye, ed., *The Face of the Crowd,* p. 58.

33. G. Rudé, *The Crowd in the French Revolution,* p. 178.

34. G. Rudé, *Paris and London,* pp. 298–99.

35. Ibid., p. 129; *The Crowd in the French Revolution,* p. 181; and *Wilkes and Liberty,* p. 183.

36. G. Rudé, *Paris and London,* p. 19.

37. G. Rudé, *The Crowd in History*, pp. 5–6.

38. Ibid., pp. 259–60. This theme is further developed by E. P. Thompson in *The Making of the English Working Class* (London, 1963).

39. G. Rudé, "The French Revolution and Participation," in Kaye ed., *The Face of the Crowd*, pp. 146–47.

40. The term is taken from Charles Tilly, *The Contentious French* (Cambridge, Mass., 1986).

41. See Rudé's remarks in "The Changing Face of the Crowd" where he also discusses other criticisms of his work.

42. See E. J. Hobsbawm's *Primitive Rebels* (1959; rev. ed. Manchester, 1971), and *Labouring Men* (London, 1968). On Hobsbawm's work, see Kaye, *The British Marxist Historians*, chapter 5, pp. 131–76.

43. See Rudé's comments in "The Changing Face of the Crowd."

44. E. J. Hobsbawm and G. Rudé, *Captain Swing*, pp. xvii–xviii.

45. On the Hammonds, see Hobsbawm's introduction to J. Hammond and B. Hammond, *The Village Labourer* (New York, 1970), and G. Rudé's introduction in J. Hammond and B. Hammond, *The Skilled Labourer* (New York, 1970).

46. E. J. Hobsbawm and G. Rudé, *Captain Swing*, pp. xx–xxiii.

47. F. Krantz, " '*Sans erudition, pas d'histoire*,' " p. 14.

48. E. J. Hobsbawm and G. Rudé, *Captain Swing*, pp. 201–11.

49. Ibid., pp. 242, 258. Also, see Rudé's article "English Rural and Urban Disturbances on the Eve of the First Reform Bill, 1830–1831," in Kaye, ed., *The Face of the Crowd*, pp. 167–82.

50. Ibid., pp. 224–45.

51. G. Rudé, *Protest and Punishment*, p. 1.

52. Ibid., pp. 2–4.

53. Ibid., p. 10.

54. Ibid., p. 247.

55. G. Rudé, *Criminal and Victim*, pp. 78–79.

56. Ibid., pp. 117, 118–21.

57. Ibid., pp. 124–26.

58. G. Rudé, *Paris and London*, pp. 136–37.

59. Ibid., pp. 302–3.

60. Ibid., p. 304.

61. See note 15 above.

62. H. Lefebvre, "Revolutionary Crowds," in J. Kaplow, ed., *New Perspectives on the French Revolution* (New York, 1965), p. 175.

63. G. Rudé, *Paris and London*, esp. "Prices, Wages and Popular Movements in Paris during the French Revolution," pp. 163–77.

64. G. Rudé, *The Crowd in the French Revolution,* p. 200, and *Wilkes and Liberty,* p. 188.

65. G. Rudé, *The Crowd in the French Revolution,* pp. 210–19.

66. Ibid., pp. 199, 200, and note 3 on p. 200.

67. Ibid., p. 225.

68. G. Rudé, "Society and Conflict in London and Paris in the Eighteenth Century" (1969), in *Paris and London,* pp. 35–60.

69. G. Rudé, *Wilkes and Liberty,* chapter 6, pp. 90–104.

70. Ibid., p. 190.

71. Ibid., p. 187.

72. Ibid., p. 197.

73. Ibid., p. 12.

74. G. Rudé, *Paris and London,* pp. 289–90.

75. G. Rudé, *Ideology and Popular Protest,* p. 7.

76. The most comprehensive treatment of Western Marxism is offered in Martin Jay, *Marxism and Totality* (Oxford, 1985).

77. G. Rudé, "Marxism and History," p. 49.

78. On Gramsci, see Joseph Femia, *Gramsci's Political Thought* (Oxford, 1981); and for a survey to 1981 of Gramsci Studies in English, see H. J. Kaye, "Antonio Gramsci: An Annotated Bibliography of Studies in English," *Politics and Society* 10 (1981), pp. 335–53, which is being updated by the Gramsci Study Circle (NYC), under the direction of Frank Rosengarten, et al. Also, on Gramsci and the British Marxist historians see chapter 1 of the present book.

79. G. Rudé, "The Changing Face of the Crowd," and "The Pre-Industrial Crowd" (1969), in *Paris and London,* pp. 31–3.

80. Also see the articles in Section II of Kaye, ed., *The Face of the Crowd:* "European Popular Protest and Ideology on the Eve of the French Revolution"; "The Germination of a Revolutionary Ideology among the Urban *menu peuple* of 1789"; and "Ideology and Popular Protest."

81. See chapter 1 of the present work.

82. G. Rudé, *Ideology and Popular Protest,* pp. 15–25.

83. A. Gramsci, *Selections from the Prison Notebooks,* ed. Q. Hoare and G. Smith (London, 1971).

84. G. Rudé, *Ideology and Popular Protest,* pp. 20–24.

85. Again, chapter 1 above, and Jerome Karabel, "Revolutionary Contradictions: Antonio Gramsci and the Problem of Intellectuals," *Politics and Society* 6 (1976), pp. 123–72.

86. G. Rudé, *Ideology and Popular Protest,* p. 28.

87. Ibid., pp. 31–36.

88. Ibid., pp. 36–37.

89. G. Rudé, *Debate on Europe, 1815–1850* (New York, 1972).

90. These essays are included in Section I of Kaye, ed., *The Face of the Crowd.*

91. H. Stretton, "George Rudé," p. 52.

92. G. Rudé, *Debate on Empire,* pp. viii, x, xiii.

93. Ibid., pp. xii, xv, 69, 179, 210–12.

94. Ibid., p. 102. Consider the resurgence of "conservative" historiography and the political ascendance of the New Right in both Britain and the United States. See Harvey J. Kaye, *The Powers of the Past* (London, 1991).

95. See his comments in "The Changing Face of the Crowd."

96. G. Rudé, *Revolutionary Europe,* p. 104.

97. G. Rudé, *Robespierre,* pp. 197–208, 151.

98. Ibid., p. 213. Also, see his essay, "Robespierre as Seen by British Historians," in Kaye, ed., *The Face of the Crowd,* pp. 115–23.

99. G. Rudé, *Europe in the Eighteenth Century,* pp. 11–14.

100. Ibid., pp. 239; and 129–35, 140, 153–54, 305.

101. G. Rudé, *Hanoverian London,* p. 70.

102. For example, see Alfred Cobban's *The Social Interpretation of the French Revolution* (London, 1968). For Rudé's comments on the "revisionist challenge," see the concluding remarks to "Interpretations of the French Revolution," in Kaye, ed., *The Face of the Crowd,* and, especially, his discussions in *The French Revolution.*

103. G. Rudé, "The French Revolution," in N. Cantor, ed., *Perspectives on the European Past* (New York, 1971), pp. 47–48.

104. G. Comninel, *Rethinking the French Revolution* (London, 1987).

105. G. Rudé, foreword to ibid., p. x.

106. Comninel's work is also heavily influenced by the work of Robert Brenner in *The Brenner Debate* (Cambridge, 1985).

107. G. Rudé, foreword to G. Comninel, *Rethinking the French Revolution,* p. xii. Also, see Rudé's thoughts on the "transition" in France in his essay, "Feudalism and the French Revolution."

108. For example, see William Reddy, *Money and Liberty in Modern Europe* (Cambridge, 1987).

109. See E. P. Thompson, "Eighteenth-century English Society: Class Struggle Without Class?" *Social History* 3 (May 1978), pp. 133–65; his forthcoming book, *Customs in Common* (New York, 1992); and, of course, *The Making of the English Working Class.* On Thompson's work, see H. J. Kaye, *The British Marxist Historians,* chapter 6, pp. 167–220; the contributions to H. J. Kaye and K. McClelland, eds., *E. P. Thompson: Critical Perspectives* (Oxford, 1990); and chapter 4 of the present book. Also, see Hans Medick, "Plebeian Culture in the Transition to Capitalism," in R. Samuel and G. Stedman Jones, eds., *Culture, Ideology and Politics,* pp. 84–112, and Ellen Wood, "The Politics of

Theory and the Concept of Class: E. P. Thompson and His Critics," *Studies in Political Economy* 9 (Fall 1982), pp. 57–58.

110. Kaye, *The British Marxist Historians,* pp. 246–49, and chapter 1 of the present work.

111. For a selection of Gramsci's *Letters from Prison,* see the collection edited by Lynne Lawner (New York, 1973).

112. See, for example, J. Stevenson, "The 'Moral Economy' of the English Crowd: Myth and Reality," in A. Fletcher and J. Stevenson, eds., *Order and Disorder in Early Modern England* (Cambridge, 1985), pp. 218–38, and Tim Harris, *London Crowds in the Reign of Charles II* (Cambridge, 1987).

Chapter Three

This chapter originated as my introduction to *History, Classes and Nation-States: Selected Writings of V. G. Kiernan* (Oxford: Polity Press/Basil Blackwell, 1988). It has been significantly added to by the incorporation of arguments from my introduction to *Poets, Politics and the People: Selected Essays of V. G. Kiernan* (London: Verso, 1989). I should add here that I plan to produce two additional volumes of Kiernan's Selected Writings: *Imperialism and Its Contradictions,* and *Intellectuals and the Making of History.*

1. V. G. Kiernan, *The Lords of Human Kind* (Harmondsworth, 1972, rev. ed.); *European Empires from Conquest to Collapse, 1815-1860* (London, 1982); *Marxism and Imperialism* (London, 1974); *America: The New Imperialism* (London, 1978); *British Diplomacy in China, 1880-1885* (Cambridge, 1939; reprinted with new foreword, New York, 1970); and *Metcalfe's Mission to Lahore, 1808-1809* (Lahore, Punjab Government Record Office, Monograph 21, 1943).

2. V. G. Kiernan, "Foreign Interests in the War of the Pacific," *Hispanis American Historical Review* 35 (February 1955), pp. 14–36; "India, China, and Sikkim: 1886–1890," *Indian Historical Quarterly* 31 (March 1955), pp. 32–51; "India, China and Tibet: 1885–1886," *Journal of the Greater Indian Historical Society* 14 (1955), pp. 117–42; "Kashgar and the Politics of Central Asia: 1868–1878," *Cambridge Historical Journal* 11 (1955), pp. 317–42; "Colonial Africa and its Armies," in B. Bond and I. Roy, eds., *War and Society,* vol. 2 (London, 1977), pp. 20–39; "The Old Alliance: England and Portugal," in R. Miliband and J. Saville, eds., *The Socialist Register 1973* (London, 1973), pp. 261–81; and "India and Pakistan: Twenty Years After," in R. Miliband and J. Saville, eds., *The Socialist Register 1966* (London, 1966), pp. 305–20. For a complete bibliography of Kiernan's writings to 1977, see the special issue of *New Edinburgh Review* 38–39, "History and Humanism," prepared in his honor (Summer–Autumn 1977), pp. 77–79.

3. Tom Bottomore, et al., eds., *A Dictionary of Marxist Thought* (Oxford, 1983, new ed., 1991).

4. See, for examples, V. G. Kiernan, "Intellectuals in History," *Winchester Research Papers in the Humanities* (Winchester, King Alfred's College, 1979); "Class and Ideology: The Bourgeoisie and its Historians," *History of European Ideas* 6

(1985), pp. 267–86; and "Evangelicalism and the French Revolution," reprinted in Kaye, ed., *Poets, Politics and the People,* pp. 65–77.

5.   See V. G. Kiernan, "Working Class and Nation in Nineteenth-century Britain" (1978), in Kaye, ed., *History, Classes and Nation-States,* pp. 186–98; also, "Victorian London: Unending Purgatory," *New Left Review* 76 (November–December 1972), pp. 73–90; and "Labour and the Literate in Nineteenth-century Britain" (1979), in Kaye, ed., *Poets, Politics and the People,* pp. 152–77.

6.   See, for example, V. G. Kiernan, "Wordsworth and the People" (1956), and "Human Relations in Shakespeare" (1964), in Kaye, ed., *Poets, Politics and the People;* "Art and the Necessity of History," in R. Miliband and J. Saville, eds., *The Socialist Register 1965* (London, 1965), pp. 216–36; "Civilisation and the Dance," *Dunfermline College of Physical Education Occasional Papers* 2 (April 1976); and "Private Property in History," in J. Goody, J. Thirsk, and E. P. Thompson, eds., *Family and Inheritance: Rural Society in Western Europe, 1200–1800* (Cambridge, 1976), pp. 361–98.

7.   V. G. Kiernan, trans. and ed., *Poems from Iqbal* (Bombay, 1947; rev. ed. London, 1955); *Poems from Faiz* (New Delhi, 1958; rev. ed. London, 1971); and *From Volga to Ganga* (Bombay, 1947).

8.   Harvey J. Kaye, *The British Marxist Historians: An Introductory Analysis* (Oxford, 1984), pp. 8–18; and E. J. Hobsbawm, "The Historians' Group of the Communist Party," in M. Cornforth, ed., *Rebels and Their Causes* (London, 1978), pp. 21–47.

9.   Kiernan's article is "Evangelicalism and the French Revolution." Also, see the retrospective in the 100th issue of *Past & Present* by Christopher Hill, Rodney Hilton, and Eric Hobsbawm.

10. Barrington Moore, Jr., *Social Origins of Dictatorship and Democracy* (Boston, 1966), pp. 522–23.

11. See the selection in *Poets, Politics and the People* to be discussed below.

12. Perry Anderson, *Lineages of the Absolutist State* (London, 1974), p. 11, and Kaye, *The British Marxist Historians,* p. 229.

13. One cannot help but note once again the biographical relationship between Nonconformism and socialism found in the lives of Kiernan, Christopher Hill, E. P. Thompson, and Sheila Rowbotham. See my references in *The British Marxist Historians,* p. 103. It should be added that Kiernan has for many years kept notes towards a book to be called *Religion in History.*

14. H. S. Ferns, *Reading from Left to Right* (Toronto, 1983), pp. 76–77. These recollections and others were restated by Professor Ferns in a series of very enjoyable and helpful conversations with me at the University of Birmingham in the winter term 1987.

15. See T. E. B. Howarth, *Cambridge Between Two Wars* (London, 1978). For a recent fictional representation, see Raymond Williams, *Loyalties* (London, 1985). For Kiernan's own thoughts on Cambridge in the 1930s, see his piece, "Herbert Norman's Cambridge," in Kaye, ed., *Poets, Politics and the People.* Also

see Noel Annan, *Our Age: English Intellectuals Between Two World Wars—A Group Portrait* (London, 1990).

16. Ibid. Cornford died fighting for the Republican cause in the Spanish Civil War. Klugmann remained a party activist and official until his death in 1977. On Cornford, see Kiernan's "Recollections," in P. Sloan, ed., *John Cornford: A Memoir* (London, 1938), pp. 116–24; and Peter Stansky and William Abrahams, *Journey to the Frontier: Two Roads to the Spanish Civil War* (Boston, 1966). Herbert Norman returned to Canada to pursue an outstanding career as a diplomat and scholar until his death in 1957, when he committed suicide, having been hounded by McCarthyite witch-hunters. See R. W. Bowen, ed., *E. H. Norman: His Life and Scholarship* (Toronto, 1984); also, Reg Whitaker, "Return to the Crucible—the Persecution of E. H. Norman," *The Canadian Forum* (November 1986), pp. 11–28.

17. Ibid., especially Kiernan, "Herbert Norman's Cambridge."

18. See note 9. Also, see with regard to Kiernan's work in this area his contributions to Ali Sardar Jaffri and K. S. Duggal, eds., *Iqbal Commemorative Volume* (Delhi, 1980); these are "Iqbal as Prophet of Change," "Iqbal and Milton," and "Iqbal and Wordsworth." And, for his own recollections of the years in India, see Kiernan, "The Communist Party of India and the Second World War–Some Reminiscences," *South Asia* 5 (December 1987), pp. 61–73.

19. V. G. Kiernan, *The March of Time* (Lahore, 1946); *Castanets* (Lahore, 1941); and "Brockle" and "The Senorita" in *Longman's Miscellany* 3, 4 (Calcutta, 1945 and 1946).

20. Hobsbawm, "The Historians' Group of the Communist Party."

21. See V. G. Kiernan, *State and Society in Europe, 1550–1650* (Oxford, 1980).

22. Hobsbawm, "The Historians' Group of the Communist Party," p. 24—a point often repeated in conversation with the author (HJK).

23. For examples: in Britain, David Cannadine, "The State of British History," *Times Literary Supplement,* 10 October 1986, pp. 1139–40; and in the United States, Thomas Bender, "Making History Whole Again," *New York Times Book Review,* 6 October 1985, pp. 1, 42–43. On this question, see Harvey J. Kaye, *The Powers of the Past* (London, 1991). I should add that Kiernan has recently authored a "popular" book titled *Tobacco* (London, 1991) in which, he says, that having given up smoking he turned to writing about it.

24. E. H. Carr, *What is History?* (New York, 1961), p. 69.

25. V. G. Kiernan, "Notes on Marxism in 1968," in R. Miliband and J. Saville, eds., *The Socialist Register 1968* (London, 1968), p. 182.

26. Kiernan, "Class and Ideology," p. 268.

27. Kiernan, "Notes on Marxism in 1968," p. 184.

28. From Kiernan, *The Lords of Human Kind,* p. xiv; a point made in a similar fashion is found in a letter to the author of 8 June 1986.

29. V. G. Kiernan, "Problems of Marxist History," *New Left Review* 161 (Jan.–Feb. 1987), p. 106.

30. Kiernan, "Notes on Marxism in 1968," pp. 186, 208. Indeed, the opening words of Kiernan's first book, *British Diplomacy in China,* are: "All abstraction falsifies" (p. xxvii).

31. Hobsbawm, "The Historians' Group of the Communist Party," p. 31; and Christopher Hill in conversation with the author in January, 1987.

32. Maurice Dobb, *Studies in the Development of Capitalism* (London, 1946), e.g., pp. 17–18.

33. Keith Tribe, "The Problem of Transition and Question of Origin," in his *Genealogies of Capitalism* (London, 1981), pp. 19–21; also, clearly revealed in papers in the possession of V. G. Kiernan. The group's "position" was stated in "State and Revolution in Tudor and Stuart England.," *Communist Review* (July 1948), pp. 207–14.

34. See Kaye, *The British Marxist Historians,* chapter 2, pp. 23–69.

35. See T. H. Aston and C. H. E. Philpin, eds., *The Brenner Debate: Agrarian Class Structure and Economic Development in Pre-Industrial Europe* (Cambridge, 1985); and Philip Corrigan and Derek Sayer, *The Great Arch* (Oxford, 1985). Christopher Hill's own "bourgeois revolution thesis" has been much revised; see Kaye, *The British Marxist Historians,* chapter 4, pp. 99–130.

36. See Kaye, ibid., esp. pp. 36–40, 51–53. It should be noted, however, that Kiernan's general position on merchant vs. industrial capital has also been revised; see his *Development, Imperialism and Some Misconceptions* (University College of Swansea, Centre for Development Studies, 1981), Occasional Paper 13, p. 25.

37. Though, of course, so too have Eric Hobsbawm and E. P. Thompson. For examples, see Hobsbawm's "Karl Marx's Contribution to Historiography," in R. Blackburn, ed., *Ideology in Social Science* (London, 1972), pp. 265–83, and Thompson's *The Poverty of Theory and Other Essays* (London, 1978).

38. Kiernan, "History," in Kaye, ed., *History, Classes and Nation-States,* pp. 29–65; also, see Kiernan's essay in *Marxism and Imperialism.*

39. Kiernan, "Notes on Marxism in 1968," pp. 178, 183.

40. F. Engels, *The Peasant War in Germany* (New York, 1966). Kiernan, "History," p. 43. Also, see Kiernan's foreword to F. Engels, *The Condition of the Working Class in England* (Harmondsworth, 1987), pp. 9–25.

41. V. G. Kiernan, "Gramsci and Marxism," in Kaye, ed., *History, Classes and Nation-States,* pp. 66–101; and "The Socialism of Antonio Gramsci," in K. Coates, ed., *Essays on Socialist Humanism* (Nottingham, 1972), pp. 63–86. Also, see his article "Gramsci and the Other Continents," *New Edinburgh Review* 27 (1985), pp. 19–23. For Gramsci's writings, see *Selections from the Prison Notebooks.,* trans. and ed. Q. Hoare and G. Nowell Smith (New York, 1971); and Lynne Lawner, ed., *Letters from Prison* (New York, 1973).

42. Kiernan, "The Socialism of Antonio Gramsci," p. 75; and "Gramsci and Marxism," p. 45. On Gramsci and the British Marxist historians, see chapter 1 of the present work.

43. Kiernan, "Gramsci and Marxism," p. 73.

44. Kiernan, "Art and the Necessity of History," see note 6 above.

45. V. G. Kiernan, "Reflections on Braudel," *Social History* 4 (January 1977), p. 522.

46. This part of *British Diplomacy in China*, which would normally appear first, is situated rather late in the text. This is probably due to the fact that the work was attuned to the requirements of diplomatic history, the latter section added by a young Marxist interested in questions of social and political structure, change and development.

47. V. G. Kiernan, foreword to the 1970 edition, *British Diplomacy in China, 1880–1885*, p. xii. See note 2 above for references to his postwar and later diplomatic studies, though additionally should be noted his article "Diplomats in Exile," in R. Hatton and M. S. Anderson, eds., *Studies in Diplomatic History* (London, 1970), pp. 301–21, one of the things which he says he most enjoyed writing.

48. This concern also led him to write "Britons Old and New," in Colin Holmes, ed., *Immigrants and Minorities in British Society* (London, 1978), pp. 23–59. This article surveys British historical development in terms of its being a receiver of immigrants and refugees. Also, see Kiernan's pugnacious piece, "After Empire," *New Edinburgh Review* 37 (Spring 1977), pp. 23–35.

49. Kiernan, *European Empires*, p. 230. Another similarity between this book and *The Lords of Human Kind* is the style in which they are written. A British reviewer of *The Lords* refers to it as "historical impressionism"; the reviewer of *European Empires* in the *American Historical Review* (June 1983), describes its form as "pointillist." I would agree with the latter, applying his description to both books for, indeed, the two are characterized by numerous "capsule accounts" of incidents, episodes, and battles drawn by Kiernan from the entire geography of imperialism to provide particular pictures of its landscape.

50. For an example of a related article, see V. G. Kiernan, "American Hegemony under Revision," in R. Miliband and J. Saville, eds., *The Socialist Register 1974* (London, 1974), pp. 302–30.

51. Kiernan, *America: The New Imperialism*, p. 1.

52. Kiernan, "Imperialism, American and European," in his *Marxism and Imperialism*, p. 130.

53. Kiernan, *Marxism and Imperialism*, pp. viii, 67.

54. Ibid., p. viii. "The Marxist Theory of Imperialism and its Historical Formation" is the first essay in *Marxism and Imperialism*, pp. 1–68.

55. Kiernan, *European Empires*, p. 227. Unfortunately, Kiernan provides no estimates here; nor do we know if he is including the African slave trade prior to the nineteenth century (which, admittedly, Africans themselves participated in quite actively).

56. V. G. Kiernan, "Imperialism and Revolution," in R. Porter and M. Teich, eds., *Revolution in History* (Cambridge, 1986), p. 129.

57. Ibid., p. 121; and V. G. Kiernan, "Tennyson, King Arthur and Imperialism," in Kaye, ed., *Poets, Politics, and the People*, pp. 129–51.

58. Kiernan, *The Lords of Human Kind,* p. xxvi. Also, for example, see Kiernan, *Development, Imperialism and some Misconceptions.*

59. V. G. Kiernan, "Europe and the World: The Imperial Record," in M. Wright, ed., *Rights and Observations in North-South Relations* (New York, 1986), p. 38; and "Tennyson, King Arthur and Imperialism," p. 150.

60. Kiernan, "Imperialism and Revolution," p. 137.

61. Kiernan, "Notes on Marxism in 1968," p. 195, 190–191.

62. Ibid., p. 196.

63. V. G. Kiernan, *The Duel in European History* (Oxford, 1988).

64. For examples of these renewed interests, see Benedict Anderson, *Imagined Communities: Reflections on the Origin and Spread of Nationalism* (London, 1983); Ernest Gellner, *Nations and Nationalism* (Ithaca, 1983); Anthony Giddens, *The Nation-State and Violence* (Oxford, 1986); and J. A. Hall, ed., *States in History* (Oxford, 1986). Moreover, with the breakup of the Soviet bloc/empire we should expect many more.

65. "State and Nation in Western Europe" (1965), in Kaye, ed., *History, Classes and Nation-States,* pp. 102–17. It should be noted that in the book, *State and Society in Europe, 1550–1650,* he notes the work's similarity to Perry Anderson's *Lineages of the Absolutist State.*

66. Kiernan, *State and Society in Europe, 1550–1650,* pp. 5–6.

67. Kiernan, "State and Nation in Western Europe," p. 109.

68. Ibid., p. 114.

69. Kiernan, *State and Society in Europe, 1550–1650,* p. 12.

70. Kiernan, "Foreign Mercenaries and Absolute Monarchies" (1957), reprinted in Kaye, ed., *History, Classes and Nation-States,* pp. 118–37.

71. Kiernan, "State and Nation in Western Europe," p. 117.

72. See V. G. Kiernan, "Marx, Engels, and the Indian Mutiny," in his *Marxism and Imperialism,* esp. pp. 227–34.

73. Kiernan, "Notes on Marxism in 1968," p. 204.

74. Kiernan, "Nationalist Movements and Social Classes" (1976), and "Conscription and Society in Europe before the War of 1914–1918" (1973), are both reprinted in Kaye, ed., *History, Classes and Nation-States,* pp. 138–65, and 166–85.

75. Kiernan, "Nationalist Movements and Social Classes," p. 139.

76. Ibid., p. 154. Also, see V. G. Kiernan, "On the Development of a Marxist Approach to Nationalism," *Science and Society* 34 (Spring 1970), pp. 92–98.

77. V. G. Kiernan, "Revolution" (1979), in Kaye, ed., *History, Classes and Nation-States,* pp. 201, 205, 263, note 5.

78. V. G. Kiernan, *The Revolution of 1854 in Spanish History* (Oxford, 1966).

79. See Kiernan's introduction to I. MacDougall, ed., *Voices from the Spanish Civil War* (Edinburgh, 1986), and his review of Ronald Fraser's *The Blood of Spain,* in *New Left Review* 120 (March–April 1980), pp. 97–107.

80. Kiernan, *The Revolution of 1854,* p. 1.

81. For examples of his calls for history from the bottom up, see Kiernan's review of Raymond Williams's *Culture and Society,* in *The New Reasoner* 9 (Summer 1959), pp. 75–83, and his review of Christopher Hill's *The Century of Revolution,* in *New Left Review* 11 (September–October, 1961), pp. 62–65.

82. Kiernan, "History," p. 31, and "Revolution," p. 205.

83. V. G. Kiernan, "Patterns of Protest in English History," in Kaye, ed., *Poets, Politics and the People,* pp. 18–39.

84. V. G. Kiernan, "The Covenanters: A Problem of Creed and Class," in ibid., pp. 40–64.

85. John Saville, ed., *Democracy and the Labour Movement* (London, 1954), p. 8. Both of Kiernan's essays, "Wordsworth and the People," and "Socialism, the Prophetic Memory," are reprinted in Kaye, ed., *Poets, Politics and the People,* pp. 96–128, and 204–28.

86. V. G. Kiernan, "Wordsworth Revisited," *The New Reasoner* 7 (Winter 1958–59), pp. 62–74.

87. See A. L. Morton, *The English Utopia* (London, 1952). Also, see chapter 5 of the present work on Morton.

88. Kiernan, "Socialism, the Prophetic Memory," p. 204.

89. Kiernan, "The Covenanters," p. 51.

90. V. G. Kiernan, "Labour and the Literate in Nineteenth-Century Britain," in Kaye, ed., *Poets, Politics and the People,* pp. 152–77.

91. See E. P. Thompson, *The Making of the English Working Class* (London, 1963), and Dorothy Thompson, *The Chartists* (London, 1984).

92. Kiernan, "Patterns of Protest in English History," pp. 165, 168. Also crucial on this point is Kiernan's essay, "Working Class and Nation in Nineteenth-Century Britain," pp. 186–98. And, it should be noted, the concept of "labourism" is derived from the work of his longtime friend and comrade, John Saville. See Saville's "Ideology of Labourism," in R. Benewick, et al., eds., *Knowledge and Belief in Politics* (London, 1973), and more recently in his books, *1848: The British State and Chartism* (Cambridge, 1987), and *The British Labour Movement* (London, 1988).

93. James Young, *Socialism and the English Working Class, 1883–1939* (London, 1988); and, for the U.S.A., see the works of David Montgomery, *Workers' Control in America* (Cambridge, 1979) and *The Fall of the House of Labor* (Cambridge, 1987).

94. See, for example, J. Saville, *1848: The British State and Chartism.*

95. V. G. Kiernan, "Problems of Marxist History," *New Left Review* 161 (January–February 1987), p. 117.

96. Eric Hobsbawm, "Methodism and the Threat of Revolution in Britain" (1957), in *Labouring Men* (London, 1964), and Thompson, *The Making of the English Working Class,* pp. 411–17.

97. V. G. Kiernan, "After Empire," p. 30 (my italics). On the relation between Kiernan's view of culture and that of Gramsci, see Kiernan's own essay, "The Socialism of Antonio Gramsci."

98. For example, see Kiernan, "Intellectuals in History."

99. Kiernan, "Labour and the Literate," p. 165.

100. V. G. Kiernan, "On Treason," reprinted in Kaye, ed., *Poets, Politics and the People,* pp. 193–203. See also his review of David Caute's *The Fellow Travellers* (1973), in *The Times Literary Supplement,* 16 February 1973.

101. Kiernan, "The Socialism of Antonio Gramsci," p. 75.

102. Kiernan, "Socialism, the Prophetic Memory," p. 216.

103. V. G. Kiernan, "Revolution and Reaction, 1789–1848 (a review of Eric Hobsbawm's *The Age of Revolution*)," in *New Left Review* 19 (March–April 1963), p. 75. Also, see Kiernan's contributions to *A Dictionary of Marxist Thought,* in particular "Christianity," "Hinduism," and "Religion."

104. Ibid., p. 76. Also, see his review of Christopher Hill's *Century of Revolution* (noted above), pp. 62–66 on Protestantism and popular protest.

105. See, on this issue, David McLellan, *Marxism and Religion* (London, 1987).

106. V. G. Kiernan, "Religion," in *A Dictionary of Marxist Thought,* p. 416.

107. Kiernan, "Notes on Marxism in 1968," pp. 207–8.

108. Ibid., p. 207. For E. P. Thompson's argument, see *The Poverty of Theory* (London, 1978), esp. pp. 171–76.

109. Margot Heinemann, "How the Words Got on the Page," in G. Eley and W. Hunt, eds., *Reviving the English Revolution* (London, 1988), p. 73. For an example of Heinemann's own historical literary criticism, see her *Puritanism and Theatre* (Cambridge, 1980). Also included in the volume, *Reviving the English Revolution,* is Kiernan's essay, "Milton in Heaven," pp. 161–80.

110. S. S. Prawer, *Karl Marx and World Literature* (Oxford, 1978), and Fred Inglis, *Radical Earnestness* (Oxford, 1982), p. 21.

111. Bill Schwarz, "'The People' in History: The Communist Party Historians' Group, 1946–56," in R. Johnson, et al., eds., *Making Histories* (London, 1982), esp. pp. 76–77.

112. Thompson, *The Making of the English Working Class,* p. 915. It should also be noted that Thompson himself has been working for many years on a book on Blake and Wordsworth. See his articles "Disenchantment or Default? A Lay Sermon," in C. Cruise O'Brien and W. Dean Vanech, eds., *Power and Consciousness* (London, 1969), pp. 149–81, and "London," in M. Philips, ed., *Interpreting Blake* (Cambridge, 1978), pp. 5–31. Also, with reference to the British Marxist historians' interest in and commitment to poets and poetry, see Christopher Hill's masterpiece *Milton and the English Revolution* (London, 1977), and the pamphlet by a senior figure of the historians' group, the classicist and professor of Greek, George Thomson, *Marxism and Poetry,* (London, 1945; reprinted 1980).

113. Postscript is included with Kiernan, "Wordsworth and the People," in Kaye, ed., *Poets, Politics and the People.*

114. Kiernan, "The Socialism of Antonio Gramsci," p. 75, and "Labour and the Literate," p. 174.

115. Kiernan, "Gramsci and Marxism," p. 93; "Problems of Marxist History," p. 118; and "Notes on Marxism in 1968," p. 198.

116. Kiernan, "Human Relations in Shakespeare," p. 79.

117. Margot Heinemann, "Shakespearean Contradictions and Social Change," *Science and Society* 41 (Spring 1977), p. 16.

118. For a most critical assessment of these currents, see Ellen Meiksins Wood, *The Retreat from Class* (London, 1985).

119. V. G. Kiernan, "Notes on the Intelligentsia," in R. Miliband and J. Saville, eds., *The Socialist Register, 1969* (London, 1969), pp. 81, 76.

120. Ibid., and "Socialism, the Prophetic Memory."

121. Kiernan, "Notes on Marxism in 1968," p. 208.

122. Kiernan, "After Empire," p. 33; "Labour and the Literate," p. 175; and "Working Class and Nation in Nineteenth-Century Britain," p. 198.

123. See chapter 1 above.

124. Kiernan, "Review of Raymond Williams's *Culture and Society*," p. 79.

125. W. Benjamin, "Theses on the Philosophy of History," in his *Illuminations* (New York, 1969), pp. 257, 255.

Chapter Four

This chapter was first published in H. J. Kaye and K. McClelland, eds., *E. P. Thompson: Critical Perspectives* (Oxford: Polity Press, 1990). It originated as a talk presented at the conference "Back to the Future" held in London in July 1988.

1. On this "historical crisis," see Harvey J. Kaye, *The Powers of the Past: Reflections on the Crisis and the Promise of History* (London, 1991).

2. The dissertation was titled "The Political Economy of Seigneurialism" (Louisiana State University, 1976).

3. Barrington Moore, Jr., *Social Origins of Dictatorship and Democracy* (Boston, 1966); and the writings of Eugene Genovese are: *The Political Economy of Slavery* (New York, 1967), *The World the Slaveholders Made* (New York, 1971), *In Red and Black* (New York, 1972), and *Roll, Jordan, Roll: The World the Slaves Made* (New York, 1974).

4. See Raphael Samuel, "British Marxist Historians, 1880–1980," *New Left Review* 120 (March–April 1980), pp. 42–55, and Harvey J. Kaye, *The British Marxist Historians: An Introductory Analysis* (Oxford, 1984), p. 103.

5. Maurice Dobb, *Studies in the Development of Capitalism* (London, 1946), and R. H. Hilton, ed., *The Transition from Feudalism to Capitalism* (London, 1976).

6. A. L. Morton, *A People's History of England* (London, 1979, rev. ed.) on which see chapter 5 of the present work, and Dona Torr, *Tom Mann and His Times* (London, 1954).

7. See the *Bulletin of the Society for the Study of Labour History.*

8. E. P. Thompson, *The Making of the English Working Class* (Harmondsworth, 1968, rev. ed.). See Stuart Hall, "Cultural Studies and the Centre," in S. Hall, et al., eds., *Culture, Media and Language* (London, 1980), pp. 15–47.

9. Bill Schwarz, "The People in History: The Communist Party Historians' Group, 1946–56," in R. Johnson, et al., eds., *Making Histories* (London, 1982), pp. 44–95.

10. W. Benjamin, "Theses in the Philosophy of History," in his *Illuminations* (New York, 1969), p. 255.

11. Thompson, *The Making of the English Working Class,* p. 12.

12. Ellen Wood, "Marxism and the Course of History," *New Left Review* 147 (September–October 1984), pp. 95–108.

13. For examples, see Alan Dawley, *Class and Community: The Industrial Revolution in Lynn* (Cambridge, 1976); Sean Wilentz, *Chants Democratic: New York City and the Rise of the American Working Class* (New York, 1984); Herbert Gutman, *Work, Culture and Society in Industrializing America* (New York, 1977); the works of Genovese cited above in note 3; and Scott G. McNall, *The Road to Rebellion: Class Formation and Populism, 1865–1900* (Chicago, 1988).

14. For examples, see: Steven Stern, *Peru's Indian Peoples and the Challenge of Spanish Conquest* (Madison, Wis., 1982); James Scott, *Weapons of the Weak* (New Haven, 1986); T. H. Aston and C. H. E. Philpin, eds., *The Brenner Debate* (Cambridge, 1985); and Immanuel Wallerstein, *The Modern World-System* (New York, 1974).

15. In literary studies, see Michael Fischer, "The Literary Importance of E. P. Thompson's Marxism," *English Literary History* 50 (Winter 1983), pp. 811–29; and on "critical legal studies," see Mark Kelman, *A Guide to Critical Legal Studies* (Cambridge, 1987).

16. This is especially true regarding the writings of E. P. Thompson; for example, on Genovese's influence, see "Eighteenth-century English Society: Class Struggle Without Class?" *Social History* 3 (May 1978), pp. 133–65.

17. See Kaye, *The Powers of the Past,* esp. chapter 3.

18. Himmelfarb's article is reprinted in her collection of essays titled *The New History and the Old* (Cambridge, 1987). The MARHO interviews are published as H. Abelove, et al., eds., *Visions of History* (New York, 1984).

19. In the U.K., see G. Himmelfarb, *Victorian Values and 20th-Century Condescension* (London, Centre for Policy Studies, 1987). In the U.S.A., see her "Manners into Morals: What the Victorians Knew," *The American Scholar* 57 (Spring 1988), pp. 223–32, and "Of Heaven, Villains and Valets," *Commentary* (June 1991), pp. 20–26.

20. January 1992: Thatcher is gone . . . John Major is in. Elections approach.

21. I refer the reader to *The Observer,* 22 May 1988, p. 1; G. Marshall, et al., eds., *Social Class in Modern Britain* (London, 1988); and *The Guardian,* 17 September 1988, p. 4.

22. Christopher Hill, *The Experience of Defeat* (New York, 1984). Also, see V. G. Kiernan, "Problems of Marxist History," *New Left Review* 161 (January–February 1987), pp. 105–18.

23. For example, Sheila Rowbotham, *Hidden From History* (London, 1983), and L. Davidoff and C. Hall, *Family Fortunes: Men and Women of the English Middle Class, 1750–1850* (Chicago, 1987). Catherine Hall's statement is in H. J. Kaye and K. McClelland, eds., *E. P. Thompson: Critical Perspectives* (Oxford, 1990), p. 99.

24. For example, see the essays collected in Herbert Gutman, *Power and Culture* (New York, 1987), and chapters of David Montgomery, *The Fall of the House of Labor* (New York, 1987).

25. V. G. Kiernan, "Britons Old and New," in Colin Holmes, ed., *Immigrants and Minorities in British Society* (London, 1978), pp. 23–59.

26. Robin Blackburn, *The Overthrow of Colonial Slavery, 1776–1848* (London, 1988).

27. Barrington Moore, Jr., *Social Origins of Dictatorship and Democracy,* pp. 522–23.

28. F. Stirton Weaver is the author of *Class, State and Industrial Structure* (Westport, Conn., 1980). The remark by Victor Kiernan was made in a letter to the author in June 1988.

29. For examples, see C. Wright Mills, *The Power Elite* (New York, 1956); Paul Baran and Paul Sweezy, *Monopoly Capital* (New York, 1966); Harry Braverman, *Labor and Monopoly Capital* (New York, 1974); William Appleman Williams, *The Tragedy of American Diplomacy* (New York, 1962, rev. ed.); James Weinstein, *The Corporate Ideal in the Liberal State* (Boston, 1968); Gabriel Kolko, *The Roots of American Foreign Policy* (Boston, 1969); G. William Domhoff, *Who Rules America?* (Englewood Cliffs, N.J., 1967); and Christopher Lasch, *Haven in a Heartless World* (New York, 1977).

30. V. G. Kiernan, *The Lords of Human Kind* (London, reprinted 1988); *State and Society in Europe, 1550–1650* (Oxford, 1980); and *The Duel in European History* (Oxford, 1988). On Kiernan, see chapter 3 of the present work. Also, see his collected essays, Harvey J. Kaye, ed., *History, Classes and Nation-States* (Oxford, 1988), and *Poets, Politics and the People* (London, 1989).

31. Perry Anderson, *Passages from Antiquity to Feudalism,* and *Lineages of the Absolutist State* (both books: London, 1974); P. Corrigan and D. Sayer, *The Great Arch* (Oxford, 1985); and John Saville, *1848: The British State and Chartism* (Cambridge, 1987).

32. Christopher Hill, *Economic Problems of the Church* (Oxford, 1956); Rodney Hilton, *A Medieval Society* (Cambridge, 1983); E. P. Thompson, *Whigs and Hunters* (Harmondsworth, 1977, rev. ed.); and E. J. Hobsbawm, *The Age of Revolution, 1789–1848, The Age of Capital, 1848–1875,* and *The Age of Empire, 1875–1914* (London, 1960, 1975, and 1987).

33. Benjamin, "Theses in the Philosophy of History," p. 262.

34. Terry Eagleton, "Marxism and the Past," *Salmagundi* 68–69 (Fall 1985–Winter 1986), pp. 291–311.

35. Here I must call attention to two outstanding works in the historical demysti-fication of industrial development by American historian, David Noble: whereas the first, *America by Design* (New York, 1977), is a power-structure study of the rise of the engineering profession in the Second Industrial Revolution, the second, *Forces of Production* (New York, 1985), is a study of the class-structuration of technology in the machine tools industry. Also, for excellent examples of studies of a ruling class and the structuration of power by the oppressed, see James Oakes, *The Ruling Race* (New York, 1982), and his article "The Political Significance of Slave Resistance," *History Workshop* 22 (Autumn 1986), pp. 89–107.

36. See, for example, the discussions in Russell Jacoby, *The Last Intellectuals* (New York, 1987), and Norman Birnbaum *The Radical Renewal* (New York, 1988).

37. See, for example, E. Laclau and C. Mouffe, *Hegemony and Socialist Strategy* (London, 1985). For a critical Marxist rebuttal (with which I sympathize) to the "post-Marxists," see Ellen Wood, *The Retreat from Class* (London, 1985).

38. John Keane, *Democracy and Civil Society* (London, 1988), p. 33.

39. Michael Walzer, *Interpretation and Social Criticism* (Cambridge, 1987), and Antonio Gramsci, *Selections from the Prison Notebooks,* ed. and trans. Q. Hoare and G. Nowell-Smith (New York, 1971), p. 155; quoted in Walzer, *Interpretation and Social Criticism,* p. 42. Also, see Walzer's book, *The Company of Critics* (New York, 1988).

40. R. H. Hilton, "Wat Tyler, John Ball and the English Rising of 1381," *Marxism Today,* June 1981, p. 19, and "The English Rising of 1381," *New Society,* 30 April 1981, p. 173.

41. See Christopher Hill's books: *Society and Puritanism in Pre-Revolutionary England* (London, 1964); *Intellectual Origins of the English Revolution* (Oxford, 1965); and *The World Turned Upside Down* (Harmondsworth, 1972, rev. ed.).

42. Terry Eagleton, *The Function of Criticism* (London, 1984), p. 36.

43. E. P. Thompson, *The Making of the English Working Class,* pp. 84–110.

44. E. P. Thompson, "Homage to Tom Maguire," in A. Briggs and J. Saville, eds., *Essays in Labour History* (London, 1960), p. 314.

45. Marcus Rediker, "Getting Out of the Graveyard: Perry Anderson, Edward Thompson, and the Arguments of English Marxism," a review of Perry Anderson's *Arguments Within English Marxism* (London, 1980), in *Radical History Review* 26 (1982), pp. 120–131. Also see, for a most appreciative reference to Thompson, Jim Merod, *The Political Responsibility of the Critic* (Ithaca, 1987), pp. 5, 201–2.

46. E. P. Thompson, preface to S. Lynd, *Class Conflict, Slavery and the United States Constitution* (Indianapolis, 1967), p. xii.

47. E. P. Thompson, "Interview," in H. Abelove, et al., eds., *Visions of History,* p. 7, and F. Inglis, *Radical Earnestness* (Oxford, 1982), p. 199. I am very much in agreement with Inglis's presentation of Thompson (pp. 193–204). Also, see Renato Rosaldo's contribution to Kaye and McClelland, eds., *E. P. Thompson: Critical Perspectives,* pp. 103–24.

48. G. D. H. Cole, "William Cobbett (1762–1835)," in his *Persons and Periods* (Harmondsworth, 1945), pp. 116–18.

49. See E. P. Thompson's "William Morris and the Moral Issues of To-day," *Arena* 2 (June/July 1951), pp. 25–30; his contributions to *The New Reasoner*, the dissident communist journal which he organized with John Saville; and his edited volume, *Out of Apathy* (London, 1960).

50. See "The Peculiarities of the English" (1965), reprinted in E. P. Thompson, *The Poverty of Theory and Other Essays* (London, 1978). On the Anderson-Thompson exchange, see Keith Nield, "A Symptomatic Dispute? Notes on the Relation between Marxian Theory and Historical Practice in Britain," *Social Research* 47 (Autumn 1980), pp. 479–506.

51. See E. P. Thompson's *Warwick University Limited* (Harmondsworth, 1970); *Writing by Candlelight* (London, 1980); "The Poverty of Theory" (1978), in E. P. Thompson, *The Poverty of Theory and Other Essays*, pp. 1–210; and *The Heavy Dancers* (London, 1985).

52. See E. P. Thompson's *Protest and Survive* (Harmondsworth, 1980), co-edited with Dan Smith; *Beyond the Cold War* (New York, 1982); *Exterminism and Cold War* (London, 1982); *Star Wars* (Harmondsworth, 1985); *Mad Dogs* (London, 1986); and, again with Dan Smith, *Prospectus for a Habitable Planet* (Harmondsworth, 1987). For an admittedly more comprehensive and "critical" examination of Thompson's "politics," see Perry Anderson's *Arguments Within English Marxism*, esp. pp. 100–207. Anderson discusses Thompson's practice in comparison with Althusser's and, also, that of the *New Left Review* which he headed.

53. E. P. Thompson, "Revolution," in *Out of Apathy*, p. 308.

54. Thompson, "Peculiarities of the English," pp. 274, 267.

55. E. P. Thompson, "An Open Letter to Leszek Kolakowski" (1973), in *The Poverty of Theory and Other Essays*, pp. 319, 333, 385.

56. Thompson, foreword to *The Poverty of Theory and Other Essays*, p. iv.

57. Thompson, "An Open Letter to Leszek Kolakowski," p. 319; *Whigs and Hunters*, p. 266, and "The Poverty of Theory," p. 192.

58. E. P. Thompson, *The Sykaos Papers* (London, 1988) (pronounced "Psychaos").

59. Walzer, *Interpretation and Social Criticism*, p. 39. Of course, Thompson also writes social criticism for the American weekly, *The Nation*. Here he speaks as a cultural cousin and comrade of the American Left; but also he reminds us that his mother's side of the family was American. Thus, even in the States he attempts a degree of "connectedness." In this regard I recommend "Remembering C. Wright Mills," and "Homage to Thomas McGrath," in *The Heavy Dancers*, pp. 261–74 and 279–337; "The Passing of the Old Order," *The Nation*, 22 March 1986, pp. 377–81; and "The Reasons of the Yahoo," *The Yale Review* 75 (Summer 1986), pp. 481–502. I should add that however much I am stressing Thompson's attempts to ground his criticism in an "English idiom" I would not for a moment deny his commitment to "socialist internationalism."

60. E. P. Thompson, "A Special Case," in *Writing by Candlelight*, p. 75.

61. E. P. Thompson, "The Secret State" (1977), in *Writing by Candlelight*, p. 163, and *The Heavy Dancers*, pp. 6, 4–5.

62. Thompson, "Homage to Thomas McGrath," p. 284. McGrath was an American friend and Thompson's favorite contemporary poet. See Thomas McGrath, *Letter to an Imaginary Friend: Part I and II* and *Parts III and IV* (Chicago, 1962 and Port Townsend, Washington, 1985).

63. V. G. Kiernan, "Socialism, The Prophetic Memory," in Kaye, ed., *Poets, Politics and the People*. I also recommend Walter L. Adamson, *Marx and the Disillusionment of Marxism* (Berkeley, 1985), esp. pp. 228–43, and Henry Giroux, *Schooling and the Struggle for Public Life* (Minneapolis, 1988).

64. Antonio Gramsci, *Selections from the Prison Notebooks*, pp. 34–35.

65. I have elsewhere proposed (as a modest act of social criticism) in the wake of a third Thatcher election victory that a new grand narrative of British history be built around the theme of "lost rights" and the radical-democratic tradition: "Our Island Story Retold," *The Guardian*, 3 August 1987, p. 7. I have incorporated this piece into chapter 5 of the present work.

Chapter Five

This chapter originated as two related, but separate, articles written in the wake of the British General Election of June 1987: "History from the Bottom Up," *Times Higher Education Supplement*, 28 August 1987, and (the section headed Past and Present: A Challenge to Socialists . . .) "Our Island Story Retold," *The Guardian* (the British national daily newspaper), 3 August 1987. I wrote the articles while my family and I were on sabbatical and resident in Britain from December 1986 to August 1987. Although my wife, Lorna, is British, and my young daughters are dual nationals, I am an American ever since my birth in New Jersey. Nevertheless, the editor who commissioned the piece for *The Guardian* gave it the title "Our Island . . ."—which made it appear that I was British. Indeed, a year later, that same editor wrote an article reporting on the "Back to the Future" conference (see note 12 below) in which I was referred to—and he thought he was clarifying things!—as a Canadian. Proof of the original confusion came when I was sitting in an audience at the 1988 American Historical Association Meetings in Washington, D.C. listening to an address by the American historical geographer, David Lowenthal (himself a resident of London for the past twenty years), for there I heard myself referred to as an "Englishman" when he quoted me from my *Guardian* essay. I introduced myself to him after the talk and we had a good laugh. I should add here that the only revisions I have made to the articles were those necessary to reconstruct them as a single chapter; however, I have appended notes both to provide the necessary references absent from the original newspaper versions and to make several comments afforded me by hindsight.

1. William Morris, "How I Became a Socialist," in *Political Writings of William Morris*, ed. A. L. Morton (London, 1973), p. 244.

2. Russell Jacoby, *Social Amnesia* (Boston, 1975), p. 4. On the "crisis of history," see Harvey J. Kaye, *The Powers of the Past* (London, 1991).

3. On the Heritage Industry, see Patrick Wright, *On Living in an Old Country* (London, 1985), and Robert Hewison, *The Heritage Industry* (London, 1987).

4. See Kaye, *The Powers of the Past.*

5. David Cannadine, "The State of British History," *Times Literary Supplement,* 10 October 1986, pp. 1139–40, and "British History: Past, Present—and Future?" *Past & Present* 116 (August 1987), pp. 169–91. For responses to Cannadine, see "Debate: British History: Past, Present—and Future?" *Past & Present* 119 (May 1988), pp. 171–203. Since this essay first appeared, David Cannadine has joined the British academic "brain drain" and taken up a professorship in the United States, at Columbia University.

6. See Ruth Dudley Edwards, *Victor Gollancz: A Biography* (London, 1987), and Sheila Hodges, *Gollancz: The Story of a Publishing House, 1928–1978* (London, 1978).

7. Maurice Cornforth, "A. L. Morton—Portrait of a Marxist Historian," in M. Cornforth, ed., *Rebels and Their Causes: Essays in Honour of A. L. Morton* (London, 1978), p. 8.

8. Ibid., p. 13.

9. All of Morton's postwar works were published by Lawrence and Wishart (London). Most recently they have issued *History and the Imagination: Selected Writings of A. L. Morton,* ed. Margot Heinemann and Willie Thompson, with introductions by Christopher Hill and Raphael Samuel (London, 1990). Also of interest is the pamphlet, *Speeches at the Memorial Meeting for Leslie Morton* (issued by the Communist Party Historians' Group, 1988).

10. See Eric Hobsbawm, "The Historians' Group of the Communist Party," in M. Cornforth, ed., *Rebels and Their Causes,* pp. 21–48.

11. Fortunately, the final product was not at all as bad as the British producer had led me to fear. See Benjamin Barber and Patrick Watson, *The Struggle for Democracy* (Boston, 1988), for the companion volume to the television series.

12. Indeed, my suggestion inspired Morton's own publishers to organize such a conference, and with the sponsorship of Lawrence and Wishart, History Workshop, the Communist Party Historians' Group, and the Society for the Study of Labour History, "Back to the Future" was convened in London on 9 July 1988, with five hundred people in attendance. Sadly, Leslie Morton had died in October, 1987, not long after my essay on his book appeared.

13. As I was preparing this chapter for the present volume the respective republics were declaring their independence from the Soviet State in the wake of the failed coup of August 1991. Now, in January 1992, as I proceed to deliver the entire manuscript to the publishers, it must be added that the Soviet Union is dissolved and the Soviet State is, as they say, "history." These events have yet to be fully comprehended.

14. See T. H. Marshall, "Citizenship and Social Class," in *Class, Citizenship and Social Development* (New York, 1964).

15. See Harvey J. Kaye, *The British Marxist Historians: An Introductory Analysis* (Oxford, 1984), esp. pp. 242–46.

16. Christopher Hill, "The Norman Yoke," originally published in J. Saville, ed., *Democracy and the Labour Movement* (London, 1954), and Dona Torr, *Tom Mann and His Times* (London, 1956). The latter was actually completed by Christopher Hill and A. L. Morton due to the ill-health of Dona Torr.

17. On 1381, see Rodney Hilton, *Bond Men Made Free* (London, 1973). For my American readers I should note that the possibility of a new poll tax was placed on the British political agenda in the mid-1980s by the Conservative party and that its imposition, first in Scotland and then in the rest of Britain, seriously contributed to the "fall" of Margaret Thatcher, that is, to her stepping down as prime minister in favor of John Major in late 1990.

Chapter Six

This chapter originated as two related, but separate, articles published as: "Capitalism and Democracy: A Retrospective on Leo Huberman's *We, The People*," *Our History Journal* 15 (April 1990), and the first part of "A Radical Theology for Democratic Education: A Review of Henry A. Giroux's *Schooling and the Struggle for Public Life*," *Educational Theory* 39 (Summer 1989). Although I have made some revisions for the sake of creating a single piece, I have not changed the arguments presented there.

1. George Scialabba, "A Thousand Points of Blight," *Voice Literary Supplement*, December 1988, p. 30.

2. Allen Hunter, "The Politics of Resentment and the Construction of Middle America" (unpublished paper, 1987), quoted in Michael W. Apple, "Redefining Equality: Authoritarian Populism and the Conservative Restoration," *Teachers College Record* 90, no. 2 (Winter, 1988), pp. 173–74.

3. See M. Crozier, S. Huntington, and J. Watanuki, *The Crisis of Democracy: The Trilateral Commission Report* (New York, 1975), and L. Silk and D. Vogel, *Ethics and Profits: Crisis of Confidence in American Business* (New York, 1976).

4. See Harvey J. Kaye, *The Powers of the Past: Reflections on the Crisis and the Promise of History* (London, 1991).

5. See the symposium on Jackson's candidacy in *Dissent*, Summer 1988, pp. 262–68. Also, see on the electoral chances for a Left Democratic candidate: Vicente Navarro, "The 1980 and 1984 U.S. Elections and the New Deal," R. Miliband, L. Panitch, and J. Saville, eds., *Socialist Register 1985–86* (London, 1986).

6. Russell Jacoby, *The Last Intellectuals* (New York, 1987), p. 190.

7. For example, see "Conservative Scholars Call for Movement to 'Reclaim the Academy,'" *The Chronicle of Higher Education*, 23 November 1988, and Jon Wiener, "Campus Voices Right and Left," *The Nation*, 12 December 1988. Also, for a rebuttal to the conservative National Association of Scholars, see Donald Lazere, "Conservative Critics Have a Distorted View of What Constitutes Ideological Bias in Academe," *The Chronicle of Higher Education*, 9 November 1988. (Of course, since I first wrote these lines there has erupted the "pc" [as in, political correctness] controversy which has been the central theme of just about every cultural magazine these past few months of 1991. Whatever the original problem might have been, the chance of really addressing it has

been lost as a consequence of the New Right seeking to turn the issue into a national political crusade against the Left.)

8. I should note that this "generation" has not been without senior figures such as Michael Harrington, Norman Birnbaum, and Michael Walzer. But, to be clear about it, the generation I am thinking of are those who were in undergraduate studies or, perhaps, grad school in the 1960s and early 1970s. (For the record, I was an undergraduate in the years 1967–71 and a graduate student in 1971–76.)

9. For excellent examples of such, see Paul Buhle and Alan Dawley, eds., *Working for Democracy* (Urbana, Ill., 1985).

10. S. Bowles and H. Gintis, *Democracy and Capitalism* (New York, 1986); F. Fox Piven and R. Cloward, *The New Class War* (New York, 1985, rev. ed.), and R. Flacks, *Making History* (New York, 1988).

11. M. Walzer, *Interpretation and Social Criticism* (Cambridge, 1987) and *The Company of Critics* (New York, 1988); J. Merod, *The Political Responsibility of the Critic* (Ithaca, 1987); Henry A. Giroux, *Schooling and the Struggling for Public Life* (Minneapolis, 1987); and W. Adamson, *Marx and the Disillusionment of Marxism* (Berkeley, 1985).

12. See, especially, Walzer's discussion in *Interpretation and Social Criticism*.

13. N. Birnbaum, *Radical Renewal* (New York, 1988), p. 199.

14. C. Wright Mills, *The Sociological Imagination* (New York, 1959).

15. Leo Huberman, *We, the People* (New York, 1932; rev. ed., 1947; paperback ed., 1970). Page references to the book are indicated in the text in parentheses.

16. D. W. Noble, *The End of American History* (Minneapolis, 1985), esp. chapters 2 and 3. Also, see Frederick Jackson Turner, *The Frontier in American History* (New York, 1920, 1962).

17. Ibid. (Noble), pp. 41–60. Also, see Ellen Nore, *Charles A. Beard: An Intellectual Biography* (Carbondale, Ill., 1983), esp. pp. 116–19.

18. These notes are to be found in *Leo Huberman: A Memorial Service and Meeting of Friends* (2 December 1968), a pamphlet issued by Monthly Review Press, pp. 6–8.

19. "Leo Huberman: October 17, 1903–November 8, 1968," *Monthly Review* 20 (December 1968). On *Monthly Review*, see Peter Clecak, "Monthly Review: An Assessment," *Monthly Review* 20 (November 1968), pp. 1–17.

20. Reprinted in *Leo Huberman, A Memorial Service,* p. 8, 27.

21. R. Jacoby, *The Last Intellectuals,* pp. 164, 176.

22. Paul Sweezy's remarks in *Leo Huberman: A Memorial Service,* p. 47.

23. H. Adams, *Thomas Hart Benton: An American Original* (New York, 1989), p. 168.

24. R. Pells, *Radical Visions and American Dreams: Culture and Social Thought in the Depression Years* (New York, 1974), p. 313.

25. See the critical but appreciative surveys of the current sate of American historiography provided in Eric Foner, ed., *The New American History* (Philadelphia,

1990). It must be noted that one particular mythic theme in American history and historiography, that of the "frontier and the making of the American West" (which, as I have noted, Huberman's *We, the People* also reproduced), recently became the subject of major controversy centered around an art exhibition at the Smithsonian Institution's National Museum of American Art. The show in question was "The West as America: Reinterpreting Images of the Frontier, 1820–1920." See Eric Foner and Jon Weiner, "Fighting for the West," *The Nation*, 29 July 1991, pp. 163–66.

26.	Here I must note the two volumes produced by the American Social History Project which originated under the direction of Herbert Gutman: Bruce Levine, et al., eds., *Who Built America?: Working People and the Nation's Economy, Politics, Culture and Society* (New York, 1989 and 1992). Also, I should not fail to mention Howard Zinn's *A People's History of the United States*(New York, 1980).

27.	L. Ribuffo, "The Burdens of Contemporary History," *American Quarterly* 35 (Spring–Summer 1983), pp. 10–11.

28.	See Harvey J. Kaye, "Colleges Must Prepare the Next Generation of Public Intellectuals," *The Chronicle of Higher Education* (Point of View), 12 June 1991.

29.	For examples, see note 10 above.

Chapter Seven

This chapter is a recomposition of three previously published articles: "Another Way of Seeing Peasants: The Work of John Berger," *Peasant Studies* (1982); "Historical Consciousness and Storytelling: John Berger's Fiction," *Mosaic: Journal for the Interdisciplinary Study of Literature* (1983); and "A Question of History: John Berger's Recent Labours," *Journal of Historical Sociology* (1988).

1.	Gerald Marzorati, "Living and Writing the Peasant Life," *The New York Times Magazine*, 29 November 1987, pp. 39–45, 50, 54. Also, see Adam Hochschild, "Another Way of Seeing Life," *Mother Jones*, December 1981, pp. 20–24, 47–53. For examples of academic discussions of Berger's works, see the special issues of *Critique, Studies in Modern Fiction*, Spring 1984; *Edinburgh Review*, November 1986; and *The Minnesota Review*, 28 (Spring 1987).

2.	Geoff Dyer, *Ways of Telling: The Work of John Berger* (London, 1986). I myself discussed the idea of writing a short book on Berger's work and historical thought with an interested British publisher.

3.	John Berger, *Permanent Red* (London, 1981; originally published in 1960), pp. 15, 18, 105, 151, and *A Painter of Our Time,* (London, 1976; originally published in 1958), p. 63.

4.	Berger, *A Painter of Our Time*, pp. 81, 148.

5.	John Berger, "'Che' Guevara," in *The Look of Things* (New York, 1971), p. 51; John Berger, *Art and Revolution: Ernst Neizvestny and the Role of the Artist in the USSR* (New York, 1969), pp. 156–57; and John Berger, "Between Two Colmars," in *About Looking* (New York, 1980), p. 127.

6. Berger, *Ways of Seeing* (Harmondsworth, 1972), pp. 11 and 13. Also see Peter Fuller, *Seeing Berger—A Revaluation* (London, 1980); and *Art-Language* 4 (October 1978), "Ways of Seeing."

7. John Berger, *G.* (New York, 1980; originally published in 1972).

8. Berger, *G.*, pp. 104–5. Also, see Ian Craib, "Sociological Literature and Literary Sociology: Some Notes on *G.* by John Berger," *The Sociological Review* 22 (1974), pp. 321–33.

9. Ibid., pp. 306, 119.

10. Berger, *About Looking*, p. 133.

11. On Berger's and Tanner's films, see Michael Tarantina, "Tanner and Berger: The Voice Off-Screen," *Film Quarterly* 23 (1979–80), pp. 32–43. And for Berger's thoughts on the subject, see "The Screenwriter as Collaborator—An Interview with John Berger," by Richard Appignanesi, *Cineaste* 10 (1980), pp. 15–19. The script of *Jonah, who will be 25 in the year 2000* was translated into English by Michael Palmer (Berkeley, 1983).

12. John Berger, "Retinal Dialectics—An Interview with Richard Appignanesi, part 2," *In These Times,* 28 May–3 June 1980, p. 16.

13. Not to be confused with Fernand Braudel's geo-environmental *longue durée.*

14. John Berger and Jean Mohr, *A Fortunate Man: The Story of a Country Doctor* (Harmondsworth, 1969), and *A Seventh Man: The Story of a Migrant Worker in Europe* (Harmondsworth, 1975). Also, see Jean Mohr's work on women migrants in Europe in World Council of Churches' Committee on Migrant Workers, *Migrant Women Speak* (London, 1978); and Mohr's work with Kenneth Brown, "Journey through the Labyrinth: A Photographic Essay of Israel/Palestine," *Studies in Visual Communication* 8 (Spring 1982), pp. 2–81, and with Edward Said, *After the Last Sky* (New York, 1986). For an interview with John Berger and Jean Mohr by Paul Willis, see *Screen Education,* 1979–80, "The Authentic Image," curated by P. Corrigan.

15. John Berger and Jean Mohr, *Another Way of Telling* (New York, 1982); and John Berger, *The Sense of Sight* (New York, 1985; British ed., *The White Bird*, London), and *And our faces, my heart, brief as photos* (New York, 1984).

16. John Berger, *Pig Earth* (New York, 1970), and *Once in Europa* (New York, 1987).

17. John Berger and Teodor Shanin, "Can Peasant Society Survive?" *The Listener,* 21 June 1979, p. 847.

18. Berger, *Pig Earth*, p. 196.

19. Berger, *Art and Revolution*, pp. 130–31.

20. Berger, *Pig Earth*, p. 196, and Berger and Shanin, "Can Peasant Society Survive?" p. 847. Also by Shanin, see "The Peasants are Coming: Migrants Who Labour, Peasants Who Travel, and Marxists Who Write," *Race and Class* 19 (Winter 1974), pp. 277–88.

21. Berger, *Pig Earth*, pp. 212, 208.

22. John Berger, "Uses of Photography," in *About Looking,* pp. 54–55.

23. Berger, *Pig Earth,* pp. 6, 97–98, 75, 30, 8.

24. Walter Benjamin, "The Work of Art in the Age of Mechanical Reproduction," and "The Storyteller: Reflections on the Work of Nikolai Leskov," in *Illuminations,* ed. H. Arendt (New York, 1969). For Berger on Benjamin, see John Berger, "Walter Benjamin," in *The Look of Things,* pp. 87–93.

25. Berger, *Pig Earth,* p. 212.

26. Barrington Moore, Jr., *Social Origins of Dictatorship and Democracy* (Boston, 1966), p. 505.

27. Berger, "Uses of Photography," in *About Looking,* p. 59.

28. Berger and Mohr, *Another Way of Telling,* p. 105.

29. James O'Connor, "The Crisis of History as the Present," *Contemporary Crises* 11 (1987), pp. 97–106.

30. Berger and Mohr, *Another Way of Telling,* pp. 106, 108.

31. These questions are posed in a similar fashion in Bruce Robbins, "Feeling Global: John Berger and Experience," in J. Arac, ed., *Postmodernism and Politics* (Minneapolis, 1986), pp.; 153–54.

32. Berger, "Uses of Photography," in *About Looking,* p. 61 (my italics).

33. Susan Meiselas, *Nicaragua, June 1978–July 1979* (New York, 1981). Also, see Berger's review of the book, "Restoring Dignity," *New Society,* 5 November 1981, pp. 243–44; and my review, "Photography and Historical Consciousness," *Studies in Visual Communication* 8 (Summer 1982), pp. 90–93.

34. Richard Appignanesi, "Seeing Red—An Interview with John Berger," *In These Times,* 21–27 May 1980, p. 13.

35. Berger, *And our faces,* pp. 65–67.

36. Fred Inglis, *Radical Earnestness: English Social Theory, 1880–1980* (Oxford, 1982), p. 192.

37. Bruce Robbins, "John Berger's Disappearing Peasants," *The Minnesota Review* 28 (Spring 1987), pp. 65–66. Quotes from *Once in Europa,* pp. 14, 27.

38. Berger, *Once in Europa,* p. 104.

39. Robbins, "John Berger's Disappearing Peasants," p. 66. This in fact connects to a very orthodox position on the peasantry which sees in them nothing but "backwardness." Cf. P. Corrigan "On the Politics of the Peasantry," *Journal of Peasant Studies* 2 (1975), and P. Corrigan and D. Sayer, "Socialist Reconstruction," *Utafiti,* Dar Es Salaam (Summer 1984).

40. Berger, *And our faces,* p. 41.

41. John Berger and Nella Bielski, "A Question of Geography," *Granta* 13 (Autumn 1984), pp. 73–114. Berger translated Bielski's novel, *Oranges for the Son of Alexander Levy* into English (London, 1982).

42. Berger and Bielski, "A Question of Geography," pp. 75, 96–97, 105. On "survival" in the Nazi death camps and the Gulag, see Terrence Des Pres, *The Survivor* (New York, 1978).

43. In particular, and respectively, I contested the views of Irene Oppenheim, "Revolutionizing Art," *The Threepenny Review* 5 (Spring 1981), p. 5, and Fred Pfeil, "Review of *Pig Earth* and *About Looking*," *The Minnesota Review* 15 (1980), pp. 125–26.

44. Berger, *Pig Earth*, pp. 212–13.

45. Dyer, *Ways of Telling*, p. 156, Robbins, "Feeling Global," p. 161.

46. See Berger's articles, "Manhattan" (1975), and "The Theatre of Indifference" (1975), in *The Sense of Sight*, pp. 61–73.

47. John Berger, "From 'Who governs' to 'How to survive,'" *New Statesman* 11 March 1988, pp. 28–29. Berger's essay was written in memory of Raymond Williams.

48. Berger's "exile" and "emigration" to the European countryside instigated changes in his historical perspective but not, apparently, in his assessment of contemporary democratic politics as having "failed." Such a view is ahistorical and will not do.

49. Berger's trilogy is now complete. See the final volume of *Into Their Labours*, titled *Lilac and Flag* (New York, 1990). Also, see his collection of articles, *Keeping a Rendezvous* (New York, 1992).

Chapter Eight

This final chapter is composed of three previously published short articles: "Looking Back," *The Times Higher Education Supplement*, 6 October 1989; "The Concept of the 'End of History' Constitutes a Challenge to the Liberal Consensus in Scholarship and Public Life," *The Chronicle of Higher Education*, 25 October 1989; and "Hard Times?" *History Today*, July 1991. "Hard Times?" was commissioned by Gordon Marsden, the editor of *History Today*, as a contribution to a series of articles on "The Death of Marxism and the End of History?" Originally, I was requested to write on either American historiography or the history of ideas in the wake of "1989" and in the face of the ongoing collapse of Soviet Communism. Antagonized by the equation of Soviet ideology with Marxist historical thought, I replied with a letter challenging the basic assumption of the series. Smart editor that he is, Gordon Marsden responded by inviting me to turn my letter into an article. It should be noted that I have made several minor revisions to all three of the pieces including the addition of references.

1. J. H. Plumb, *The Death of the Past* (London, 1969). Also, see *The Collected Essays of J. H. Plumb: Volume One, The Making of An Historian* (London, 1988), and *Volume Two, The American Experience* (London, 1989). And, on J. H. Plumb, see Robert C. Braddock, "J. H. Plumb and the Whig Tradition," in Walter Arnstein, ed., *Recent Historians of Great Britain* (Ames, Iowa, 1990).

2. Terrence Des Pres, "On Governing Narratives," *The Yale Review* 4 (1986), p. 517.

3. Plumb, *The Death of the Past*, pp. 17, 60.

4. Ibid., p. 40.

5. Ibid., pp. 41–44, 93.

6. Ibid., pp. 12–13, 136.

7. Ibid., pp. 140–45.

8. See David Lowenthal, *The Past is a Foreign Country* (Cambridge, 1985), p. 7.

9. See R. W. Davies, *Soviet History in the Gorbachev Revolution* (Bloomington, 1989).

10. See, for example, The Committee for Historical Justice, "We Want Historical Justice," *Across Frontiers* 4 (1989), pp. 33–35.

11. On the New Right German historians and the "historians' debate," see Richard J. Evans, *In Hitler's Shadow* (New York, 1989); Charles S. Maier, *The Unmasterable Past* (Cambridge, 1988); and Peter Baldwin, ed., *Reworking the Past: Hitler, the Holocaust and the Historians' Debate* (New York, 1990).

12. See Barry Buzan, "Japan's Future: Old History versus New Roles," *International Affairs* 4 (Autumn 1988), pp. 557–73.

13. Daniel Singer, "On Revolution," *Monthly Review,* June 1989, p. 33. On Thatcherism, Reaganism, and history see Harvey J. Kaye, *The Powers of the Past* (London, 1991).

14. Francis Fukuyama, "The End of History?" *The National Interest* 16 (Summer 1989), pp. 3–18.

15. Fukuyama left the State Department in 1991 in favor of a post at a conservative think tank. Also, he has returned to defend (or advance) the end-of-history thesis. See his forthcoming book, *The End of History and The Last Man* (New York, 1992).

16. Again, for a fully developed discussion of, and response to, the New Right and the crisis of history see Kaye, *The Powers of the Past.*

17. Fukuyama, "The End of History?" pp. 3–4.

18. See R. Miliband, L. Panitch, and J. Saville, eds., *Socialist Register 1987: Conservatism in Britain and America* (London, 1987).

19. For an intriguing analysis of Solidarity see Roman Laba, *The Roots of Solidarity: A Political Sociology of Poland's Working-Class Democratization* (Princeton, 1991).

Index